Isaac Schwab

The Sabbath in History

Isaac Schwab

The Sabbath in History

ISBN/EAN: 9783743324947

Manufactured in Europe, USA, Canada, Australia, Japa

Cover: Foto ©ninafisch / pixelio.de

Manufactured and distributed by brebook publishing software (www.brebook.com)

Isaac Schwab

The Sabbath in History

The Sabbath in History

BY

Dr. ISAAC SCHWAB,

RABBI

OF

ST. JOSEPH, MO.

PART I.

Copyright, December, 1888,
by
Dr. Isaac Schwab.

PREFACE.

The present work has grown out of the nucleus of a few articles contributed to a Jewish Weekly. It has now assumed the dimension of a book, in which form it is and will further be given to the world. The author has, for several reasons, seen fit to publish the first part separately at present, and let the remainder follow in a short time. Whether this will be divided into two more parts, or appear at once in one volume, will be decided hereafter. In the sequel of the present publication the author deals with the following subjects: The Sabbath with Jesus, as to doctrine and practice; the Sabbath in the Apostolic age; the Sabbath with the Jewish Christian sects, the Nazarenes and Ebionites; the Sabbath in Pauline and Gentile Christianity.

The object he has in view in putting his work before a larger public is twofold, religious and scientific. The Sabbath, most sacred as it is in its significance, and as yet theoretically planted hard and fast in the consciousness of the generality of Israel as the "perpetual sign between them and God," has yet practically lost in modern days much of its pristine awfulness, and even of the fervid reverence paid to it in ages not so long gone by. Notwithstanding that it is yet generally exalted as a prominently distinctive mark of Judaism, and valued as one of the few remaining bonds of Israel's union, it is alas! too often made to yield to the so-called pressure of modern business relations, and thus compromised as to its sanctity and validity; or it is paltered with and bartered away on various grounds of expediency. On these painful issues of modern Judaism we cannot here dwell. It lies moreover beyond the purpose of these prefatory lines to find fault and point out the different manifest decrease of true attachment for the Sabbath in our day.

The writer is, on the whole, aiming at and inspired by the hope of quickening again, by the light of historical data witnessing to an incomparable self-devotion and loyalty of Israel in the past to the *royal bride Sabbath*, that sense of superior estimation of this sacred day, which should be the pride and glory of our people at the present, no less than it was in previous times. He aims to rekindle, by the various illustrations put forth in his work, a zealous concern for the Sabbath of the Decalogue in the minds of those, with whom it has slacked through an undue addiction to worldly things and business advantages, and to possibly arrest the Neshamah yetherah "additional soul," formerly so closely attending the Israelite on the Sabbath, on its sorrowful flight from those too deeply immersed in their temporal pursuits and the material strifes of our *racing* age, or those too flightily temporizing in their attitude towards the "sign" that is to be "perpetual," and on the perpetuity of which our forefathers, as well of the middle ages as of antiquity (Jewish new-Christians of Spain, who would continue to observe the Sabbath secretly despite the baptism forced on them, were by the inquisitors singled out by the observation, from elevated places, that no smoke came out of their houses on the Sabbath, even in rigorous winter; see 'Shebhet Jehudah,' p. 96), staked their lives from their spontaneous piety and faithfulness to the Law.

On his scientific purpose the author need not spend many words. No production in any department of science, resulting from an aspiration to enrich, in some way and measure, the extant stores of knowledge, requires an apology for itself. In the domain of the intellect every original literary creation, or only newly arranged and explained subject-matter, justifies itself, even without the grounded prospect of its meeting a certain desideratum. How much more warranted is an attempt, like our own, by which a real want, however moderately, is to be supplied!

For it will be allowed by all, that a thorough-going research into the observance of the Sabbath by our ancestors in the historical ages of the second Commonwealth ; also into the opinions which prevailed in antiquity among non-Jews upon the Jewish religion, and the Sabbath in particular ; furthermore, into the mode of the Sabbatic rest and the theories held on it by the chief persons of primitive Christianity, and, in general, by the various parties of the ancient Jewish Christian Church ; and, lastly, into the position which the earlier and later Gentile Christians of those remote ages held towards the Sabbath, has thus far not been brought to light in any comprehensive literary effort. The author's relative investigations and his resolve to step before the world with their result, will therefore, he expects, be acknowledged as a timely attempt.

As to the historical merits of his work, also its tone and diction, he trusts that critics will pass on them with fairness and forbearance. The shortcomings that may strike them at its perusal, may be manifold, but they will not likely be found as originating from any haste or forwardness in forming or proposing his arguments, for he presumes to rank himself among the very cautious reasoners, which circumstance, too, accounts for his rare literary appearance before the public.

May Providence speed his work, and vouchsafe that it accomplish its combined instructive and religiously restorative purpose.

May the Sabbath, that priceless gem in the crown of the Torah, again become as bright with the lustre of Israel's spontaneous devotion to it, as it was of yore. May the reverence for it, blended with the reverence for the memories of our martyrs of the past, who endured tortures or offered up life in its honor and for the "sanctification of God," be profoundly reanimated in us, and help promoting in our midst an untarnished life of holiness.

CONTENTS.

	PAGE
CHAPTER I.	
From Nehemiah to the Age of the Antonines . .	11
CHAPTER II.	
Pagan Writers on the Jewish Religion and the Sabbath	22
CHAPTER III.	
Pagan Writers on the Jewish Religion and the Sabbath	31
CHAPTER IV.	
Roman Writers on the Jewish Sabbath	72
Notes to these Chapters	 85–132

THE SABBATH IN HISTORY.

CHAPTER I.

FROM NEHEMIAH TO THE AGE OF THE ANTONINES.

The stern and striking reproof which Nehemiah, the governor appointed by Artaxerxes Longimanus over Judea, dealt, on his second return from Persia, about 425 B. C., to the municipal authorities of the province for the violation of the Sabbath, with which he met not only in the city of Jerusalem, but in various towns of Judea, and in especial, his vigilant measure of closing the gates of the capital against any traffic on the sacred day of rest, seem to have been fraught with the best results. Ezra, his great co-laborer in the restoration of the ancient theocratic forms and regulations of national religious life, had, it is supposed, died during the years of his absence. The lack of an energetic guide standing at the helm of religious affairs, seems to have caused several grave abuses and infractions of Law to creep in and go unavenged. Among them Nehemiah had discovered a scandalous dereliction of the Sabbatic rest. Some of the Jews were found by him treading wine-presses, and others loading provisions on their wagons to bring them to Jerusalem (though they would probably not sell any before the Sabbath was over), and others buying articles of food and other commodities of Tyrian traders on the Sabbath. His authoritative remonstrance and decided interference against such profanation of the Sabbath, are recorded in Neh. ch. xiii. Thenceforth, we justly suppose, the persuasive authority of the Sopherim "Scribes" will have sufficed to ward off such flagrant lawlessness.

These, composed of Temple functionaries as well as learned persons from the lay classes of Israel, who are assumed to have begun their activity with Ezra, venerated in tradition as the restorer of Judaism, have made it their noble task to infuse a zealous spirit of religious life into the masses, and will doubtless also have largely contributed towards strengthening in their minds more and more the sense of the sacred significance of the Sabbath, by expounding the Mosaic Sabbath ordinances in the public devotional gatherings, at first held occasionally and later regularly on Sabbaths and holy days, to which were added even the Mondays and Thursdays, these days being improved by reading and commenting on the Law before the people. (See B. Baba Kamma f. 82, and comp. Herzfeld, History of Israel i. 28).[1] The work of propagating a due understanding of the Mosaic enactments was carried on by those Scribes, either as members of an organized body comprised in the "Men of the Great Assembly," or severally in their capacity as copyists, teachers and expositors of Scripture.

The Sabbath law formed with them undoubtedly a prominent subject of interpretation, for the paramount sacredness and inviolability with which it is invested in the Pentateuch. The definition of common labor prohibited on the Sabbath, and its classification into chief and minor operations, was without doubt the task those men had undertaken in their noble zeal for the advancement of practical reverence to the ancestral trust. Little by little new restrictions were passed by councils of the learned, to serve as fences of protection to the main ordinances of the Sabbath of the Decalogue. And they, too, coming from the representative 'Wise,' were reverently heeded by the bulk of the Jewish people.

An awful austerity was thus, as time progressed, woven around the Sabbath, to violate which was deemed a mark of utter religious debasement and degeneracy.

For this austerity there is historical evidence even outside of the Rabbinical works, and for a period as early as the first quarter of the fourth century B. C. Josephus reports, from Grecian histories that lay before him, particularly, it seems, the work of Agatharchides that, when Ptolemy Lagi came with his army to take possession of Jerusalem, but met with determined resistance from the inhabitants, he purposely approached the city on a Sabbath day, on which he knew the Jews would not make use of arms, nor do any other common work, and easily succeeded to take it (Ant. xii. 1, 1 ; Against Apion i. 22 ; see•also Herzfeld, l. c. p. 210). Agatharchides, like most other Grecian and Roman writers on Jewish religious institutions, could only scoff at this conscientious adherence of the Jews to their religious precepts, which they maintained even at the risk of losing their possessions and lives. To him this custom of avoiding armed engagements on a Sabbath was another of the superstitions for which he had only scathing taunt. The Sabbath observance of the Jews he pronounced a "mad custom," a "foolish practice." It is likely that Plutarch,[2] a Grecian writer of the first and second centuries C. E., in his treatise on the "Fear of the gods," or, as it is usually designated, on "Superstition," alluded in ch. viii. to that fact, when he, criticising a bootless piety, consisting in mere trust in Divine aid without that human efforts to attain the objects prayed for accompany it, puts forth as an example of it "the Jews, sitting still, in unbleached clothes. because it was the Sabbath, and suffering the enemy to plant ladders and seize upon the walls, they themselves not rising, but remaining inactive, like (fishes) in a net, (though) fettered only by their superstition."

In the Hibbert edition of that treatise the translator suggests in a note, that Plutarch had in his mind another event, that, namely, of the time of the religious persecution of Antiochus Epiphanes, when the Jews hidden in caverns of the Judean desert to escape the miseries of the persecution (the author of 2 Macc. construes their object of hiding there to have been, that they might "keep the Sabbath secretly"), were assaulted by the troops of the Syrian commander (Philippus, 2 Macc.) on a Sabbath, and perished together at the hands of the enemy (I Macc. ii. 37; Jos. Ant. xii. 6, 2).

He might also have observed, as belonging to the same period, the like instance of the resolute refusal of the Jews to fight on the Sabbath, when Apollonius, turning this day, on which he found the Jews at religious rest, to his account, had a large number of them massacred—an event that happened already before the publication of Antiochus' edict (2 Macc. v. 24 sq.); compare the case narrated there, ch. xv., 2-6.

But we have to object, that the tenor of Plutarch's description comports decidedly more with the capture of the Temple and its fortifications by Pompey, 63 B. C., when he took advantage of the Sabbath days for laying siege to it, and raising and completing the bank, from which he would batter those strongholds, the Jews making no armed opposition, but allowing him to proceed with his hostile preparations, rather than desecrate the day by active attempts of repulsion (Ant. xiv. 4, 2; see also Wars ii. 16, 4). This occurrence was doubtless matter of record in various works of history, alongside the successful conquest accomplished by Pompey, of which an historian of his acts naturally took note.

Be that as it may, and whether or not Plutarch adverted in his treatise to the last-named occurrence, we have at all events thus far adduced reliable historical attestation, that the Jews exhibited from the beginning of the Greek period to that of the Roman rule over Judea, an exemplary pious fortitude, a true simplicity of faith (comp. 1 Macc. ii. 37), in obeying what they were convinced to be the law of God rather than the dictate of self-preservation, otherwise so natural and justifiable, when it conflicted in their conscience with the allegiance they felt themselves owing to their God.

It is true, that the extreme rigor with regard to military actions on the Sabbath was, since the above-mentioned calamity in the Syrian epoch, somewhat relaxed through the intervention of Mattathias and his friends, in so far that they concluded that armed defence against hostile attacks did not come under the head of forbidden work (1 Macc. ii. 39 sq.), and that, judging from Jonathan, his brave son's proceeding against Bacchides,(ib. ix. 43), and from Josephus' statement in Ant. xii. 6, 2; xiv. 4, 2, the rule seems to have prevailed up to the latter's time, that the Sabbath law had to give way before such "necessity," as this historian denotes such cases of critical extremity. But, let us reply, was there nevertheless not enough of the former rigor left even in Josephus' time? He reflects in Ant. xii. 6, 2, upon the inactivity on Sabbaths during Pompey's invasion as not only observed at that juncture, but as still obtaining as a rule in his own day, in the following: "The law does not permit us to meddle with our enemies while they do anything else" (than make a direct assault). Offensive warfare against pagan enemies was then practically shunned on the Sabbath. This shows conclusively the religious anxiety holding sway all along over the consciences of the Jews, lest they might transgress the Sabbath law by military operations, although such inactivity might be fraught with serious disadvantages and even losses to them.[3]

That this anxiety was not lessened during the centuries of the Roman dominion subsequent to Josephus' time, may be gathered from ancient Rabbinical sources.

It is known that the Syro-Greek inhabitants of many cities of Palestine and Syria cherished an intense hatred and bitter prejudice against the Jews. Cases of mob violence by the spiteful Grecians, were specially frequent under Nero and Titus, (see Josephus, Wars ii, 14, 4 sq; 20, 2; 18, 1, 2, 5; Life § 5). That such tumults were not only fomented and enacted in larger cities having a preponderant heathen population, but spread also among the smaller places of the surrounding districts, we may conclude with sufficient assurance. The relations of the Jews to the Syro-Greeks in cities of mixed population grew doubtless yet more strained, causing occasional outbreaks, since the last deadly thrust was given to the Jewish State by the Roman colossus, and the disasters of the Jews attendant upon it. To the envy and hatred already before nourished by those fanatical pagans, there was now joined a vile contempt for the humiliated down-trodden matron, Judea.

As instances in point may be mentioned the request of the heathens of Antioch, the capital of Syria, to Titus, when he had come there after the fall of Jerusalem, to eject the Jewish people from the city (Wars vii. 5, 2), where they had lived in large numbers, enjoying since early days equal rights with the Greeks (ib. 3, 3); also the prayer of the Alexandrians to Vespasian and Titus to take away the citizenship from the Jews of that city (Ant. xii, 3, 1).

The Jews had through the loss of their State to the Romans in that fatal revolutionary struggle become strangers in their native land. All that reminded them that they had some sort of citizenship left, was the exorbitant taxation levied on them by the Roman authorities. The insolent Roman soldiers and officers, and the malicious heathen inhabitants of Palestine and Syria could now with greater impunity than ever before offer any affront to the Jews, as they were prostrate and discouraged by the disasters through which they had passed. That those heathens would under such circumstances often attack the more defenceless Jews on the Sabbath, coming on them unawares for objects of molestation, spoliation or murder, may be derived by way of induction from some passages of the old Rabbinical literature, which we can safely set down as bearing on the Jewish affairs of the Roman period, at least to the latter part of the second century C. E.

The fact that Rabbinical authorities of the first century C. E. had to legislate regarding those Jews "going out to rescue brethren from the assaults of (heathen) hordes " on the Sabbath (see Mishnah Rosh Hashanah ii. 5 and comp. Erubin iv. 3), and that sundry regulations concerning warfare to repulse heathen attacks on the Sabbath occur in another Rabbinical code (Tosifta Erubin iii. 5 sq.; comp. B. Erubin f. 45), shows evidently the practical occurrence, from time to time, of such hostile irruptions during the Roman rule.

And yet for all the sympathy for the oppressed and distressed brethren that moved and actuated those Rabbinical legislators, and for all their pious jealousy for the integrity of Jewish territory and its freedom from the pollutions of godless heathens, the scruple of violating the Sabbath by exceeding the line of lawfulness, already extended by way of dispensation for cases of inevitable necessity, would not vanish from their minds, and we may safely presume from the minds of the pious lay people, either.

Armed movements and acts on the Sabbath were held unlawful for various reasons, chief among them seems to have been, first, the need of journeying beyond the Sabbath limit from one's habitation (see Ant. xiii. 8, 4), which was traditionally set at 2,000 cubits (B. Erubin f. 51; comp. Acts i. 12), and secondly, the carrying of arms from private precincts to public thoroughfares and roads, and the reverse, which was regarded as a burden, rangeable among the principal kinds of common labor (see Mishnah Sabb. f. 73). The former consideration is confirmed as historical even by non-Jewish testimony (see Ant. l. c.), and that not later than the first half of the second century B. C.

Now, while the Rabbis of antiquity seem to have been agreed that for rescuing brethren living in the neighborhood of a town, or for defending a place attacked by heathen enemies, those Sabbath restraints may be set aside, they would yet, in their austere piety, not even leave such allowances unrestricted, permitting to rescuing parties, after they would have completed their noble work of relieving imperiled brethren, only to return a distance of 2,000 cubits, but not the entire length of their journey to their homes, wherefrom they had started on the Sabbath (comp. Mishnah Rosh Hash. l. c. with B. Erubin f. 45).

The other consideration, the violation of the Sabbath by bearing one's armor, and consequently a burden on public roads, weighed also so heavily with them in questions of defence and rescue that, although they deemed the preservation of lives and country paramount to the obligation of that traditional religious observance, they would yet place a restriction even on this dispensation, which was only later abolished through the sad experience of serious grief entailed by such anxious application of the Sabbath injunction.

To such a degree, then, the anxiety and scrupulosity as to Sabbath restraints were developed in the Rabbinical ages of antiquity! While those pious teachers saw themselves induced, in ill-fated times, to make some concessions when there was immediate or imminent danger of life, they would yet make them with timid minds and the attachment of cautious limitations. The awe of the Sabbath had permeated the Jewish consciences so completely, that only preservation of life and country was judged worthy of being put in the balance against the settled religious restraints. And while the weight of inevitable *necessity* made the opposite scale tardily rise, it was surely not a sense of levity or a disposition to compromise, that was active in making such modifications of some parts of the acknowledged Sabbath law. Dreadful contingencies urged their temporary yielding to the mandate of preservation of Jewish lives and habitations.

The sacred earnestness which we have thus far seen to have prevailed as to the Sabbath observance, inspired not only the teachers, but unquestionably also the people at large. The successive training and usage of centuries had established such deep reverence for this weekly day of rest, and created, so to speak, such an air of holiness in the Jewish sphere of life, that equally the common people and the learned class were possessed of an unbidden reverent devotedness to it.

And they would equally with the doctors of the Law imperil their lives for the sake of the Sabbath observance, in days of religious persecution. This they did, not only in the Maccabean period, but also again during the cruel proscription visited on the Jews by the emperor Hadrian, in the year 135 or 136 C. E.

In those bloody days of religious proscription, which comprised not only the occupation of the teachers with Scripture interpretation, lecturing on themes of traditional law, and the ordination of scholars for the Rabbinical office, but also the practice of any Jewish rite by the people (see B. Baba Bathra f. 60), chiefly the Abrahamic rite, the Sabbath, the reading of Scripture (Megillath Taanith ch xii.), also the observances on the festivals of Passover and Tabernacles (Midr. Rabb. Lev. xxxii.; Mechilta Jethro vi.), the daily recitation of the Shema-chapter, which was the most obligatory portion of the Jewish ritual (Tosifta Berach. ii.) etc., the intrepid devotion to the ancestral religion was proved by laymen as well as teachers. Many of them bore a zealous and glorifying testimony to the unalterable obligation of the Law of God, by discharging their religious duties, while they knew the penalty of death impending on them, if they should be apprehended in the act. Not only have a number of them endured tortures unto death for disobeying openly the imperial interdict by exercising the Abrahamic rite and refusing to serve idols (see B. Sabbath f. 130)—the latter of which we will elsewhere establish as having also been enjoined by Hadrian, only that it was probably not enforced so generally — but some of the stalwart religionists continued to put their lives in jeopardy by practicing the various essential ceremonies of religion in defiance of the prohibitory edict. They were not daunted by the risk of being detected by the imperial myrmidons or informers of their own race — for there were some Jewish renegades wicked enough to play the vile part of delators in those fatal days. They would, it is true, attempt as much as possible to conceal, by different secret devices, their religious observances from the Argus eyes of the ubiquitous spies, as they would also relax, in some instances, certain minor ceremonial restrictions, traditionally observed in connection with the essentials of their religion. Yet for all their measures of precaution they were constantly bearing their lives in their hands, while attending to ceremonial functions.

That the threatened penalty of death did not deter such Israelites from keeping the Sabbath holy, is attested by the before-quoted passages of Rabb. Lev., and the Mechilta. They would, further, do the Pentateuch reading of the Sabbath on the roofs of the houses, the attendance at the synagogues or the lower apartments of their houses being too insecure (see Jer. Erubin ix. 1), though even there they might be discovered and seized to await an atrocious visitation for offending against the Roman tyrant's authority. With heroic steadfastness they would acknowledge their reverence to the Divinely instituted Sabbath in those troubled times, which lasted long enough, indeed. It was not until some time in the reign of Antoninus Pius that, through the intercession of Rabbi Meir's pupil, Judah ben Shamua—if we may credit the testimony of a relative Rabbinical tradition (Megill. Taan. l. c.)—the cruel edict of the prohibition of the Jewish religion was revoked.

The Sabbath was then re-instated in its pristine freedom. The pious fervor with which it had been customarily observed, was yet increased, now the oppressive ban was removed, and intensified by a deep sense of gratitude to the Divine Ruler who had in his mercy disposed, that his servants should again be able to bear the "yoke of the sacred commands," without fear of human punishment.

Hadrian's war of extermination (Shemad) was another "iron furnace," in which Israel's indomitable, iron tenacity to their religion was severely tested and found proof. He had indeed struck a grievous blow at the root of Israel's proud existence, their religion, aiming by such barbarous deeds at the total overthrow of the trunk that had breasted so successfully the raging storms of the past. But that "ridiculous sophist and jealous tyrant" erred in his calculation. Israel's vitality was too vigorous to succumb to his unrelenting furor. They again came forth victoriously as to the preservation of their religion, holding aloft its banner with the inscription of "Jehovah is One," ensanguined though it was through the martyrdom of those upholding the authority of the law of God, in open or secret defiance of that of a human tyrant.

Alas! once more should the freedom of the Sabbath be disturbed by Roman interference. It was in the reign of Marcus Aurelius and Aelius Verus, the successors of Antoninus Pius, that the Hadrianic proscription of the fundamental and essential rites of the Jewish religion was renewed, about 165-69 C. E. (B. Meilah f. 17, and see Muenter, The Jewish War, etc.; also Graetz, History). Again it was, so the Talmud relates, a Rabbinical doctor, Rabbi Simeon ben Jochai, who accomplished the repeal of the interdict. It seems, however, in view of the fact that Marcus Aurelius was not at heart an enemy of the Jews (see Muenter l. c. p. 100), having also, as we prefer to assume with Rappaport, befriended the eminent Jewish patriarch, Judah I., to have lasted only a short time. From the day of its revocation we meet with no more imperial prohibitions of the Sabbath. The civil condition of the Jews improved henceforth more and more with the accession of rulers of the Roman world, who had sufficient respect and toleration for their religious institutions, not to vex them in their earnest efforts to maintain them intact. And thus could also the Sabbath obtain back its royal glory and solemn grandeur, so much dimmed during the past ages of persecution. The sceptre the Sabbath had since centuries borne and swayed so freely and so blissfully for those yielding implicit obedience to it, was from that time on no more wrested from it by unholy attempts of cruel rulers. They had, however, to contend yet with other adversaries, not materially aggressive, but none the less aiming with set purpose at the honor and validity of the Jewish Sabbath — I mean the pagan writers who treated the Jewish religious rites, among them the Sabbath, with haughty scorn and heartless derision; the Jewish Christians, making light of some traditional Sabbath injunctions; and further, the Gentile Christians, who attempted to detract more and more from the obligation of the Sabbath of the Decalogue, and enthrone in its stead another day, the first of the week. These points we will now discuss severally.

CHAPTER II.

PAGAN WRITERS ON THE JEWISH RELIGION AND THE SABBATH.

We have already before cited the utterances of Agatharchides and Plutarch on the Jewish Sabbath rest. We will now deal with the fabulous allegations and odious allusions which the bitterest libeler of the nationality and religion of the Jews ever produced in a Greek-speaking country, Apion, a grammarian and rhetor of Alexandria, attempted concerning it. He flourished at a period most unfortunate to the Jews of that city, the first half of the first century C. E. He was a native of the rural part of Egypt, yet pretended to Alexandrian-Greek birth and citizenship, and made it his prime object to work upon the "ancient and as it were innate enmity" of the Grecian inhabitants to their Jewish fellow-citizens (see Philo, Against Flaccus § 5), which was particularly aroused to a fierce degree about that period, and to scatter, with flattering prospect of universal credence, in his several writings the most scurrilous and fabulous invectives against them as to their national origin, their ancestors' departure from Egypt, and their various religious rites and customs. Following in the main those hostile authors who had before written with the same object and in the same strain, as Manetho (about B. C. 250), Molo (B. C. 90), Posidonius (B. C. 70), Cheremon (B. C. 50), Lysimachus (B. C. 30) and others, he yet added from his own mind some "very frigid and contemptible things" (Josephus, Against Apion, ii. 1). He made of the Jews original Egyptians, in order to dispute their claim to Greek citizenship, and to represent them before the vulgar as aliens in the city of Alexandria. Transcribing the older Jew-hating writers as to Israel's expulsion from Egypt, he put forth, on his own account, a most fictitious representation of their journey from there to Judea, with which he connects the malignantly absurd story of the origin of the name Sabbath. "When the Jews had traveled a six days' journey," he declares, "they had buboes in their groins." It was "on this account that they rested on the seventh day, as having got safely to that country which is now called Judea; they preserved the language of the Egyptians, and called that day the Sabbath, for that malady of buboes in their groin was named Sabbatosis by the Egyptians." Josephus undertook to write an apology of his co-religionists to controvert some of the most preposterous and at the same time grievous misrepresentations of Jews and Judaism made in previous works of Grecian writers, and particularly to confute a number of contemptuous slanders hurled against the Jews in his time by that literary mountebank, Apion. Josephus had no difficulty in dispelling his senseless insinuation regarding the Sabbath. "If Sabbo," he rejoins, "really meant that malady in the Egyptian language, it was yet so widely different from Sabbath, which is Hebrew and denotes "rest" (ib. ii. 2). But how many of the Asiatic and African Greeks or Romans of that century were inclined to hear and read a vindication of anything Jewish, and be disabused of erroneous notions on Judaism formed and fostered in their minds with obdurate partiality? Few, indeed, would be influenced by Jewish apologetical writings to give up their prejudices and ill-will nurtured against the Jews in those days. In Alexandria, where Jews had resided since centuries, enjoying guaranteed rights and privileges with the rest of the Greek citizens (ib. ii. 4), and occupying, in Philo's time, two, out of the five districts into which the city was divided (Against Flaccus, § 8), the heathen populace cherished a profound chagrin at that equality which entitled them to every public distinction and social prominence. Under Cæsar, whose fair treatment of the Jews of Alexandria stood embodied in a documentary grant publicly exhibited on a certain pillar of that city (Ag. Ap. l. c.), as also in the reigns of Augustus and Tiberius, who were firmly protecting its Jewish inhabitants against any injury, as well as strongly guarding the religious liberty of the Jews in the whole empire (Philo, Ag. Flacc. § 7, 10 ; Legatio § 8, 40 ; Josephus, Ant. xix. 5, 3), the Alexandrian populace could not vent their ill-will to the Jews by any palpable acts of violence. They could harbor deep prejudice against them, scorn and envy them at heart, but further they might not dare to go, knowing that a willing Cæsar was always prepared to chastise mutinous mobs. Things took a different turn, however, with the accession of that frantic monster, Caligula. Under this Herod-like emperor unspeakable mischief and indignities were visited on the Jews of Alexandria.

The governor, Flaccus, who had for five years, as long as Tiberius was on the throne, behaved himself tolerantly to the Jews, suddenly changed his policy when the empire came into the hands of that furious tyrant, Caligula. Riotous attacks upon the Jews were schemed by the Alexandrian mob — and they were not an inconsiderable portion of the population — and Flaccus conspired with them. They knew that the Jews could be provoked by no insult to a higher pitch than by idolatrous intrusions. So they concluded to erect images and statues, representing the reigning emperor, in the synagogues, "putting forth the name of the emperor as a screen" (Ag. Flacc. § 6).

This was surely a false pretense, for Caligula had then given no such orders. His deification and orders of erection of statues of himself in places of worship, were of a later date. But the Grecian mob knew well, that the Jewish heart was implacable against interference with their monotheistic belief, and that their abhorrence of image-worship was too intense to allow any trifling with it. To make sure that the peaceful Jews would be violently roused and thus get involved in a riotous disturbance, as well as to wound them most severely at the vital nerve of their spiritual existence, nothing could be designed as having so prompt an effect as an attempt at profaning their houses of worship with idols.[4] A synagogue in which idols were forced, was indeed held by the Jews equal to being destroyed. This is evident from various passages in Philo's "Flaccus" and "Legatio."

Flaccus was not satisfied with the defilement of the synagogues alone. He further issued an ordinance declaring the Jews as "foreigners and aliens," and gave also license to the heathens to exterminate them (Flacc. § 8). A furious onset by the mob ensued. Plunder, destruction of life and property, unnameable cruelties were perpetrated upon the helpless Jews of Alexandria. Fortunately for them, Agrippa I., the Jewish tetrarch bearing the title of King, had come there a second time during this year of persecution, and succeeded to bring about a cessation of the hostilities and to "rectify things." This, however, meant only a truce for awhile. For a new governor was sent there after the removal of Flaccus, in 38 C. E., whose fierce antagonism to the Jews did not much fall short of that of his predecessor. Moreover, his administration fell in with his master's order of deification of himself, in which the Jews could never acquiesce, so that they could not have expected a more lenient treatment from him, had he even individually been favorably disposed towards them. Caius Caligula, after dispensing cruel death to a friendly adviser, to his father-in-law, also to his cousin, and banishment to his sisters after blasting their honor (Suetonius, Caligula, § 24), aspired to be adored as a god. He commenced with presenting himself in the garb of demi-gods, such as Hercules, Castor and Pollux, Bacchus; then pretended to the dignity of such divinities as Mercury, Apollo, Mars (Philo, Leg. §§ 11, 13), till lastly he claimed to be Jupiter incarnate (ib. § 29), and had a temple erected to his own deity, in which he placed a golden statue of himself, dressed in the same vestments he would wear in person every day (Suetonius l. c. § 22).

What the Jews could expect under the rule of such a frenzied autocrat, was easy to predict. The mania of his godship possessed him so thoroughly, that no other consideration of policy or humanity could prevail against it. Suspecting the Jews, at the outset of his claim of divinity, as opposing it obstinately (Leg. §§ 16, 30),[5] he conceived a bitter hatred to them which, becoming soon known to the pagan Alexandrians (ib. §§ 18, 20), was improved by them to commit the most barbarous hostilities against their Jewish fellow-citizens. Alas! they were to be citizens no more, but held as "the very lowest of slaves" (ib. § 16). The infamous populace could now, without fear of punishment, turn their fury against them. And they did so. Philo has described their fearful suffering, the most grievous part of it, in his own eyes as well as in those of his co-religionists, was the dedication of the synagogues to the worship of Caius! To curry the favor of the emperor, they ostentatiously published, in their "journals" which he delighted so much to read, that they had transformed the synagogues to his temples (ib. § 25), whereby they had crushed the Jews to the dust, whom they knew to prefer death to such profanation of their synagogues.

The governor, whose name is not given, looked inactively on while the many atrocities were perpetrated upon the Jews, "allowing the mob to carry on the war against them without any restraint" (ib. § 20). It seems even that, inspired by the central authority of Rome, he was himself very active in oppressing the Jews with religious prohibitions. We learn from Philo ("On Dreams" § 18), that a certain governor had endeavored to change and abolish the Jewish laws and customs, and to this end began with forcing them to violate the Sabbath, "thinking that this measure would be the beginning of the departure from the whole ancestral Judaism." There is indeed no historical evidence that this governor was identical with the one under notice. But the language he used in his cruel mockery of the Jews, when he found them determined not to transgress the pivotal law of the Sabbath, savors much of the spirit then predominating at the imperial court. The governor, in his harangue to the Jews, gave himself out as a combination and concentration of all thinkable evils and dangers to life, before which the Sabbath should give way even to the pious Jews, as he thought it otherwise customarily yielded in such cases of extremity. Are we by it not reminded of Caligula's pretension to be himself the embodiment of law, against which no other human will or time-honored statute counted for anything? It was but natural, from the truism of 'like master, like servant,' that his subordinates should be congenial to him, and act with the same arrogance of power and a claim of irresponsibility, lesser in degree than the master's, only inasmuch as the governors had also, on their part, to conform to the emperor's one-man will.

The Alexandrian Jews sought again relief through the medium of Agrippa, who was a most intimate friend and favorite of Caligula. They addressed a petition to him, in which they extensively set forth their profound loyalty, as well as the violent treatment they had received from the governors and the populace. Soon after they determined to send an embassy of representative men to Rome to plead their cause before the emperor, or rather, as it would appear from the passage in Leg. § 29, that the delegates themselves could not forbear to be "involved in the lawlessness of which all the rest made themselves guilty" (by having, namely, in their midst synagogues profaned by images of a deified man), these offered their services of their own accord and voluntary resolution. One of them was the philosopher of world-wide fame, Philo, a brother to the alabarch or imperially authorized president of the Alexandrian Jewish community, Alexander, who had, without doubt for his stanch fidelity to God and refusing to own the Roman monster as deity, incurred his displeasure and was put in prison, from which he was not released till the accession of Claudius (Ant. xix. 5, 1). The ambassadors, five in number according to Philo—who certainly knew better than Josephus how many they were, the latter having perhaps drawn his relative information from a more distant pagan source, in which the delegation was stated as consisting of three men—set sail in midwinter of 38-39 C. E., embarking on their awful mission with resolute hearts, and doubly staking their lives, as they really did, in committing themselves to the doubtful mercy of the waves and the undoubted frenzy of an all-powerful ruler, for the vindication of their ancestral religion[6] and their cruelly insulted brethren.

The Alexandrian populace, too, had dispatched representatives to plead before the emperor in defence of their actions, and at the same time to denounce, with every possible calumniation, their Jewish fellow-residents. Josephus (ib. xviii. 8, 1) states their number also to have been three, and lets, moreover, the two delegations be chosen by agreement of the two parties at feud. This sounds, however, utterly incredible, when we consider the many violent acts and enormous indignities inflicted on the Jewish community by the hateful populace for at least two years, and consequently the implacable resentment the former must have felt towards their persecutors. Can it then, in view of the deepest animosity existing between the two parties, be imagined that they arranged a peaceable meeting, in which either of them should have proposed and agreed upon a submission of their quarrel to the imperial tribunal? And what point of dissension could it have been that was to be submitted? The civil rights of the Jews, disannulled by Caius' governors, and disputed by the envious and hateful populace? Surely the gravely insulted Jews would not have condescended and given them the satisfaction of being a party in a suit, in which they had not in the least any legitimate voice, and of co-operating towards settling a question and resolving a doubt that practically existed not, the Jewish rights being matter of governmental record, to interpret which not the pagan Alexandrians, but the imperial tribunal was the proper authority. Or should the Jews have suggested to their enemies a joint deputation, and acted so much against their own best interests, by giving the fanatical, rapacious and murderous populace yet a chance of extenuating, in the course of a controversial suit, their enormous crimes committed against them? No, indeed. We therefore presume as much more likely under the then circumstances, that no understanding at all was had between the Jews and pagans of Alexandria, but that the Jewish delegation was resolved on without the knowledge of the latter, for fear of forcible interference from them and, perhaps, the governor, whose power of forbidding their departure was unquestioned. By some prudent arrangements, we suppose, they escaped discovery, and succeeded to set out on their voyage unhindered. Their departure must however, we further suggest, soon have become known. This made the Alexandrian populace hastily move to send on also a delegation of their own, in order not to be overreached by the Jews.

Josephus states that the above-named libeler, Apion, was one of the heathen delegation, presenting him as a sort of spokesman of the opposition. Having no evidence to the contrary, we must not dispute the accuracy of this statement. We can, however, not help wondering, why, if Apion had really been such a prominent member of the heathen delegation, Philo has not once mentioned him as such. From Philo's report it would, further, appear as rather more likely that not Apion, but Isidorus, a most dangerous demagogue of Alexandria, was the main speaker of the opposition at the ambassadors' meeting with the emperor (see Leg. § 45). But what matter, who of the heathen Alexandrians present was the loudest and most forward in the denunciation of the Jews? It is sufficient to know that all of them were united as to the charge of disloyalty and disobedience to the emperor. This accusation had, under the circumstances, no need of even being formulated in speeches. Caligula's mind was already filled completely with this most aggravating supposition, before the embassy arrived at Rome. The information of Capito, a collector of imperial revenues in Judea, against the Jews, that they had torn down an altar erected at Jamnia to the worship of the god Caius (ib. § 30), and the hostile insinuations of such courtiers as Helicon and Apelles (see ib.), had sufficiently confirmed him in it. What this fresh set of maligners could accomplish, was merely adding some fuel to the already burning rage of the emperor at the refusal of the Jews to acquiesce in his pretension to be God.

His mind was withal, as we suppose, already at a previous and early period irritated against the Jews through the insidious work of that Alexandrian sycophant Helicon, who was "chamberlain and chief body-guard" to him, and who, as Philo further observes, "discharged all his Egyptian venom against the Jews," (ib.), "exciting and exasperating his master against them" (ib. § 28). Having risen from a slave to the dignity of influential courtier under Caligula, he used his influence extensively to instil his, in a manner, native ill-feeling and antagonism to the Jews into his susceptible spirit. His "satirical and quizzing observations mingled with his more formal and serious accusations" (ib. § 27), formed no doubt a most frequent subject of his conversation with the emperor, to whom he was a constant companion. He could, too, talk so largely to him about Jewish customs, from his early notice of them in his native city, Alexandria, where he had as instructors the "chattering part of the population" (ib. § 26)—those rhetorical and literary mountebanks of the type of Apion—that the master would easily look to him as an authority upon everything pertaining to Jews and their religion. We think not to judge amiss in attributing the failure of the Alexandrian Jewish delegation to vindicate their nation and national religion before the emperor, for the most part to this perfidious sycophant, who would systematically and assiduously undermine the ground of defence and apology, on which those earnest Jewish men could place themselves to support their cause.

CHAPTER III.

PAGAN WRITERS ON THE JEWISH RELIGION AND THE SABBATH.—CONTINUED.

That the Alexandrian and other Greek works in which notices of Jewish history and religious rites occur, had some influence on the Roman writers who also presented Jewish accounts in their various compositions, we are far from disputing, although it is demonstrable in Tacitus only. This "grave personage" had evidently read and made use of a number of those Grecian works. Instead, however, of consulting for a true historical purpose the universally accessible Greek version of the Bible, and also the works of Philo and Josephus that had long before his time of writing been published, he preferred, from his haughty contempt for the Jewish people, to draw his information from those heathen sources, however turbid[7] and incongruent with one another they were in regard to the description of the ancient historical events of the nation of Israel. He particularly copied, as we will later see, Lysimachus and Apion, Alexandrian authors whose names appeared already in our previous discussion.

But that the hatred to the Jews which was found among the generality of the pagans, and is also encountered in Roman literature, should originally have emanated from Egypt, that is, from the Alexandrian writings of Manetho, Cheremon, Lysimachus, Apion, and others, as Dr. Joel, "*Blicke in die Religionsgeschichte*," ii. p. 106; 116-19, suggests, we cannot accept as resting on any plausible grounds. Nor can we agree with him as to his conjoined proposition, that Greek authors, such as Posidonius and Apollonius Molo who also wrote on Jewish matters, had already "long (before Apion) thrown the Alexandrian fables, passed as Jewish history, on the Roman market, so that it need not be wondered at that, as once Cicero who, as an adherent of Pompey, had the Jews against himself, was edified by them, so later Tacitus propounded, on the strength of such authorities, his opinions on Jews and Judaism, opinions that are surely all but creditable to him."

As to the delight which Joel lets Cicero have felt over the reproductions, by Posidonius, Molo and others, of the Alexandrian stories about the Jews, we have to object, first, that there is to our knowledge no evidence at all adducible that either one of those writers had spread them in Rome. That Cicero had Molo,[8] the rhetorician, for his teacher, whose school at Rhodes, Greece, he attended even twice, is true. Yet it proves nothing as to the question of his acceptance of Jew-hating sentiments from him, a theory also advanced by Graetz (History of the Jews, iii. p. 171), who attributes Cicero's antagonism to Jews to the influence excited by that Greek mentor on this, his Roman pupil. Such conjecture is, however, too far-fetched. Hatred to Jews was a sentiment which required no cultivation at the hands of a teacher. Nor can it be supposed that it constituted a subject in the course of study at that particular school. Had we to assume that such was the case, we would consistently have to expect to meet with the same aversion to Jews in Cæsar's documents and acts recorded in historical works, for he, too, studied under that Greek master. But we know to the contrary, that he had shown a constant favorable disposition to the Jews. Secondly and mainly we object, that it is altogether insupportable to account for Cicero's position towards the Jews by Grecian influence. Let us now inquire whether such influence is discernible anywhere in his extant writings.

The frothy pun which he flung out in his Oration as prosecutor of Verres,—a man who, as senatorial governor of Sicily, was to its inhabitants what Florus, in the subsequent century, proved himself as imperial procurator of Judea, namely, a villainous grinder of the people and defrauder of their substance and privileges,—" What has a Jew to do with pork?" will surely not be held out as a reasonable indication of his settled antagonism to the Jews.

Nor can we discern in his Oration for Flaccus who had been charged with various acts of official malpractice while he was governor of Asia Minor, one of the charges having been the confiscation of the annual contributions of the Jews of that province to the temple of Jerusalem, any acquaintance with Alexandrian or other Grecian Jew-hating literature at all.

In the defence of his client before the court at Rome, Cicero had to deal with three sets of charges brought against Flaccus by Laelius who, having contracted a deep grudge against him and being besides, as it is intimated in the oration itself, probably abetted by Pompey, had at great expense procured Asiatic witnesses to testify against the accused, acting at the same time as his prosecutor. The charges were, first, those of Greek witnesses from Phrygia and Mysia; secondly, those of Jewish witnesses, probably from those cities in which Flaccus had seized the Jewish sacred money, as Apamea, Laodicea, Adramyttium and Pergamus, or, if none such had come to Rome from their native places (Cicero does indeed not mention any Asiatic Jews as present at the court), of Roman Jewish representatives who voluntarily and out of sympathy undertook to plead the cause of their Asiatic brethren, or, possibly, of Laelius himself, who may have individually assumed to act as champion of the grievance of those Jews and to prefer their charges as their witness; and lastly, of Roman citizens who had brought complaints against him.

At the outset we may state, that the assault which Cicero made upon the Jews in his oration, does by far not equal in vehemence and acrimony his contemptuous arraignment of pagan Greeks in the same address. This point is too important to be left out of consideration in the question before us. We will refer to it again later, in treating of Juvenal's remarks on Jewish customs. Compared with the striking reproaches which Cicero in his oration threw on the Greeks of Asia in general, the contumelious sallies against the Jews must be pronounced mild, indeed. The butt of his attack on the Jews was their religion, and in particular that religious custom on which the charged dereliction of his client turned — the contribution of sacred money to the Temple treasury — rather than they themselves as a nation, whom he would accuse of nothing else than of enmity to his country,[9] and this, on account of their armed resistance to Pompey's forces, and by it to the Roman supremacy, and of lack of patriotism towards Rome, because they were " at times unruly in the assemblies in defence of the interests of the republic." Not a word of disparagement of their general or individual character did he put forth, however, unless we account his charge of their want of patriotic attachment for Rome, for which he indeed proposes that " it would be wisdom to despise them," as such. But we would venture the assertion, that not even in the innermost mind of Cicero the case of the Jews in conquered provinces and anywhere in the Roman empire, where they were not treated as equal citizens, could fall under the category of a real moral delinquency. An unpatriotic position could be reprehensible only in those cases where people had been granted the complete benefits of Roman citizenship.

How different, however, was his language regarding the Greeks! He not only denounced their witnesses present at the trial, but their entire race in Asia, as worthless, because faithless, creatures. Not only did he declare them enemies of Rome in much stronger terms than the Jews, saying about them, that they " abominate the sight of our faces and detest our name," and that " it was their power and not their inclination that was unequal to the destruction of the republic." He even branded them unreservedly, in equivalent words, as a nation of liars and perjurers (see Oration §§ 4, 5, 15).

Again, while he has no hesitancy in loudly stigmatizing the whole class of the Asiatic Greeks to which the witnesses belonged, as faithless and having no regard to truth, he finds himself, by the " great unanimity " of the Jews as a body, and the " weight they carry in the popular assemblies," constrained to utter his opprobrious invective against them " in a low voice, just so as to let the judges hear him," afraid of their becoming "excited against himself and against every eminent man," if those of their race who attended at the trial should hear his reproachful declamations about them.

This is assuredly a tacit admission, on the part of Cicero, that the Jews, though now subdued by the Romans, were yet to be feared for their compact moral force, by which they could easily be incited to resent unremittingly any offence aimed at their name and religion. Is this admission, we ask, not really a commendation of the Jewish character, although we own that Cicero was far from intending it as such?

But, aside from this point of view, it will have to be admitted by every reader of the Oration, that the Jews stand out therein, in his whole argument, in prominent favorable relief against the Greeks, in so far, at least, that he had seriously to recognize and notice them as solid factors, whereas he would not accord even this much to the despised Greek nation, in denouncing which he used no caution or guarded evasion whatever, paying not the least regard to the sentiments of its people, might they be ever so severely outraged by his speech.

This comparative prominence is further evident from the fact, that he degraded the Asiatic Greeks, toward the end of his argument against their witnesses, by holding out in scathing illustrations their several inferiority, by which he wished to urge implicitly upon the judges, that they were altogether too insignificant to deserve even a transitory attention by the judges in the suit they had brought. No such sort of vilifying reflection upon the Jews, as to their social and human merits in general, was attempted by him, however. He declares them, indeed, forsaken by the "immortal gods," in that they were then subjugated to the Roman power. But this he did only, as is obvious from the context, to demonstrate to the judges, that the Jewish religious customs need not be respected by the all-powerful Rome. The truth of the Roman worship was to him proved by the long series of eminent successes with which his country was crowned. Its guardian gods were consequently the only true ones. The Jewish religion, he wished to insinuate on the other hand, could by no means be true, or the Jews must have succeeded to so propitiate their Deity, that they would be spared the defeat which they had, as it was then fresh in the memory of the Romans, actually suffered.

Having thus far, by the parallel of Cicero's position towards the Greeks and Jews in his oration, seen that the latter fared incomparably better at his hands than the former, we will now investigate the real nature of the invectives he launched out against them, to ascertain whether there is truly any influence of Grecian anti-Jewish literature discoverable in it. Is it perhaps, we ask, to be found in the circumstance that he denounced their annual gifts of sacred money (Shekel tribute) as a "barbarous superstition?" There is in fact nothing foreign noticeable in it. The sharp antagonism to the exportation of that money was genuinely Roman. This custom of the Jews was, for fiscal and economical reasons alone, obnoxious to the Roman magistrates. The Senate had, so Cicero at least brings forward in the same oration, already before his consulship, and afterwards again while he was consul, prohibited it. Relying, perhaps, on the Roman intolerance against that Jewish custom, the spiteful and fanatical Greeks of the eastern provinces had later, under Augustus, repeatedly prevented the exportation of that money to the holy city. It happened then that the money—designated, by the way, 'first fruit,' in judicial Roman decrees; see Ant. xvi. 6, 7, and Philo, Leg. §40—was, on or after having been collected in various cities of Asia Minor and Libya, either directly stolen from the Jews, or confiscated under pretense of taxes, which the Jews had practically not owed (Ant. ib. 4, 5). Augustus, from his fair and generous mind, sent decrees to all the Roman provinces, that no magistrate should permit any impediment being laid in the way of the Jews either assembling together (which assemblies were always eyed with suspicion by Roman authorities; cp. Philo ib. §40) to make arrangements for forwarding the sacred contributions to Jerusalem, or actually conveying it thither (cp. Ant. ib. 6 with Philo l. c.). Marcus Agrippa, the general and son-in-law of Augustus, declared in a separate order, doubtless consequently upon the emperor's own strict injunction, the violent dispossession of the Jews of their sacred money as sacrilege and punishable as such a crime (Ant. ib. 4).

Cicero was indeed not so fair-minded as to tolerantly appreciate that pious custom, anxiously cherished by the Jews of the dispersion. Nay, he was bigoted enough to stigmatize it before the board of judges as "a barbarous superstition that it were an act of dignity to resist." He surely evinced a large degree of malicious prejudice in this denunciation. Yet we have to bear in mind, that his speech was that of a barrister, and not of a judicial functionary. He was in need of points of argument in favor of his client, and in the predicament of a want of personal accusations or insinuations to be used against his antagonists, he would resort to vituperating generalities, such as the religion confessed by the entire class to which the plaintiffs at court belonged. That even from this view his abusive language was, judged by our modern principle of religious tolerance, a cruel trespass against the freedom and peace of conscience of a large class of people under the Roman dominion, and to be condemned in the bitterest terms of indignation, no one is readier than we to admit. But not only must we not put a modern critical estimate on intolerant utterances of persons of remote barbarous ages, the language of a barrister calls even at all times for its own peculiar estimate, and can never be quoted as a reliable standard of the thought and sentiment of his contemporary fellow-citizens, nor even of his own mind and disposition as man, independently of the practice of his profession. Thus we must not judge too harshly of Cicero's invective in question. The less so when we consider, that the mode employed by him is not eschewed entirely in our own day, even in civilized, Christian countries. Lawyers still usurp the privilege of assailing and derogating an opponent at court in any possible manner. If they cannot arraign his personal character, they are, if not restrained by a genuine spirit of tolerance and its ascendency over the role they assume at court, apt to perpetrate the nuisance of holding out his racial descent or religious communion to a reproach, which bigotry and prejudice have always ready to hand. That such a course is most reprehensible, will be conceded by all fair-minded people. Yet it still exists, and often passes uncensured by our tribunals.

As to Cicero's branding that Jewish religious custom a "barbarous superstition," we have to remark, further, that he was not the only Roman employing the last-named epithet at least, when speaking of the religious usages of the Jews. Almost every known Roman writer speaks thus disdainfully of them. It was even peculiar to the bigoted Roman, to stigmatize every foreign worship, not the Jewish alone, as a worthless superstition.[10] No matter how lofty in its fundamental conceptions of the Divine such worship might be, it had to be condemned as unworthy and treated with contempt, because it was in opposition to his own venerated "immortal gods."

The exorbitant pride and conceitful patriotism of the high-born Roman bigot were the chief motives for the haughty scorn, not unfrequently mingled with jealousy[11] as well, which he held constantly in store for all non-Roman forms and modes of worship. From this point of view the monstrosity of Cicero's attack on the Jewish religion certainly loses the offensive force of peculiarity. Nay, the following circumstance may even have the virtue of somewhat mitigating it. In speaking of the religion of the Jews we find the term "superstition" used by Romans of even avowed friendly disposition to them, and that in such connections, in which it cannot possibly be supposed to have been inspired by an invidious or slanderous mood of mind. It practically occurs in decrees issued in their favor; see those published in behalf of the Asiatic Jews under Cæsar's government, in the ethnarchy of Hyrcanus II, in which freedom from military service is awarded them for their objection of having to violate in it the laws of the Sabbath and festivals, also the food restraints, which observances are therein denoted as the "superstition the Jews are under" (Ant. xiv, 10, 13, 14, 16).

Consistently with such Roman habit of expression, the annual contributions of the Jews to the Temple treasury might have been termed a superstition, without necessarily implying a derogatory intent and giving offence to a Jewish hearer. As positive we can only assume that Cicero's adding, in his oration, the adjective "barbarous," and withal his railing at the Jewish religion and nation, must have trenchantly affected the sensibilities of the Jewish people then present at the court.

Be all this as it may, this much will be admitted generally as beyond any doubt, that Cicero's entire assault on the Jews in that oration shows not the slightest vestige of an influence of extraneous literature, such as the Alexandrian, or that of Apollonius Molo, his teacher, on his mind as to his estimation of the institutions of the Jewish people. There is positively nothing in it that could not be accounted for by his mere Roman position, virtually independent of any Jew-hating remarks made in writings or verbal aspersions of any Grecian literator.

As to Tacitus whom Dr. Joel also points out as having drawn his anti-Judaic sentiments from Grecian sources, we admit that he, at once the most circumstantial and venomous Roman writer on Jewish subjects, had indeed got his information about the history of the Jews, that is, their origin and the cause of their exodus from Egypt, from a medley of Alexandrian Greek accounts. But does this circumstance indicate in the least, that his prejudice against the Jews was aroused and inspired by them? Should we not assume rather, that, as a bigoted and conceited Roman, he had cherished a deep contempt for the Jews, before he ever read any of those works, and that it was just this previous antagonism to them that made him look to that pagan literature for information as to their ancient history, when "about to relate the catastrophe of that celebrated city?" (Hist. v. 2.) This Grecian literature with its Jew-detesting fables must indeed have been found most convenient to him, for it completely accorded with his own *animus* regarding the Jews.

The story of their violent expulsion from Egypt he adopted from "very many authors," who "agree" that it happened under the king Bocchoris, when "a pestilential disease had spread over Egypt." Those authors were not only Lysimachus (see Ewald, Hist. of Israel, in Joel 1. c. p. 116), but must have been, since Josephus credits only the latter with fixing the period of the expulsion at the reign of said king (Ag. Ap. ii. 2), other Grecian writers besides him—unless it be that Tacitus scrupled not to give out Lysimachus' individual opinion as that of "very many authors." This is indeed not unlikely, considering that, much as his own report in Hist. v. 3, resembles in the outlines the description which Josephus produces as that of Lysimachus, he practically deviates from him in about the same proportion in some points, as he is found to agree with him in others. It might accordingly be that he followed Lysimachus in general, but garbled his accounts to suit his own temper and whim, when he was about to improve them in his Histories.

His perusal of Apion's writings is also traceable therein. The literary calumnies about the Jewish people of that Egyptian writer were spread broadcast in the latter part of the first century, C. E. Tacitus rehearses the grotesque fable reiterated by Apion from the works of Posidonius and Apollonius Molo (see Ag. Ap. ii. 7), that the figure of an ass was consecrated in the sanctuary of the Jewish temple (Hist. v. 5), although he declares in the subsequent chapter according to the truth, that they "allow no images whatever in their cities, not to say in their temples," and exhibits later, in ch. ix., the "generally known fact" that, since Pompey had on his entrance in the Jewish temple found no effigy of a god in it, it was in all its apartments empty of any such material representation of a deity.

His use of Apion's compositions may, further, be inferred from his notice, that "they do not bestow this adulation (of setting up or venerating their likenesses) to kings, nor this honor to the Cæsars," which sounds much like a censure. He may have come by it through the correlative note of that Egyptian libeler who, as Josephus reports, (Ag. Ap. ii. 6), had charged the Jews with criminal disloyalty for not erecting images to the emperors.

He had also apparently copied from Apion the story of a six days' journey of the Jews (from the Arabian desert), at the end of which they landed in the country "now called Judea." He based like him, in the subsequent chapter, the origin of the Sabbath on the termination of that journey and "the rest from their toils," not reproducing, however, that furious calumniator's etymological feat of the Sabbath being named after the malady in their groins—Sabbatosis in Egyptian. He would not decide upon and directly adopt that derivation, either. Indecision was, on the whole, a prominent mark of his historical excellence. He prefers many a time to enumerate various opinions on a certain question, and then to let the reader trouble himself about the one meriting choice out of the rest. This mode can be tracked through his entire range of histories. As to the Sabbath he narrates side by side with the above derivation the views of others, that, namely, the seventh day received its distinction by the Jews from the honor they paid to Saturn, or the venerated number seven by which "most of the heavenly bodies complete their effects and course" (Hist. v. 3, 4; cp. Ag. Ap. ii. 2).

There may be possibly, we suggest, some more parallels to be discovered between both those writers as to subjects of Jewish religious or historical import. And lastly, Tacitus may, we admit in the premises, have read every line of literature composed by Grecian writers on and against Jews that was extant in his time. But, we have to ask, does all this indicate in the remotest way, that he learned from those authors contempt for Jews and Judaism, as Dr. Joel advances? This contempt was, as we expect to demonstrate convincingly to every reader in the sequel, as much a home-growth at Rome, as it was in Alexandria, and had no need of being "imported into that city from abroad," viz., from Alexandria, as that learned author insists.

History shows variously that the antagonism to the Jewish people in pagan countries was not alone domesticated in the latter city, but also in other large centres of Greek-speaking countries, such as Antioch, Syria, Cæsarea, Palestine, different cities of Asia Minor, etc. All that can be imputed to the influence exerted by the Alexandrian pagan writers of Apion's ilk with regard to the Jews is, that they have more or less contributed towards widening the chasm between Jewish and Gentile populations in cities of the Roman empire having such mixture of inhabitants. The calumnies they embodied in their works, may have found their way into the minds of many heathens, and made of them still fiercer opponents of the Jews than they were before. Their story of the expulsion of the ancient Israelites from Egypt on account of leprosy, may in particular have been spread broadcast, and seized upon with keen relish by the Grecian barbarians. 'This can be deduced from the instance mentioned by Josephus, Wars ii. 14, 5. Yet, we contend, the real and original causes of pagan hatred and contempt for Jews are not to be sought in contagious transplantation. Such view is too narrow, and, in fact, as we will presently begin to prove, thoroughly erroneous.

We are able to account for the pagan aversion to the Jews, first, by the peculiarity of their religious usages and their diverse worship ; secondly, their separateness, caused for the most part by that diversity ; thirdly, their unconcealed disdain for pagan polytheism ; and fourthly, their attempts at propogating their religion and making converts of polytheists and idolaters. An acrid envy at Jewish success and prosperity — and "envy soon curdles into hate " (Froude) — is moreover in all cases to be presupposed as a ground-sentiment among the generality of pagans. And it may, lastly, be noted that such Roman writers of the empire as Juvenal and Tacitus, who flourished after the bloody Jewish revolutionary war, and partly witnessed yet the insurrections under Trajan and Hadrian, must, from their intense proud patriotism, have bitterly resented the ever challenging attempts of the pertinacious small Jewish nation, attempts that repeatedly compelled the Romans to expend endless sums and spend enormous forces, that they might retain hold of it. The rancorous indignation at the continuous troubles, and serious and heavy losses that the Romans had to suffer from the Jews, may have been not the least of the elements of the virulent hate that made up the general sentiment and disposition of those men against them. If the reader will patiently follow us as we will produce the relative illustrations, he will, we hope, be convinced of the correctness of our view and, on the other hand, also of the eccentricity of having to look to Alexandria as the hot-bed of all pagan Jew-hating. He will with us attribute such deplorable excrescence, whether existing in Alexandria or Rome, to the causes just noted, either combinedly or severally, as the case might at each juncture have been.

From Haman to Tacitus the diversity of the Jewish religious Law had formed a most serious object of pagan vexation. Joel had evidently judged too rashly in assigning to it only a "semblance of foundation," by which the aversion nourished by the heathen against the Jewish people might be explained ('Blicke,' etc., ii. p. 107). Haman's famous charge was re-echoed by Tacitus who states (Hist. v. 4): "In order to bind the people to him for the time to come, Moses prescribed to them a new form of worship, and (one) opposed to those of all the world beside. Whatever is held sacred by the Romans, with the Jews is profane ; and what in other nations is unlawful and impure, with them is permitted." We cannot afford to enlarge here on the malicious falsehood of the latter assertion, by which he outmatched even the rancorous Haman of old. As to the former, we have no doubt that it was the malevolent expression of a sentiment of chagrin harbored by thousands of pagans of his and other times before and after him. Those "new rites, contrary to all other mortals," annoyed them pungently to the core. They stood forth in continuous and conspicuous opposition to their polytheism, and impressed themselves, on the intelligent of them at least, as an abashing testimony of their own inferior worship and rites. That they were constantly chafed by it, may be gathered from Josephus' rejoinder to Apion (i. 25), in which he states as one of the causes of the reproaches which the Egyptians cast upon the Jews, "the difference of our religion from theirs, etc." It is surely not a vague supposition of the historian that a hostile sentiment against the Jews grew upon the thinking Egyptians, when they contrasted their own inferior animal worship with the imageless worship of those who would think themselves superior by allowing no material representations of the Divine. They may never have owned their feeling of shame, as little as the learned Roman would own his, on comparing his national polytheism with the purely spiritual Jewish Monotheism; but it existed nevertheless in their heart of hearts, pricking them constantly and exciting a sharp odium against the confessors of Judaism. The haughty disdain which the one or the other of them vented against the Jewish religion and rites from the tower of their pantheon was, we believe, never entirely unmixed with a certain degree of that feeling, overshadowed though it was by the irrepressible national egotism, and sense of superiority over all the rest of mankind, almost physically peculiar to the Roman patrician. The same sentiments may properly be assumed to have prevailed to a large degree with all other heathens of antiquity.

The diversity of the religion of the Jews which scandalized them so thoroughly, was as a rule accompanied by the two other moments mentioned above, viz., their separation and open disdain of polytheism, which combination must have vexed them the more strongly, and confirmed the more enduringly the breach and alienation between the two classes.

As to the Jewish separateness, Tacitus has given vent to his intense annoyance over it, specially their being "separate as to meats and marriage with others" (Hist. v. 5), which he, as it would appear from the context with the preceding sentence, "but against all others they have a hostile ill-will," attributed in his mind to a mere national and social aversion to other nations, not being capable, or, at any rate, disposed, like many modern decriers of the Jewish clannishness so-called, to account for it by merely religious and ethical causes. Even the initiatory rite of the Jews he would not explain in a purely religious bearing, asserting of it that "it was instituted by them, that they might be known by this distinctive mark" (ib). The trend of this insinuation logically agrees with his previous accusation, that the Jews have a "hostile ill-will against all others."

The same nationally antagonistic separateness Juvenal imputes to the Jews, or rather the fully Judaized children of proselytes from polytheism, when he says (Sat. xiv. 103-4): "They show the way to none who does not observe the same religious rites with them; and they lead to the sought-for fountain only the circumcised." In about the same strain the before-mentioned Lysimachus had charged the Jews. He imputed to Moses that he urged the Israelites "to have no kind regards for any man, nor give good counsel to any, but always to advise them for the worst" (Ag. Ap. i. 34). As to Juvenal's strictures it may be observed here in passing, that they were not so much directly aimed at Jews and Judaizers, as at Roman parents as such, against whom he inveighs in that satire for the evil examples they were, as he claims, setting to their children. As a specimen of them he produces, among others, that Judaizing peculiarity. Moreover, it must be owned, as we will more explicitly notice hereafter, that he was by far no such virulent hater of the Jews as Tacitus.

From the times of those pagan writers to the modern era in which a Goldwin Smith and his congenial brethren in prejudice and malice flourish, an immense line of accusers of the Jews of a hostilly exclusive disposition towards Gentiles has thriven, all of them blinded by the obdurate prepossession, or at all events working on the pretext, that the Jewish separation as to eating and connubial observances was due to an hereditary and invidiously cherished antipathy to all other people not belonging to the Jewish race or religious community. The distance of nearly eighteen hundred years between the life of

Tacitus and Goldwin Smith has not essentially altered that main accusation. The last-named celebrity, in an article published a decade ago, basing on the refusal of the Jews to intermarry with the Gentile English people his assumption that they cannot be real patriots, argues as follows: "Nothing is more destructive of those relations with the rest of the community on which patriotism depends, than the refusal of intermarriage." And he charges them with being a "jealously separate race * * * refusing to mingle with humanity, and drawing on themselves the hatred of the nations." He has proved himself in perfect accord with old Tacitus, differing from him only in this respect that the latter, not having before him a bloodstained volume of records of Gentile persecutions of the Jews, such as the seventeen hundred years subsequent to his lifetime exhibit, did not feel himself called upon to deal with the problem, how the Jews "drew on themselves the hatred of the nations" so much, as to note the "hostile ill-will (he imagined) the Jews bore to all others."

For our present purpose we suggest in this connection that, as little as Dr. Joel would be inclined to pronounce Goldwin Smith's Jew-hating erudition as derived from Alexandrian sources, so little must Tacitus be supposed to have drawn his antagonism to Jews from them. There is indeed no conceivable warrant for such a supposition. The Gentiles, everywhere on the globe, whether in the east or west, have ever taken offence at the Jewish separation, mainly evinced by their refusal of participating in their meals or intermarrying with them. They accounted for it by a national or personal aversion, believing or at least representing it as inherent in the minds, and continuously fostered through the optional and intentional practice of the Jews. That religious and ethical motives were the real cause of that separatism, to which came considerations of ceremonial purity, impeding and forbidding the mutual intercourse of both classes more or less seriously, according to the greater or lesser rigor with which those considerations were popularly heeded in the various periods of Jewish history, they could or would not accept and realize.

A third concurrent element in the growth of pagan hatred to Jews, equally in Rome and Alexandria, and one of decided moment, although modern Jewish writers as a rule take no note of it, was their implacable and irrepressible abhorrence of the pagan polytheism and idolatry. Tacitus was truly correct in stating (Hist. v. 5), that those Gentiles who embrace the Jewish religion (as genuine converts) are early impressed with nothing sooner than to "contemn the gods etc." The first thing inculcated on the mind of the pagan applicant for reception into Judaism, was indeed invariably, and in all countries, the abandonment of polytheistic worship and total abstraction of the mind from such worship. This was the absolute, indispensable condition, under which any one heathen could ever expect to be permitted to enter the fold of Judaism. The negation of polytheism and idolatry was, too, valued so highly, that Rabbinism raised it, rather hyperbolically, it is true, to a state of positive, practical profession of Judaism. See B. Megillah f. 13 : "He who rejects false worship is called a Jew." Compare also Sifre, Numb. § 111: "He who denies idolatry, owns (implicitly) the (obligation of the) entire Torah," or, as this frequently employed sentence is construed in B. Nedarim f. 25: "One who denies idolatry, is accounted a practical observer of all the laws of the Torah." Monotheism being the foundation-principle of Judaism, a proselyte had indeed, as Tacitus alleges, to be taught first to contemn the gods of heathenism. The unparalleled jealousy of the Jews for their pure monotheistic creed had, moreover, raised that contempt to a fierce, horror-like sentiment, of which they made no secret, wherever in the Graeco-Roman world they witnessed the practical folly of idolatry. At times it would even develop into a polemical position, and this in particular, when they were provoked by hostile treatment at the hands of their polytheistic neighbors. This is not only reasonably to be supposed, but can be deduced from the following report of Josephus (Ant. xix. 5, 3). The emperor Claudius issued an edict to all the cities of the empire, enjoining the pagan populations to respect the Jewish rights and privileges, that is, not to "hinder" them in the observance of their "hereditary (religious) customs," adding advisedly: "And I do charge them (the Jews) also to use this my kindness rather modestly, and not to show a contempt of the religious rites (deisidaimonias) of the other nations, but to keep their own laws" (without, namely, at the same time disparaging the worship of others). The like allusion seems to have been intended by the same emperor in his special order for the city of Alexandria (ib. 2), that both parties, the Jews and Gentiles, should "employ the greatest care that no dissension should arise (between one another) after the promulgation of this edict."

Are we not entitled to discover in this circumstance an example, that the Jews were not always merely apologetic as to their own creed, but now and then also aggressive against the dignity of heathen divinities and religious usages? We admit that this state of aggressiveness was, as a rule, brought on by the frequent outrages perpetrated by the rancorous Grecians on the Jews and the enormous scorn constantly exhibited towards them in society. They would through such insulting treatment be embittered to such a degree, that they could not, even in the intervals of comparative peace, suppress their wounded feelings and irritated temper on those occasions, offering them a chance to retaliate on their oppressors by some scornful strictures on the extravagant folly and fallacy of their worship or impurity of their lives. Had they been ordinarily and constantly treated with indulgence by their pagan fellow-countrymen, they would possibly never have uttered a reviling word on their belief and rites. Yet this much is at least shown by the aforesaid imperial act, that the Jews living in various cities of numerous Syro-Grecian populations were then, as they were doubtless before and afterwards, not always suffering from pagan assaults and insults, but occasionally maintaining even an offensive attitude towards their worship. Comp. Hausrath, 'N. T. Times,' i. 178, who likewise maintains, from respective passages of the Apocrypha, that the Jews really derided polytheism, and that therefore Pliny's (Hist. Nat. xiii.), judgment on the

Jews as being a "nation noted for their insults to the gods," had a foundation in fact. Let us observe here in passing, that in Pliny we find another illustration of the blind hatred of the greatest Roman intellects to the Jews, a hatred that made them commit the grossest inconsistency, rather than concede to them the credit of a pure and commendable worship. Pliny himself derided the gods of the popular mythology as childish fables. He was a radical pantheist, and one not of the moderate Stoic type, for he would not think of spiritualizing the popular divinities, nor could he decide whether the belief in Providence was profitable to mankind. Nature was his god; see on his system, Friedlaender, Darstell. aus der Sittengesch. Roms, iii. 483 sq. Yet the Jews had to be held out to scorn for their contempt of the numberless gods of heathendom. He himself had declared it as a mark of human weakness to inquire after the form of the Deity — if there were any. But the Jewish rejection and detestation of idols was an insult to the gods!

The same has to be remarked on Juvenal, his contemporary. In his thirteenth satire he mocks at the immense crowd of the then national deities, and speaks of them in a manner which certainly must have shocked the religious Roman readers and appeared to them as the most blasphemous assault. Yet he had nevertheless no word of recognition for the imageless worship of the one invisible God of the Jews, and of appreciation of their religious customs. We have, on the other hand, to bear in mind that even he could not rid himself of the native Roman attachment for the immortal gods, and would not only not disadvise others from sacrificing to the divinities (see Sat. 354, '55), but once himself brought an offering to Ceres Helvina (Friedlaender, l. c. p. 490).

We may gather our supposition, further, from Rabbinical sources. Idol and polytheistic worship are by Rabbis of the first and second centuries C. E., arraigned sarcastically in disputations with cultured pagans as well in Rome as in Palestine (see B. Adodah Zarah, f. 44, 55, *et* alias; comp. also with that passage of f. 55, the identical argumentation used in the monotheistic or monarchic Jewish Christian production, the Clementine Homilies, ix. 6, by Peter, in his alleged address at Tripolis).

It seems, furthermore, to have been a settled rule among the Jews, that meats and drinks sacrificially consecrated to idols, were to be regarded not only as prohibited for use, but as ceremonially defiling as a corpse (see B. Ab. Zar. f. 30, et passim).

This Jewish horror for things sacrificed to idols passed even, we may observe here in passing, over to the Jewish Christian church. Not only do the Clementine Homilies contain a solemn interdiction of sacrificial meat of the pagans to the Gentile Christians (vii. 4, 8), which is denounced as such an abomination that it is by comparison designated "the repast of demons" (ib. 8). But the Apostolic decrees, attributed to the council of the Jewish Christian church of Jerusalem, enjoin the same abstinence on Gentile converts to Christianity (Acts. xv). Whatever may be declared against the authenticity of this narrative of Acts (see Baur, 'Paul the Apostle,' and the author of 'Supernatural Religion'), so much is at least indisputable, that those decrees reflect the Jewish Christian sentiment and determination, which these sectaries had carried over into their new affiliations. They continued to feel the same implacable horror for all things offered to idols, as they felt before they severed their connection with orthodox Judaism, and would consequently insist on those who turned to their creed from heathendom, to abstain from them likewise. It was Paul alone who would declare idol-meat an indifferent thing to those Christian believers who had "knowledge" (1 Cor. viii).

That the decided, open contempt with which alike Jews and Jewish Christians treated the idolatrous practices, feasts, and consecrated meats and drinks which they noticed among pagan worshipers, will not infrequently have led to contentious scenes, cannot be doubted. Jewish scrupulosity had, moreover, not only denounced wine really consecrated to idols as unlawful for use, but prohibited all the wine made by pagans (Mishnah Abod. Zar. ii. 3). And at a certain epoch of the first century C. E. (not during the Jewish revolutionary war though, between 65-70, as Graetz, 'Hist. etc.' iii. 575, suggests, for already in the time of Josephus' administration of Galilee the objection to the use of oil made by heathens had passed as a fixed rule, and could therefore not have been recently introduced) an interdict was put on the purchase of bread and oil from pagans.

These and the like authoritative Jewish restrictions necessarily implied to the heathen people who could not help taking note of it, the imputation to them of an abhorrible religious debasement and a deterring impurity of life by the Jewish people.

In general, it was everywhere in the Graeco-Roman world known, that the Jews despised their polytheistic worship and rites. This necessarily created and kept up a stinging grudge against the professors of Judaism. It was, as we may here add, partly from this grudge that the heathen Syro-Grecians contested the claims of the Jews to live together and enjoy equal rights with them.

Such a small number of dissenters — as they would hold the Israelites — should presume to scorn the established, almost universal worship of the gods, and set themselves with their own against the powerful nations of the earth! This was too much for them to bear without bitter resentment. They would at times object that, if the Jews wanted to enjoy equal privileges with them, they should also adopt the same worship with them ; see Ant. xii. 3, 2 ; Ag. Ap. ii. 6. The same compatriots, so they argued alike in Grecian countries and in Rome, should have the same national religion in common, which was polytheism. That the Jews would not only not recognize the national divinities and participate in the solemn rites performed in their honor, but despise the latter as irrational and reject the former as non-entities, could not but grievously offend and provoke the heathen mind (comp. Tacitus' and Pliny's reproaches mentioned before).

Lastly, we have to mention as one of the chief causes of pagan contempt for Jews, their proselytizing efforts and successes, which vexed the Roman men of letters as well as some of the bigoted emperors of the first century C. E., to an intolerable degree. The Jewish religion had at that period made stupendous headway and very marked inroads upon paganism everywhere in the Roman empire. No importation of Alexandrian literary vituperations was therefore needed, as Dr. Joel opines, to incense Roman literators against the Jews. The immense proportions Jewish propagandism had assumed, were alone sufficient to make a bigoted Tacitus pour out all his gall, or the satirists vent all their spleen, on the Jewish people. Not only was their national pride sorely offended at noticing their country deities, with their many peculiar services, festivals and ceremonies neglected, and many of their countrymen devoted to a religion so utterly antagonistic to their polytheism, and which was professed by a people held in all respects so much inferior to the Roman, and subdued under their rule. But the Jewish religion being conceived as a *law* demanding of its votaries a mode and conduct of life so different to the Roman in many essential points, they found in it a standard of civil life radically conflicting with their own, and menacing by its spread the predominance of their own *law*, which they believed should alone govern as far as the imperial dominion reached. This filled the pure-blooded, proud Roman with a sort of pious horror.

To substantiate our assertion, we will produce the respective utterances of Tacitus, Juvenal and Seneca. Tacitus, after reviewing some of the "new rites" of the Jews "contrary to the rest of the mortals," together with his interpretation of their origin and import, and setting forth their distinctiveness as to meals, marriage and circumcision, says: "Those gone over to their religion adopt the same custom (of circumcision), and they are early impressed with nothing sooner than to contemn the gods, to cast off their (allegiance to their) country, and to despise their children and brothers" (Hist. v. 5). It is evident from this description that he had seen and heard of many good Romans attached to Judaism in preference to the time-honored worship of the guardian gods, even to such an extent that they would undergo the painful rite of initiation in its faith. Not the downfall of the Jewish State, nor the temporal and social degradation of the Jewish people ensuing from it, had refrained those converts from entering the pale of the politically annihilated nation. This roused his ire to the utmost pitch. He inwardly chafed at a phenomenon so astounding, and at the same time so humiliating to the national religion of his country. Conversion to Judaism was to him a total aversion from Romanism, in its comprehensive politico-religious sense.

Juvenal, although by far not so virulent in his utterances on the Jews, censures those "happening to have a Sabbath-fearing father (that is, one converted to Judaism), and who (consequently) adore nothing but the clouds and the divinity of heaven ; * * * but they are used to contemn the Roman *laws*, and learn, observe and fear (in preference) the Jewish *law*, all that Moses has handed down in a secret volume" (Sat. xiv). Here we have a distinct arraignment of the Jewish observances, believed to be subversive of loyalty to Romanism in all its relations, which radical transformation he imputes to all those proselytes and their children, who saw fit to forsake the religion of their native country.

In the same strain had Seneca, a few decades before, cast his bitter reproach upon the Jews for their propagandism, saying : "As meanwhile the (religious) custom of that wicked nation has gained strength to such an extent, that it is already received throughout all lands, the vanquished have (thus) given laws to their conquerors" (see Augustine, De Civitate Dei, vi. 11). He noted the vast and steadily growing advancement of Jewish belief and practice in the empire, which appeared to him, as to many other Romans, as a substitution of a foreign set of laws for the Roman, and could in his indignation at such a state of affairs not but discant contemptuously on the Jewish propagandist impetuosity. It was not the Jewish religion he attacked, but the effrontery of the Jewish people to attempt supplanting the Roman worship and rites by their own among the Gentiles.

The Jewish proselytism so eminently carried on since the reign of Augustus and perhaps already before, was viewed by representative Romans with mingled rancor and jealousy. In the Augustan age we find the poet Horace already alluding to the zealous propagandism of the Jews, in the passage, "and just as the Jews, we will compel thee to join this (the poet's) crowd" (Sat. i, 4). This unmistakably shows that the zeal for spreading their faith, in Rome at least, had then been very active among Jewish enthusiasts.[12] Ovid, Horace's younger contemporary, who also flourished mainly in the period of Augustus, may too have alluded to such state of things, in his 'Remedy of Love.' In it he advises the young man suffering from the malady of voluptuousness, to strenuously engage in some kind of work, since idleness promotes sensuous passions, or to journey away from the place of temptation, and not to "fear showers, nor let the Sabbath of the stranger detain him, nor yet the Allia, so well known for its disasters" (the memorial day of a defeat which the Romans had once sustained).

While we must not press this point too far as an evidence of conversions to Judaism among the people of Rome in the poet's days, for it is possible, as Riley in his annotation to that passage observes, "that the Romans in some measure imitated the Jews in their observance of their Sabbath, by setting apart every seventh day for the worship of particular deities"—a question to which we will later recur—, and that accordingly the outward adoption of the Sabbath by some Romans was not a real, not even a half-conversion, since even this had to be attended by an unconditional surrender of every sign of polytheism; and, further, because that passage easily admits, on the other hand, of the interpretation, that the poet did not at all advert in his mind to any sort of religious observance of the Sabbath by some Romans, but merely to the circumstance that, as the seventh day was commonly known as one "not suited for the transaction of business" by the Jews (Ovid, 'Art of Love,' l. I.), it was by some superstitious Romans, who were though entirely bare of any attachment for Judaism, feared as an ill-omened season for beginning any new work or setting out on a journey on it, and that he consequently wished solely to encourage the young man, whom he addressed, not to mind such scaring delusions at all: we yet have to recognize this much as a certain result from the poet's description, that the influence of Judaism had made itself somehow felt in the Roman society of his time.

Especially so, when we hold in view that the noted passage in the Art of Love, which we reproduce later, allows the interpretation, that Roman ladies of pagan nationality were accustomed to visit synagogues on the Sabbath of the Jews. This would show from the poet's writing, that the Jewish Sabbath had actually awakened the sincere religious interest of native Romans in his time.

The Jewish propagandist zeal did not diminish under Tiberius, but seems rather to have grown apace as the empire continued. To the epoch of this emperor belongs the reproach made by Jesus to the Scribes and Pharisees, that they "compass sea and land to make one[13] proselyte" (Matt. xiii. 15). While the imputation of their traversing the whole earth to catch only one pagan soul is on its face an exaggeration, and one doubtless due to the irritated temper of Jesus; and while the student of history will at all events have to pronounce the charge of Jesus as one-sided and inspired by partisan passion, since it is an undeniable fact that the Asmonean princes were, as outspoken and fanatic Sadducees, by far the most aggressive and obtrusive propagandists Judaism ever produced, so that it cannot be seen why the one party, the Pharisaic doctors and votaries, should be charged with an excess of proselytizing zeal, and no such reproach uttered against the other; we have yet no valid reason to doubt the authenticity of Jesus' accusation in its substance, namely, that proselytism was in his time very brisk among the Jewish people.

We will at once adduce another instance from which this may be inferred for the period of Tiberius' reign. An account of a persecution of the Jews of Rome by this emperor is preserved in history. It is presented by the four authors, Josephus, Philo, Suetonius and Tacitus. The Jewish and Egyptian cults must at that time have made such rapid encroachment in the eternal city, that the authorities were deeply alarmed, and concluded to proscribe and suppress them. Tacitus (Annals ii. 85) who relates the fact, that under Tiberius " action was also taken concerning the expulsion of the Egyptian and Jewish rites," and Suetonius (Tiberius, xxxvi.) who reports of him that he " restrained the foreign religious customs, the Egyptian and Jewish rites," leave no doubt that the measures of repression related further on by those writres were puritanical[14] in their character, undertaken, namely, to cleanse the Roman polytheistic institutions of intruding foreign elements, prominent among which were the Jewish and Egyptian, which seem to have then made the largest headway in the capital. Philo who, in passing, attributes the persecution then enacted against the Roman Jews to the promptings of Tiberius' privy-councillor, Sejanus,[15] exonerating the emperor entirely from its opprobrium (Leg. § 24 ; cp. Ag. Flaccus § 1), represents indirectly its origin to some *accusations* laid against them. Of what nature they were, he does not signify. He merely states that Tiberius discovered immediately after Sejanus' death, that " the accusations which had been brought against the Jews who were dwelling in Rome, were false calumnies, inventions of Sejanus ;" and also that the emperor sent official declarations to all the governors of the provinces, comforting the Jews everywhere, that "the punishment[16] was not executed upon all, but only on the guilty ; and they were but few."

While we have to note with regret that that Jewish author who, as the contemporary of Tiberius, could have given us the best and truest information on the offence committed by or at least charged on the Jews, as also on the character of their penalty, was yet utterly silent on these points, we are nevertheless not left wholly uncertain about the reference he made in his mind in regard to them.

The analogy offered by the two before-named Gentile writers, throws sufficient light on the facts in question as they were present in Philo's mind, though he did not explicitly state them. It was undeniably the Jewish propagandism at which the Roman authorities had taken grievous umbrage, and for which they proceeded with vengeance against the Jews. This our supposition is not only not contradicted by Josephus who, in Ant. xviii. 3, 5, puts forth a very singular version of the origin of the persecution under Tiberius, but, in the main, even supported. According to him its direct cause was an act of fraud committed by a Jewish conversionist who was a fugitive from Judean justice, and his three accomplices, upon a prominent female proselyte, Fulvia, the wife of Saturninus.[17] We see that even Josephus has connected, though indirectly, the persecution of the Jews with propagandist efforts of some of them. Accordingly we may suggest that we are substantially furnished with testimony by all the four above-named writers, that the progress of the Jewish propaganda in Rome must under Tiberius have been very strong and alarming, so that either he himself, or his privy-councillor, perhaps in conjunction with the Senate, concluded to peremptorily proceed against and forcibly suppress it.[18]

That Jewish proselytism had not lessened, but rather increased under the emperors Caligula and Claudius, in whose reigns the Jewish prince Agrippa enjoyed such vast privileges, succeeding at last to become king of the Jews, in which exalted position he wielded a very potent influence under which the Jewish cause could not but have thriven freely and auspiciously, is provable from various sources. Not only does it result from Seneca's stricture quoted above, and which belongs to this and perhaps partly to Nero's period, but it is also demonstrable from the Satire of his younger contemporary, Persius — like him by-the-by a Stoic, having had Cornutus as teacher. Persius, criticising in his fifth Satire some varieties of moral slavery, which he declares as worse than bodily servitude, holds out to censure also those in the bonds of superstition, as one example of which he designates the observance of Jewish holidays. which he must have noticed or at least known to exist, among Judaizing Romans. He says: "And when Herod's days [19] have come, and lamps holding violets which are placed at the greasy window, discharge a heavy fume, and the tail of the tunny-fish swims round in a red platter, and the white bowl swells (is filled) with wine: thou movest the lips silently, and fearest the circumcised Sabbaths" (vv. 179-84). This shows incontestably that towards the middle of the first century C. E., the age of this satirist, the Jewish religion had made remarkable headway in Rome, and its rites were embraced by a number of those Roman people, who were no more satisfied by the rotary mechanism and spiritless forms of the State religion. Jewish propagandism could then flourish and extend in Rome the more, because Tiberius' edicts of repression had been revoked by Caligula (Dion Cass. lx. 6, in Renan, 'Apostles').

As to the much-mooted expulsion of the Jews from Rome by Claudius, this circumstance seems not to have materially interrupted, for any considerable length of time at least, the energical progress of the Jewish propaganda, since it is an historical fact, conceded, too, by almost every modern author who wrote on this subject, that it thrived in his reign all over the Roman world. Suetonius' report (Claudius, § 25; cp. Acts xviii. 2), "The Jews making constant tumults under an instigator, Chrestus, he expelled from Rome," is contradicted by Dion Cassius, who records of Claudius that he, "finding the Jews again overweaning, did, as they could not be banished from the city without tumult by their multitude, not drive them out, but forbade them, following their parental mode of life, to hold meetings."[20] While the edict surely appears even in Dion's version hard and oppressive enough, it yet does not seem to have prevailed long, nor markedly checked the propagandist influence and agitations of Jews in Rome. For we have the above-cited testimony of Seneca for its continuance which, while the exact date of its composition is not known, can yet safely be taken as referring to the state of things obtaining at and extending through the reigns of both Claudius and Nero.

Under the latter emperor the spread of Judaism in Rome was doubtless considerable, having also had, as may properly be surmised, a powerful champion in the person of the empress Poppaea, who is by Josephus characterized as God-fearing — a title often used for Judaizing converts from paganism. That she was a devotee of Judaism is very probable, from her solicitous intercession with the emperor in behalf of Jewish petitioners against the determination of both the king and the procurator of Judea, in a matter concerning the reverence for the temple of Jerusalem (Ant. xx. 8, 11 ; see also Winston's note ib., and Schuerer, l. c.).

That with the downfall of the Jewish State this propagandism did not abate, but perhaps rather increase, may be inferred from the invidious paragraphs of Juvenal and Tacitus, and in particular from Dion Cassius' account of Domitian's furious proceedings against Judaizers.

Captive Judea, though held down by the iron grasp of the Roman power, and smarting under the contumely poured out upon her by the heartless victors, had yet in her widowhood — mainly, we hold, by the eternal verity and unvarying vigor of her principles of belief — continued to make many spiritual captives from among the heathen. Jerusalem was destroyed, the Jewish State dissolved, but Judaism itself remained a conquering force. Its professors were politically cowed and socially scorned, yet this misery had not impaired the spiritual essence of Judaism itself. It remained intact, and proved itself powerful and triumphant in continuing to win converts to itself. As captives even, the Jews carried with them into strange lands the boon which attracted the favorable attention and desire of a number of pagans.

Domitian, though he had worked with all his might to stamp deeper and deeper on the name of the Jews the odium of their expatriation, by severely and occasionally ferociously exacting the Jewish fisc so-called — that most repulsive tax imposed by Vespasian in place of the annual sacred gift of the Shekel, as a tribute to the Capitoline Jupiter — could not hinder the vast expansion of Jewish belief and rites in the realm, and specially in Rome. His own cousin Flavius Clemens who was invested with the consulship, and his wife Flavia Domitilla, his own niece, were adherents of that Judaism which he so utterly detested. For the first time in the history of the progression of Judaism in Rome, proselytes to this faith were stigmatized with the title and charged with the crime of atheism, now that he had sworn bitter vengeance on it. Those high personages were judicially accused and condemned of that crime. Both had to pay a dire penalty. Clemens was sentenced to death, and his wife Domitilla banished to an island.[12] The same charge of atheism was brought against "many others" (see Dion Cassius) who had adopted or, as this writer is pleased to render it, "lapsed into Jewish customs." Their punishment was either death or confiscation of property.

The same writer's testimony opens to us a most unambiguous and clear view of the propagation of Judaism in heathen countries, as late even as the latter years of the first century C. E. For those vengeful proceedings of Domitian were enacted in the last year of his reign. And as his mild successor, Nerva, had decreed that no one should be harassed for his "Jewish mode of life" (Dion lxviii.), it is justly to be supposed that conversions to it became again as frequent under him as they were under Domitian.

To sum up, it cannot be questioned that these cases, occurring in the very heart of the empire and witnessed by many bigoted puritans, also by the contemporary literators Juvenal and Tacitus, will have aroused their jealous ire and intense contempt toward the pertinacious Jewish nation.

Think of the spleeny satirist Juvenal and his younger
compatriot Tacitus, the praetor, and later, under Trajan,
consul and afterwards consular, being by inevitable fate
compelled to witness for over half a century a mighty,
impulsive Judaizing activity in the capital. Imagine them
seeing thousands of homeless Jews, reduced to slavery or
beggary, in Titus' and the subsequent reigns; and on the
other side noticing, despite the crushing scorn fastened on
their nation, a continuous influence on pagans of their
religious precepts. More bitter than wormwood it must
have been to them, particularly to Tacitus, to note a goodly
number of their countrymen not only abjure the allegiance to the many immortal gods and tutelar divinities and
"contemn" them, but — scandal of scandals — fly to, and
own and worship a god "apprehended merely in the mind,
and as an only one, eternal, inimitable and imperishable
Being" (see Hist. v.); to note them, moreover, observe
the Jewish Sabbaths, holidays and fasts, dietary[22] and marriage restraints, and specially the rite of circumcision — a
rite that was, judging from the frequent derisive allusion to
it by many Roman writers of the empire, to the Roman
mind the most obnoxious of all,[23] but to which so many
neophites submitted themselves and their male children
with pious alacrity, to become fully incorporated in the
community of Israel.[24] Add to the Judaizing of Roman
converts the above-discussed grievances against the Jews
of their diversity of worship, their separateness and disdainful treatment of polytheists, supplemented by an always
ready and ample proportion of Gentile envy against them,
as also by the intense national indignation at them for causing to the Roman power such an excessive strain on men
and resources by their contests and wars; and then judge
whether Roman laureate poets or other literati by the grace
of the immortal gods, and withal high-flown patricians and
dignitaries of the city could not, through these circumstances
alone, have become Jew-haters, independently of any foreign influence, especially that of the Alexandrian literature,
as Dr. Joel has so emphatically and with such an amount of
literary diligence, as well as self-complacency, asserted?

We positively protest — and believe to have abundantly supported this our position -- that the mischief of literary slander and aspersions cast by Roman scribes on Jews and Judaism, sprang originally from those fountains flowing everywhere in the pagan world, in Rome as well as in Alexandria, with an ever fresh current. That their baleful veins were somehow sympathetically interconnected, we are ready to admit. But that they were associated through real contact, cannot be sustained by any shadow of evidence.

The diversion from our main subject which we allowed ourselves in the foregoing discussion, to refute the one-sided and overdrawn assertion of Dr. Joel, will appear of not inconsiderable moment for its illustration in the sequel. For the arguments we employed to show the various causes of pagan hatred and contempt for Jews as being everywhere home-born, enable us to account much better for the false and derisive representations of the Jewish religion and its usages in Roman literature. Consequently we will also understand better the various opinions expressed in it on the Sabbath.

It may be laid down as an axiom that it was just the contempt, in which Jews and Judaism were held by those literators, and the malevolence they cherished against the Jewish nation, that kept them in almost total ignorance of their real religious conceptions and the import of the rites practised among them. While any foreign form of worship was to the bigoted Roman a superstition, and as such held in light esteem or thoroughly despised, his own being the religion proper,[25] and for this reason to be revered, might it be ever so absurd, the Jewish was yet more offensive to him for the combined causes previously mentioned. Should such a conceited bigot, in his assumption of the Roman superiority above all the rest of mankind, take the pains of searching at the fountain-head and seeking the crystal springs, the concurrence of which made up the stream of Jewish life? That would have been expecting too much. A superficial observation of any Jewish rite practised in the capital, was to him sufficient to babble about it in his peculiar, contemptuous strain. His words or works were anyhow not intended for Gentiles sympathizing with the Jewish nation, but for those either indifferent to or possessed of ill-will towards it. Why then should he, in speaking of points of the Jewish religion, take caution lest he might pervert the truth and give forth misstatements? Reproach for any distortion of facts, not to say for incorrect statements pertaining to Jewish questions, he had surely not to fear. And as to his individual conscience, this suffered no touch of compunction about any misrepresentation of the Jews and their religion. It was overruled by the native assumption of primacy which engrossed his mind, allowing no fair judgment and justice to be awarded to any institution that was not Roman, and was especially blunted with regard to the Jews, by the force of the intense contempt he nourished against them.

When we observe an astounding ignorance betrayed by Roman writers on Jewish subjects, we will, moreover, as regards some of them, be at a loss to determine, whether it was real or only feigned. Their stable antagonism to Jews would not permit them to state those subjects in the favorable light, in which they may have appeared to themselves. They found it much easier and more gratifying to make a mockery of them in spite of their own better knowledge. As a typical ignorance of Roman literators about Jewish religious observances, Juvenal's designation of the Mosaic code as a "secret book"[26] may be cited. Such, indeed, it was and remained to the body of the Romans. Even the authorities were utterly ignorant of the real inwardness and purport of the Mosaic institutions. They noted the Jewish law as so peculiar and different from the Roman. Suspicious emperors were haunted by it as by a spectre, instilling on their minds the fear, that it might be a code enjoining an irreconcilable opposition to the temporal power of Rome, or the sovereign impersonating it. We have already above reflected on Caligula's questioning of the Jewish delegates about their "constitution," that is, as we explained it, the Mosaic Law, with regard to the worship and its obligations set forth therein. He could surely have informed himself about the principle of the immateriality of the Deity maintained by the Jews, from the extant Greek version of the Pentateuch. But he doubtless scorned the idea to read it himself, or have it interpreted by unbiased expositors.

A like instance of an imperial investigation of the statutes of the Jews, is reported in the Rabbinical literature. It shows strikingly, how little acquaintance with them the Roman authorities had got. If, as Graetz (Hist. iv. 119) maintains, it belongs to the period of Domitian's reign,[27] it might be connected with the opposition the Jews manifested against the imposition of the poll tax. They abhorred it so deeply, that "some either concealed their Jewish mode of life or dissembled their Jewish descent" (Suetonius, 'Domitian,' ch. xii.), rather than pay a tribute, by which their hearts were revolted. That furious despot may have construed the opposition as an attempt at rebellion, and consequently desired to get authoritative information, whether it could be found as grounded on or referable to some texts of the Jewish Scripture. To obtain it he may have sent those "two military ambassadors"[28] to the Jewish academy and Senate of Palestine, of whom an account is given in Sifre, Deut. § 344; the Jerus. treatise of Baba Kamma f. 4; and the Babylonian treatise of the same denomination, f. 38 (unlicensed edition). They may have been commissioned to descry that portion of the Jewish Mosaic-traditional Law, having a more or less direct bearing on the mutual relations of Jews and Gentiles, with the chief view of ascertaining whether any, or how many of its precepts indicated or implied disloyalty to foreign rule and insubordination to other laws, which were in this case the Roman.

The versions of the three just named Rabbinical passages have indeed in their present transmitted form a legendary aspect. They disagree with one another, too, on the subject-matter proposed at that imperial inquiry. In both the first and last-named places the envoys are said to have taken exception but to one Rabbinically construed ordinance of the Pentateuch, and this not identical in both. The Jerus. Talmud reports two such instances of Mosaic-traditional usage (one of which is again subdivided in two propositions), touching the mutual relations of Jews and Romans. But in the main, namely, as to the inquisition into the prevailing principles and regulations regarding the responsible interrelations of both nations, they agree. And this justifies our assumption that there is a real historical background to that differently rendered Rabbinical account of the imperial inquiry, made, once upon a time, into the Jewish Law.

Whether it was undertaken for merely political reasons, or for judicial and social objects, or to collect a general information about the principles of faith, practices of religion and ethical maxims of the Jews, is immaterial in the question now before us. Thus much we may justly infer from that account, that the emperor — whoever he was — had with his entire administration kept himself till that time in utter ignorance on the established customs of the Jews. Whether it was essentially lifted by that official inquiry, is very questionable, indeed. For we do not believe that any one of the Roman emperors cared much about knowing the intrinsic merits of those Jewish customs, not bearing in some way on the problem of the loyalty of the Jews to the imperial government. The result of the inquiry by the ambassadors will then have had very little, if any, beneficial result for the Jews. Their religion will from thence not have been better appreciated by the Roman bigots, than it was before.

They will have continued to spurn its rites as "absurd and mean" (see Tacitus, Hist. v. 5, end), and persevered in their scornful ignorance of them.

That Roman military and judicial functionaries, administering the Jewish affairs in Palestine, were during the empire, specially from the second century C. E. on, somewhat read in the Jewish Scriptures — some of them understanding, perhaps, the Hebrew language — as can be proved from many passages of the Rabbinical literature, does in truth not conflict with our opinion, that the bigoted Roman at home was ignorant on Jewish matters from his deep contempt for the Jewish nation. It was, we hold, inevitable, from their close contact and administrative dealings with the Jews. Besides, the sense of expediency must have urged that some of those officials should acquire a better knowledge of them, than their cultured or learned countrymen at home. It was their station that unavoidably made them somewhat familiar with the institutions of the Jews, so many questions of their civil law and religious custom coming under their cognizance. That therefore the governor, Tinnius Rufus, Quintus' successor in Hadrian's reign, and a few more civil and military officers of the Roman government in Palestine, showed themselves fairly versed in Scripture, does not signify aught against our supposition. And while we admit ourselves that the historical inquirer receives from several indications of literature the impression, that later in the second century, perhaps already during or after Hadrian's reign, there was an endeavor on the part of some cultured Romans and pagans in general, even those not connected with the Roman administration in Judea, to attain some better and more comprehensive knowledge of the contents of Hebrew literature, we presume to avouch, on the other hand, that it was not from any love or devotion to it, or the motive of being able to appreciate better the Jewish character and institutions, but mainly to qualify themselves for keeping up disputes on the latter with those aggressive Jews, who would press them with arguments against their polytheism. By being Scripture-proof themselves they hoped to retaliate on them with the weapons of criticism, and bring home to them, if possible, the weakness of their own position. This can be gathered in particular, as far as both Jewish and Christian polemics are concerned, from the notices preserved by Origen of the 'True Account' of Celsus, on which we cannot here enlarge.

The same ignorance that prevailed in Rome about the Law and customs of the Jews, was exhibited by its men of letters about their object of Divine worship. From Cicero to Juvenal, and beyond the latter's time into the period of Hadrian and the Antonines, we meet either with absurd misconceptions or coarse taunts of the Jewish God by many cultured Romans. Cicero, in his Oration for Flaccus, betrays a total lack of knowledge of the fixed Jewish belief of the divine Unity. For he exclaims there: "How dear it (the Jewish nation) was to the immortal gods, is proved by its having been defeated, etc." The Roman pantheon, much as his own philosophical reasoning has helped shelling it, was still his sublime ideal. About the spiritual Jehovah of the Jews he had not learned, or he could not have made the foregoing exclamation.

Juvenal makes of the Jews "adorers of clouds and the heaven"[29] as deities (Sat. xiv. 97; cp. "summi fida internuntia coeli," ib. vi. 545). Tacitus has indeed so far done justice to the Jews, that he stated according to the truth their imageless and intellectual worship of one only divine Being. But it was by no means from any sense of approbation or consent that he made this statement, but from his malignant mind and with scornful criticism. He has moreover tainted that true account by countenancing, at another place, the story of an ass's image being worshiped in the Temple (Hist. v. 4), and, further, by relating in the name of some, that a sort of service of Bacchus was carried on there, though he had for himself to find it incongruent with the known Jewish institutions.

In the Talmud we meet with many sacrilegious diatribes uttered by Romans of official rank in controversies with Rabbis. The Romans with all their intellectual refinement and even philosophical training could not disengage their mind from the attachment to their gods, nor advance towards the Jews with a tolerant valuation of their religious conceptions and practices. Custom had identified them with the national polytheism, which they recognized and demanded as the only acceptable form of worship for the various nations of the empire. However deeply decaying it was in the capital, it nevertheless predominated outwardly, and outwardly even the freethinkers made obeisance to it. Not only nature's forces were worshiped in their manifold personifications, even abstract virtues and vices had their shrines. Dead parents were held as gods, and dead emperors were pre-eminently awarded divine honor. Even a number of living emperors claimed divine adoration from the people. Fervid, high-wrought patriotism, mingled with a slavish adulation, made the soldiers worship the inanimate golden eagles in front of the legions as the 'gods of war.'

The Jewish decided and stern opposition to every form of polytheism, even the cultured Roman could not comprehend.[30] He was neither competent nor inclined to lift himself in his thought to the eminence of the purely spiritual apprehension of the Divine and, while he would not discard allegiance to his national gods for himself, to judge fairly of those among whom such apprehension was firmly established. If nevertheless true enlightenment as to the unity of God is known to have existed with some of the Roman people at certain periods of their historic life, it did not, we believe, flash on them from their self-illumined spirit, but came to them refracted through the medium of Jewish missionaries and their diligent course of propaganda.

As a characteristic specimen of the stubbornness with which leading Romans defended, on the one hand, the most ridiculous and decrepit religious institutions of their own, and spurned, on the other, all the foreign, branding them with the stigma of superstition, we may adduce Cicero's denunciation, in the above-discussed Oration for Flaccus, of the Jewish contribution of sacred money as a "barbarous superstition." When we bring this acrimonious judgment home to himself and his vaunting nation, we will meet with such a striking contrast in favor of the Jews, that we can account for his refusing to apply the same stigma to some of the most senseless institutions of his own country, merely by his immovable, blind, patriotic partiality.

The reader is without doubt in general familiar with the genuinely Roman organization of the auguries. They were held equal in importance with the sacrificial ritual. The augurs were the seers or prophets of Rome. They were the interpreters of the divine will and dispositions from certain signs. The Roman contrivances of divination were so essential and indispensable in the opinion of even the most enlightened citizens that, much as some could not help mocking at them as fallacies, or designating them at least as "inventions for the illiterate," or to "satisfy the erroneous notion of the multitude" (Cicero, De Divin. i. ch. 47), there were again others who put forth their whole armor of logical arguments and philosophy to defend them (ib. ch. 49). Even the Stoics of Rome, whose tenet of Fate or Necessity should of itself have precluded their belief in or vindication of them, were obsequious to this predominant and deeply rooted organization, arguing in its favor in this wise: "The omens from cleft livers, or peculiar sounds of birds are not due to a direct interference of God. But the universe had from the beginning been so constituted, that certain signs have to precede certain events, some in entrails, others on birds, or in lightning, portents, constellations, the vision of dreamers or the speech of soothsayers" (ib. ch. 52). It were mainly Epicurean freethinkers like Ennius, who were outspoken and independent enough to freely jeer at that Roman hocus-pocus (ib. ch. 58). The elder Cato, too, is reported to have declared—and this sentence had made such a mark that tradition preserved it for coming ages—that "he wondered how an haruspex should not laugh on meeting a colleague." Cicero agrees with this sentiment (De Divin. ii. 24; De Nat. Deor. i. 26). He, further, arraigns the Stoics strongly for their inconsistency, contending that according to their theory that nothing occurs by chance and everything that happens, however rarely, has its appointed natural cause, there could not possibly be any validity in portents (De Divin. ii. 28). He also directly assails the three departments of haruspicina, viz., divination from entrails and other marks of victims, from lightning, and from various prodigies (ib. ii. 18 sq.). His standpoint is, that there is actually no divinity in divination, that is, the gods are not connected with anything from which diviners derive their predictions and premonitions.

And yet for all that he pleaded earnestly for the retention of the institutions of divination, and the obedience due to the auspices revealed by the national college of augurs. To run counter to such "religion" and obstinately set at naught this "inherited custom," was to him most censurable and deserving of punishment (ib. ii. 33). He holds that, although the organization of the augurs was originally intended only to serve as oracles, it was yet later preserved and retained *for the sake of the commonwealth* (ib. 35). "The custom, ceremony, discipline and law of the augurs and the authority of their college," he puts forth, "are retained alike with regard to the opinion of the vulgar, and the great advantages accruing therefrom to the State" (ib. 33).

It were, as we see, motives of statecraft and indulgence of the popular belief, that prevailed on Cicero to stand up for a 'religion,' which he had otherwise to expose as so unreasonable. He could not get it over his egotistically patriotic heart to dissuade the people from its continuance, much as his clear, philosophical mind protested against it. Differently he thought, however, concerning the Jewish custom in question. It certainly was approvable by the most caustic logic. Yet to tolerantly acknowledge it as pious and proceeding from a consciousness of nationality, which he himself praised as the worthiest quality as far as the people of his own country were concerned, he had no mind. The augurs' observation of the sacred chickens kept in pens, and the way they ate, was 'religion,' strictly to be heeded. But the religio-patriotic gift of the Jewish people dispersed from the centre of their national and publicly religious life, he must stigmatize with the contumelious title of "barbarous superstition!"

In about the same manner has Tacitus pitifully compromitted himself by denouncing what was to him Jewish superstition, while he was a victim to real superstition himself. In his narration of the prodigies that appeared, during the last throes of the Jewish revolution, in 70 C. E., on the heavens in the beleaguered city of Jerusalem, he taunts the Jews as a "nation given over to superstition, but opposed to religions (religious rites)," because they held it wrong to avert the evil of which they were forewarned by those portents, either with sacrifices or vows.

Had they resorted to propitiating the divine wrath manifested by those signs, by victims, animal or human — for the latter practice was yet in vogue in Nero's time and still later; see Joel, 'Blicke etc.' ii. p. 25 — the religious historian would apparently have been satisfied. But since they did not attempt to expiate those portents (see on this point also Josephus, Wars vi. 5, 3, 4, and compare 2 Macc. v. 2-4), and would most unquestionably have with abhorrence abstained from doing so, if it were to be attempted by a human sacrifice (he seemingly wondered, too, that they held it as "criminal to kill any of the agnates," Hist. v. 4), they had to be branded as a superstitious nation!

Again, he proved himself a very credulous man by fairly believing in the Chaldean horoscopy. Deploringly he relates the continuously decaying faith in this art of the Chaldean astrologers, "of which the past as well as the present offered such illustrious examples." Even the Chaldean wisdom he could value — for its pretended benefit to the State only, it is true—, but for Jewish wisdom, the "beginning of which is the fear of God," he could not conceive the slightest regard. Their firm and unshaken religious belief was decidedly 'superstition,' whereas he had not independence of spirit enough to decide for himself, whether the Stoic Fate doctrine, or the Epicurean chance theory commended itself for acceptance (Ann. vi. 22).

CHAPTER IV.

ROMAN WRITERS ON THE JEWISH SABBATH.

Can we in view of the indiscriminate disregard for Jewish religious institutions with which we meet in the works of the literary men of Rome, expect from them a fair valuation of the Sabbath? Can we expect that those denouncing the Jewish religion as superstition, and who were purposely or carelessly ignorant about it in its various precepts from their utter contempt for its professors, should speak reverently and appreciatingly of their weekly day of rest? Contemplative rest, sacred meditations, the average Roman knew not. To have a halting day once every week on which man should pause, collect his mind, and abstract it from the turmoil and also pleasures of common life, was a perception exceeding his horizon. The Roman festivals were mostly gay holidays with plenty of exciting sensuous enjoyments. When he therefore saw the Jews and Judaizers observe the Sabbath with abstinence from labor and due sanctity, his pagan spirit must have been roused to disdainful pity for the former, and scornful spite against the latter. Many a one will have vented his disgust at this observance in derisive and reviling language. Literators have embodied this sentiment in their writings, as we will now demonstrate.

Before we review, however, the opinions on the Jewish Sabbath, uttered by writers from the Augustan age onward, we have to premise that from their contemptuous ignorance about all the Jewish solemn days, they used to confound them with the Sabbath, or, rather, comprised them all, even the fast days, under the generic name 'Sabbata.'

That the fasts were to them included in this name, can be proved from the following. Suetonius (Augustus, 76) preserved a statement of Augustus, made in a letter to Tiberius, in which that emperor boasts, as one more proof of his moderate living and continence, "not even a Jew observes the fast of the Sabbath (he employs the unusual

singular form, Sabbas) so strictly as I did (fast) to-day."
He doubtless alluded here not only to the fast of the
Atonement day, as Joel proposes (l. c. p. 133), but to other
fasts as well. The same import has Martial's jejunia
sabbatariarum, or sabbatariorum, " the fasts of the Sabbatarians" (Epigrams iv. 4). In this epigram he depicts the
incomparably unbearable smell of a certain Bassa in the
following way. Naming a number of very bad odors,
among them the "smell of the fasts of the Sabbatarians,"
he sarcastically suggests that Bassa had better smell of all
those intolerable things, than to smell as he really did.
This is reducible to the meaning, " of all these things,
Bassa, I would rather smell than smell like you;" see the
translator in Bohn's Library. The expression Sabbatarians
suggests the supposition, that he thought at the same time
of Judaizing converts from paganism, who, from Josephus'
notice (Ag. Ap. ii. 40), kept the fasts like the born Jews.

We construe Juvenal's peculiar description of the land
of Agrippa and Berenice — Judea — as the one, Observant
ubi festa mero pede sabbata reges, " where kings observe
the solemn Sabbaths with bare feet" (Sat. vi. 159), in the
same sense of fasts of the Jewish people. That he should
have had in mind that of the Atonement day only, is not
likely.[31] He can fairly be supposed to have known of the
Jewish custom of having the feet bare on many fasts. The
Roman Jews had doubtless observed it on the so-called
public fasts, pre-eminently the Ninth of Ab, and also the
communal fasts for rain, provided these properly Palestinian
days of humiliation were kept in the dispersion as well.
There is from their partial perpetuation unto our own day
all likelihood, that they were then observed also in Italy,
and that out of reverential accommodation to the mother-
country, though the rainfalls were there regular. These
fasts for rain were the Mondays, Thursdays and Mondays
following the new moon of Kislev, on which public gatherings for devotion and penitence took place, if the ' former
rain' had not fallen till then. That it was enjoined to be
barefooted on the second trio of these fast days, is attested
in the Mishnah, B. Taanith f. 12.

That the Thursday fasts of this description were not unknown to some Roman writers, may be gathered from Horace's Satire, ii. 3, in which he introduces "Jove's day" (Thursday) as the one on which this god "appoints fasts." It is the opinion of several commentators, that he alluded here to a Jewish fast, adopted also by Judaizing Romans. If it be really feasible to construe Horace's statement in this meaning, we will suggest that he either knew as well of the existence of Monday fasts, but singled out only the Thursday for its superior consecration, or that, in his superficiality as to Jewish customs and indifference to religion in general, he took no notice of the established rote of those fasts, but mentioned the Jove's day fasts merely at random, having by chance heard that the Jews and Judaizers observed fasts on Thursday.

Be this as it may, and whatever allusion Juvenal may have made in the above passage of his Satires, this much can incontestably be maintained from other sources, that Roman writers mixed up the Jewish fasts with the Sabbaths, giving them the latter designation.

That they included the Jewish festivals in the name Sabbath will, after the foregoing elucidation, not surprise us. We may deduce this, moreover, from the above-quoted paragraph of Persius who, alluding, as we have shown, to all Jewish holidays, comprises them under the general name 'Herod's days' and also 'Sabbaths.'

Even new moon's day is, by Horace at least, denoted Sabbath, as will appear from the satire on which we will, for several important reasons, enlarge in the following. In the ninth of his first book of Satires the phrase "thirtieth Sabbath" occurs. That it cannot mean any other solemn day of the Jews than that of the new moon, the reader will promptly hold evident with us. This satire had the fate of a various interpretation in several points. In order to get familiar with the treatment of religion by that leading poet of the Augustan age, we will reproduce it synoptically, offering in connection our own exposition of its chief contents.

Horace was once molested by a bore (not a Jew from the Roman Ghetto, as Mommsen, 'Provinces of the Roman Empire,' iii. p. 250, gives it) who persisted in following him beyond the Tiber — where the "poor Trastevere, the Jewish quarter, densely populated since Augustus" (Gregorovius) was situated. His friend Aristius Fuscus met him by chance. He, too, knew and at once recognized that obstrusive fellow. Horace motioned the friend to manage to rescue him from his clutches. The importuner did, however, not take the hint. Horace got exasperated, and contrived the make-shift of getting him out of the way by suggesting in the form of a question, that the friend had to communicate some secret to him. By this means he surely expected to get rid of him. Fuscus, most likely satisfied in his mind that Horace's device would be attended with no success, attempted to employ another and, as he thought, better one. He said, in the hearing of the bore, "I remember well (about what matter I have to speak to you secretly); but I will tell you it at a more opportune time (and place); to-day is the *thirtieth Sabbath :* dost thou wish to offer an affront (for this affront by-the-by Horace puts in his friend's mouth the filthiest word of the Latin vocabulary) to the curtailed (circumcised) Jews?"

We surmise that the spot where they had met, was near a synagogue or, perhaps, on the porch of one, in which the Jews, it having been Rosh Chodesh, were assembled or about to meet for worship. To his friend's objection Horace replied : "I have no religion." "But I have," the friend rejoined ; "I am somewhat weaker, one of the many. Excuse me, I shall speak to you at another time." The bore then saw fit to take his retreat.

Whether the affair described by Horace took place in reality, or is a mere product of his fancy, thus much we gather at any rate from this satire, that he was not only a rude scoffer at Jewish religious observances, but in the main an unscrupulous reviler of every religious sentiment of believers. Godless Epicurean as he was, he had no reverence for things holy, and made no conscience of disturbing other people's devotion. While in the case in point it were Jews whose religious sentiments were to have been spared, he would surely, from the language he used, not have paid any regard to those of other devotees, either. The "fear of the gods" he elsewhere characterized as the bane of society (ib. ii. 3).

We contend, further, that the friend who avows himself as "one of the many," was by no means a Jew, as Jost, 'History of Judaism,' i. 330, suggests, nor a sort of proselyte, as Schuerer (Hist. of the Jewish People, etc., ii.) thinks. There is positively, we maintain, no warrant whatever for either construction of the words "unus multorum." All that is implied in them is, that the friend confessed himself as being one of those who had religion, or at least veneration of the Divine. This would constrain him in his conscience, not to scandalize the Jews or any other class of worshipers at their place of devotional assembly, by standing in front of it and holding an animated or demonstrative conversation. We have to ask those authors inclined to make of Horace's friend a Jew or Judaizer, Was it consistent or at all possible that the poet should have imputed to his friend such a contemptuous allusion to the Jews as we note in the above, had he been one of them, or attached to them by religious belief? Would such action not have been a most barbarous outrage of a friend's feelings, of which no sensible person ever makes himself guilty?

On Ovid's mention of the Sabbath we reflected in part already above. We have seen that he called it "the Sabbath of the stranger." That he designates the Jews as strangers, though they were assuredly not treated as such by the emperor Augustus (see Philo, l. c.), must not surprise us from the pen of a Roman writer. The Roman men of letters as a class seem to have had a settled aversion to the Jews. The very tolerant regard which Augustus had manifested towards the Jews as to the observance of their Sabbath (see Philo and Josephus), was evidently not shared by our poet.

In fact, it seems, he treated it not only as the Sabbath of the stranger, but it is probable that his knowledge of Jewish matters and customs was only gathered by a superficial hearsay, and was withal limited to the rites of circumcision and the Sabbath, which formed the principal, salient points of demarcation of the Jews from the Gentiles in the eyes of the Roman public. He with other earlier and later writers of the capital, kept himself at a haughty distance from the Jews, and remained proudly ignorant of their religious institutions. This distance we may recognize also in his styling them once the "Jew(s) of Syria" (Art of Love, 1. I.), and again, later in the same book, the "Syrians of Palestine," which latter denomination he probably derived from Herodotus (comp. Mommsen, ' Provinces of the Roman Empire,' iii. p. 244).

As to Ovid's notice of the Sabbath, it occurs yet, beside the passage quoted above, in two places of the just cited 'Art of Love.' In the first place he advises the young man anxious to start a courtship, to betake himself to various public institutions and shrines, among them the temple of Venus and Jewish synagogues, concerning which latter he suggests "nor let the seventh holy-day observed by the Jew of Syria escape you."

That the poet should here have had before his mind the attraction of "numbers of Roman females to the services held in the synagogues on the Sabbath, probably by the music," as Riley (as above) remarks, is a rather far-fetched assumption. The Jewish music in the Roman synagogues was doubtless of a very primitive character, a plain chant, that can barely be thought to have attracted the notice and desire of attendance of any outsider but him, who was otherwise drawn thither by a sense of devotion to the God of Israel worshiped therein. It would, on the contrary, appear as more probable that, if Gentile Roman ladies were meant by the poet, he thought of them as seeking the Jewish places of worship with the sincere, pious purpose of adoring the true God and otherwise entering into religious relations with the Jews.

But this interpretation is by no means necessitated by the tenor of the passage in point. We have to declare it quite admissible, that he referred only to Jewish ladies visiting their own places of worship on the Sabbath, from among whom he advised the young man addressed to choose an object of love.

Later in the same book he proposes to him not to fix upon any inopportune or unlucky day for his purpose, to which sort of days he does yet not count, as he expressly states, the fatal memorial day of Allia (see above) and "the day, when the festival occurs, observed each seventh day by the Syrian of Palestine, [a day] not suited for the transaction of business."

Persius' passing on the celebration of the Jewish Sabbaths and holidays by Judaizing Romans as an instance of that kind of slavery, which consisted in allowing religious fear to sway the mind, we have already discussed above.

We will now turn to his older contemporary, Seneca. His malicious utterance regarding the extensive acceptance of Jewish laws by the Roman and other nations, the pith of which is the sentence, that they, the vanquished, have given laws to their conquerors, we have already reviewed. Let us now examine what he says on the Jewish Sabbath. He reproaches the Jews that "they injure themselves by its observance, as they lose by it almost the seventh part of their lifetime, passing it in idleness" (Augustine, l. c.).[32] That proud philosopher of the Porch who professed such sublime doctrines as " Virtue is shut out from no one, it is open to all ;" or, "the mind makes the nobleman, which enables us to rise from the basest condition above fortune ;" or, " All men have the same beginning and the same origin. No one is more noble than another, except the man of lofty genius, with talents fitted for the successful pursuit of the higher objects of life," had yet no mind to apply them so universally as to make them embrace the Jews as well. No, these were a "most criminal nation,"—an incriminating denotation which we meet with in no other Roman writer, not even the malicious Tacitus, who made out the Christians only as " hated for their crimes."

Seneca's national and religious prejudice against the Jews was evidently intensified by his notice of the rapid and large progress that their religion was then making among the Gentiles. A man of such superior intelligence, and ethical teacher of such high pretention as he was, should, we verily expect, have been free from intolerance of every description. We should think to find him a foremost champion of religious liberty and social toleration. Instead of it we meet him in the van of base and coarse haters of a people, whose national crime was no other than their tenacious adhesion to their ancestral religion.

The Sabbath, he charges, the Jews pass in idleness! Bigot as he was, he would not acknowledge the sacred rest and meditative and devotional exercises of the Jews on the Sabbath as meritorious, and at least equal to the feasts of ecstasy, which he and his colleagues would indulge themselves in with rapturous delight when they would pretend to have arrived at solutions of hard ethical problems, that had for a long time engrossed their high mental faculties!

Nor would he pause to reflect on the circumstance, that his own fast and fierce fellow-citizens lost much more time, than the Jews, in the celebration of their many public festivals. "The seven ordinary Roman festivals of the year lasted together"— towards the end of the glorious Republic —"sixty-two days, aside from the gladiatorial fights and other numerous occasional sports and amusements" (Mommsen l. c. iii. p. 496). Moreover, what a preponderantly favorable contrast with the popular festivals of Rome must not the Jewish Sabbath have offered to an unprejudiced person, in its great conduciveness to the elevation of the mind, which so prominently figured as the end of every wise man in the Stoic philosophy. As how much preferable must not have appeared to such a person the material loss of one day out of seven, when it was counterbalanced by the remarkable gain, in its stead, of refinement of thought and feeling, to the spending of series of days in idle excitement in the circuses, where barbarous spectacles were the intellectual food on which the Roman vulgar subsisted; where beasts were set to fighting not only with one another, but also with men, and the combats of gladiators with each other — those select performances with which candidates' courting the suffrages of the crowd, or grands ambitious to settle themselves in the high opinion of their fellows for glory's sake, used at times to treat the masses — formed the keenest delight offered to the populace! And, further, how incomparably more conducive to the advancement of pure morals must not to such a person have appeared the reading and study of the Law, replete as it was with the most salutary lessons for a pure and noble life, as it was customary with the Jews on the Sabbath, than the meaningless and dry heathen rites performed in the capital of the world.

Indeed, had the Hebrew Scriptures with their many rules of purity taken hold of the degenerating people of Rome during the empire, instead of the attempt of the Stoics to reform them, the chronicles would have had to record no such stupendous depravity as to cases of adultery, incest, pæderasty, patricide and infanticide. But no, the Jewish religion and its sacred literature were accorded no regard by the leading and learned men of Rome. They were too narrow and contracted in their estimation of their own country institutions, to give credit to those of the Jews, or encourage a broader influence of their sacred literature.

Juvenal [33] makes the same reproach of idleness as to the Sabbath of the Jews and Judaizers. In the above-quoted satire in which he dilates on the evil examples given by Roman parents to their children, he produces as one of them the Jewish mode of life, which the sons of Judaizing parents adopt from them. "But the father is in fault," he complains, "with whom each seventh day was a day of idleness, and did not belong to any part of active life." The harsh and contemptuous verdict of idleness by which both he and Seneca condemn the Sabbath, must not surprise us, considering that they looked at it through the darkened glass of national prejudice and bigotry, and, in particular, that they were sorely vexed at seeing a number of their Gentile compatriots find spiritual solace in the reverence for, or 'fear of the Sabbath.' Their contempt for the Jews being mingled with the deep indignation, that some of the good Romans had so glaringly estranged themselves from the custom of their mother-country, prompted them the more vehemently to denounce the Sabbath as an institution and vehicle for fostering idleness.

That Tacitus, the most malignant Roman traducer of the Jews, fell in with those two literators in denouncing the Sabbath as a day of idleness, we must not find strange. He differs from them only in being more explicit on the origin of the Sabbath, of which he enumerates, with his reputed historical excellence, several accounts gleaned from the armory of Grecian Jew-haters, such as Apion and the like. The theory that "the seventh day was fixed for rest, because that day had brought them the termination of their toils," seems to have suited him best. For he could attach to it the imputation of the preference of the Jews for idleness, which he indeed brings forward in the connected sentence: "then," those writers say, "sloth having pleased (the Jews), the seventh year, too, was given over to idleness."

We have, with this chronic, bitter Jew-hater's opinion on the Jewish Sabbath, arrived in our review at the period of Trajan. The violent commotions of oriental Jews in his and Hadrian's reign, and the latter's unexampled furious prosecution of those of Judea, were surely no opportune occasions for dissolving the prejudice against the Jews in general, and rectifying the misconceptions the bigoted Romans had cherished regarding their religious institutions, among them the Sabbath.

Nor were perhaps the times of the Antonines much more favorable for a fairer estimation of the Sabbath by them. Uprisings of smaller proportions occurred again in Palestine under Antoninus Pius and even Severus, and measures had to be taken to deal with them (Mommsen, 'The Provinces of the Roman Empire,' ii. p. 244). Such insurrections would surely not permit the cultivation of a more friendly sentiment towards the Jews by the Roman people, at least by their men of letters or of prominent political station. The emperor Pius showed himself indeed yielding to the Jews, in that he repealed for them Hadrian's interdict of circumcision. Yet for all that we do not believe that the spirit of national prejudice and antipathy will have permitted the body of representative Romans to abate their contempt for Judaism. With regard to the Sabbath, it can be equally supposed that they, though perhaps knowing a little more about it from the Hadrianic period onwards than before, did not treat it with any fairer measure of indulgence than they had formerly done. If they have not further derogated it as a day of idleness, they will doubtless have denounced it as an idle superstition.

On the whole we maintain, that it was so alien to their national consciousness, as well as to their religious dispositions and habits, that its appreciation was ordinarily not to be expected. Of its repeated proscription, too, under Marcus Aurelius and Verus, mention was made in the earlier part of this work.

As a representative heathen sentiment on the Sabbath about Hadrian's period (and thereafter), we will, before we close this chapter, adduce that of Tinnius Rufus, the governor of Judea in his reign. This personage is in the Rabbinical literature frequently credited to have been engaged in colloquies with Rabbi Akiba. He is reported to have once questioned this sage: "What can be the preference of one day before others, that the Sabbath was for your people singled out of the rest of the week days?" The striking reply of the Rabbi was: "And what distinguishes one man from others; I mean, why was Tinnius Rufus himself chosen from the rest of the Romans for the high post he presently holds?" The governor retorted: "For what other reason than because the emperor deemed it right to intrust me with it?" "In the same way," Akiba declared, "the Sabbath has been selected from the other days. God wished to honor it" (Rabb. Gen. ch. xi). The foregoing objection against the Sabbath is so likely to have been made by a genuine Roman, that the authenticity of the Midrashic narrative connecting Rufus' name with said colloquy, cannot well be questioned. For with the Romans the distinction of one day from the others of the week for objects of Divine worship and sanctification, was at best a superstitious abnormity.

NOTES.

[1] Zunz, in his "Gottesd. Vortraege," quotes Josephus, Against Apion ii. 18, and Acts xv. 21, in which passages the custom of reading the Law in public every Sabbath, is mentioned as very old.

[2] If Plutarch had taken pains to acquaint himself with a larger volume of Jewish historical facts, than he really did, he might have hit upon one instance at least, entirely similar to those cases of the Greek mythology enumerated before in the chapter of his book in point, and which he declared as so commendable, because they offer an example of prompt resoluteness to fight with material weapons, combined with prayerful reliance on divine aid. About the same thing Jonathan, the Asmonean leader, exhorted his brave warriors to do, when they were surprised by Bacchides' forces in the valley of the Jordan on the Sabbath, which day he had slyly chosen to make havoc among the Jewish army. Jonathan summoned his men "to arise and battle for their lives," though it was the Sabbath, for there was no escape, the waters of the Jordan cutting off the possibility of retreat. At the same time he urged them to "call unto God, that they might be saved out of the hands of the enemies." There was surely no "cowardice" in those Jews; their unbending religious faith was blended with an equally unbending heroism. And yet they were slow in resolving to make battle on the Sabbath even in the utmost extremity to which they were reduced, fearing God more than the destruction of their lives! (See 1. Macc. ix. 43 sq.).

[3] That the zealots had in the fight against Cestius not regarded the Sabbath, as Josephus states reproachfully (Wars ii. 19, 2), cannot well be held out as an instance of a diminution of that anxiety in the minds of the Jewish people. For not only were the zealots only a faction or factions out of the whole Jewish population, the great majority of whom were moderate and yet peacefully inclined at that point of time; but we have also to consider that those enthusiastic revolutionists could, in their fiery impulse to avenge the unheard-of outrages committed on their nation by Florus and previous

procurators, and to defend and free it from the oppressive crushing dominion of the Romans, not be expected to sit down passively and ponder scrupulously over the possibility of breaking the Sabbath, by setting out to meet the approaching army of Cestius. They could not afford, we suppose, to wait till this commander would make the first attack, losing perhaps meanwhile, during the Sabbath rest, the best advantages over him. There was in those days of fearful pressure and successive miseries too much at stake for their country to be determined by the nice distinction between offensive and defensive warfare, which at any other time themselves doubtless recognized as well. As to Josephus' animadversion, ib. 17, 10, we suggest, that the same reply holds good which we objected to the previous one, only that we know of no mitigating explanation of the act itself reported there.

I may mention here yet in passing that Graetz, History of the Jews, iii. 545, has rendered the passage of Josephus ib. ii. 19, 2, in which he observes that the Sabbath is with them kept the most holy, incorrectly. He lets him convey the notion, that the zealots were observing the Sabbath most of all. But we have to object, that Josephus did there not specially refer to the zealots, but stated merely a practice of the Jews in general. Nor does he discriminate in that place as to classes keeping the Sabbath more or less holy, so that his words might be construed to indicate "most of all." These two words do not occur in his statement at all. He solely wished to put down the Sabbath, in contradistinction to other holy days or religious rites, as being most strictly observed by the Jews.

On the tenability of his other opinion, that the Shammaites were political sympathizers of the zealots, the Hillelites favoring peace and discouraging a revolt from the Romans, we will here not pass. The reader is referred to what Jost, Hist. of Judaism, i. 327, Note, observes on this theory. Only this much we will object, as pertinent to our present subject, that to discover political zealotism in the mere theoretical exposition, credited to Shammai (not the Shammaites!) in B. Sabb. f. 19, of the two words "ad ridtah" in Deut. xx. 20, where directions are given for any future war of conquest (see Sifre, Deut. § 203), is altogether too conjectural. Moreover, Shammai's authorship of that exegetical proposition is by no means authenticated, the Tosifta Erubin, iii. 7, reporting it in the name of Hillel. Who is, in our day, competent to decide, that the version in the Babylonian Talmud is more accurate than that of the Tosifta?

⁴Comp. Ant. xix. 6, 3, where the insolent mob of Doris is reported to have, under Claudius, forced this emperor's statue in the synagogue of that city, in spite of an imperial edict previously published, that guaranteed to the Jews undisturbed, religious liberty.

⁵This suspicion was doubtless based on his knowledge of what happened under his predecessor, Tiberius, that the Jews, namely, offered desperate resistance to Pilate's attempt of placing shields dedicated to the emperor (Josephus, Ant. xviii. 3, 1, has "ensigns with the effigies of Tiberius" instead) within the city of Jerusalem (Leg. § 38-39). Philo seems to have alluded to this occurrence, together with the profanation of the Alexandrian synagogues under Flaccus' administration, when he advances with respect to the order of Caius to erect his statue in the Temple: "For you (Caius) seem not to have attempted the innovation with the Temple through ignorance of what was likely to result from it" (ib. § 31). Helicon of whom we treat in our text, and other persons of his household, the greater portion of whom were Egyptians, have undoubtedly, on their part, not failed to foster that suspicion.

⁶That the desecration of the Alexandrian synagogues was the immediate and decisive cause of the mission of the Jewish deputation to Rome, appears not only from the passage in Leg. § 29 quoted in our text, but, further, from the colloquy they held among themselves before they were summoned to a second audience with the emperor, upon receiving from a co-religionist the startling news, that the Temple of Jerusalem was destroyed (that is, as good as destroyed, because supposed to have been defiled by idols), the emperor having given the order of erecting a statue of himself in the holy of holies: "And will it be allowed to us * * to open our mouth about the synagogue before this destroyer of the most holy place?" (Leg. l. c.) That the Jewish disfranchisement during the administration of Flaccus and his successor, and the atrocious treatment from the populace, formed part of their complaint, is certainly not to be questioned. This is evident enough from Philo's statement, that the Memorial with which the envoys provided and, perhaps, wished to introduce themselves to the emperor, contained "a summary of what we had suffered, and of the way in which we considered that we deserved to be treated" (ib. § 28); as also from his later reflection (ib. § 29) upon "both the objects on account of which we were sent." Their complaint was about their religious and bodily persecutions, as well

as about the insolent encroachment on their charters of civil equality. Both objects were combined. Yet, we hold, predominant and directly urging to the voyage to Rome was not their political suffering, but the unendurable affront of the dedication of the synagogue to Caius, the deified emperor.

We consequently do not agree with Graetz, otherwise so highly deserving of the elucidation of those gloomy events in the history of the Alexandrian Jews, who (History iii. 553) insists that their "disputed equal rights were the (sole) cause of the Jewish embassy." He wishes to prove it mainly from Ant. xix. 5, 2. But the edict of Claudius presented there, has by no means an exclusive political bearing; it guarantees to the Jews religious liberty, as well as it re-secures their established rights and privileges. Nor can we for one moment entertain the supposition, that the "sedition" set forth there as having arisen between the Jews and the Greeks of Alexandria, was on account of political rights. The Alexandrian populace could not withhold these from the Jews This only the Roman government might violently do, directly or through the lord-governors. Why then should they fly to arms and fight with the Alexandrians to recover what these could neither bestow nor deny, their civil rights; specially now, after the death of their most cruel oppressor, Caius, when it was surely more practicable to seek redress for present political disabilities at the seat of the central power, Rome? But when we attribute that armed uprising of the Jews to continuous religious insults and affronts, which we know them to have endured up to that time, and also to all kinds of social chicanery to which they were daily exposed, we have found a much more reasonable motive for it. The unspeakable suffering as to their religious conscience and personal security, that seemed to them never to cease, at last incited them to armed resentment, for which they doubtless chose the absence of the resident governor, so that they had not to fear a forcible suppression of their attempt from this side.

As to the word "politeia" used by Philo, and which Graetz construes in a political sense, we contend that it has in the relative passages no such meaning at all. He meant by it the national religious constitution or law of Israel, as contained in the Mosaic code. In this sense it is incontrovertibly employed by him in 'On the Migration of Abraham,' ch. xvi., where he propounds, "A good name falls to the lot of nearly all who, rejoicing in contentment, do not overthrow any one of the existing laws (he has here in mind such laws as the Sabbath, the festivals, circumcision, of which he speaks in the immediate sequel), but observe the ancestral (or national) constitution — *ten patrion politeian* — not without thoughtfulness." Comp. also the "God-loving constitution," that is, the Mosaic Law, in 'On Monarchy' ch. vii. The same signification it has without doubt in the sentence (Leg. § 44), " * * when we were sent for (by the emperor to an audience with him, not, 'when we were delegated' by our Jewish community) to enter upon the contest concerning the politeia." And the same religious bearing, we hold, the term has in Caius' question to the delegates (ib. § 45): "I wish to know what legal principles you practically entertain as to the politeia?"

He was evidently curious to hear an authoritative interpretation of the principles of the national law, which the Jews urged so persistently in their opposition to offer worship to his godship, to ascertain whether it really conflicted organically with such compliance, or was only put forward as pretext and disguise of their inward disaffection and disobedience to him.

[7] Hausrath, 'New Testament Times', in Joel, ' Blicke, etc.' ii. p. 118, says: "Apion made his Jewish historical studies and investigations in the taverns of Alexandria, and reproduced the material gathered there with the most decided talent for everything filthy."

[8] Molo was by far not so malicious against Jews as Apion; see Josephus, Ag. Apion ii. 15.

[9] Whether Cicero succeeded in convincing the judges, that the Jews were real enemies of Rome, we do not know. The charge he advanced could certainly not apply to the remoter past. It is attested by authentic history that the Jews were, in the times previous to Pompey's invasion of the Jewish land, not averse to the Roman protectorate. From the first half of the second century B. C., the Jewish rulers were anxiously seeking friendly alliances with Rome. Judas Maccabeus made a league of friendship and assistance with the Senate, which was afterward renewed by his brothers Jonathan and Simon during their respective administrations, and again by the latter's son, the high-priest and sovereign, John Hyrcanus. Nor was surely the appeal of John's grandsons, Aristobulus and Hyrcanus II., who contended with each other for the title to the government, to Pompey for an authoritative decision of their claims, a sign of disregard for Rome or disdain of her glory. It must on the contrary appear to every one as a mark of open, respectful acknowledgment of her great power and prestige.

Aristobulus, it is true, was repugnant to Pompey's authority (Ant. xiv. 3, 3 sq.), and his men obdurately refused to peaceably surrender Jerusalem with its fortifications to him, according to the agreement made before between both (ib. 4, 1), a refusal that brought on the forcible attack and ultimate capture of Jerusalem by the Roman army.

But unbiased judges could scarcely detect any sudden national hostility to Rome in the determined endeavor of Aristobulus' military to fight off a power, attempting to usurp the possession of the capital of the Jewish nation, to which it had no claim whatever, save the flimsy one derived from the league obtaining between the two nations, and which they could not allow to interfere in disfavor of him whom they held their rightful sovereign. Even if the refusal of Aristobulus' men had to impress itself on the minds of Roman authorities as a direct affront offered to them, this could not with any shadow of right and consistency be made a charge of against the entire Jewish nation. For the multitude of the Jews were, at least since Alexander Janneus, avowed votaries of Phariseism (Ant. xiii. 10, 6), and on this account decided opponents of the Sadducean claimant, Aristobulus. Adhering to Hyrcanus (ib. xiv. 2, 1), from sectarian motives at least, they quietly submitted to Roman interference, although they practically discountenanced, on the other hand, as we may state here additionally, the assumption of kingly rule by either of the contending rivals (ib. 3, 2). They could consequently not as a body be adjudged enemies of Rome.

That the resistance to Pompey's forces had indeed not permanently been construed as an aversion from the Roman supremacy, is clear from Augustus' official testimony, that "the nation of the Jews have been found *grateful* to the Roman people * * * in times past also, and chiefly Hyrcanus the high-priest, under my father (?), Cæsar the emperor" (ib. xvi. 6, 2). The interval between this epoch and the time of Cicero's delivery of the oration in question, was only about twelve years. Blind prejudice alone could then have maintained that the whole Jewish nation was hostile to Rome. For indeed those who were grateful to Rome a short time afterwards, could not have been permeated by a spirit of enmity towards it on that day when Cicero put forth his argument in his speech.

Let us observe yet that to conclude from the apocryphal 'Psalms of Solomon,' as Hausrath did, that the sting of the wound which Pompey had inflicted on the Jewish people, was never afterwards removed, is too hazardous. The interval between Pompey's invasion and the incorporation of Judea as a Roman province under Augustus in 6 or 7 C. E., or rather the time of the census and taxation, was indeed, on the whole, agreeable between the two nations, as is evident from the foregoing.

[10] For a good Roman to embrace such a superstition was at times held really criminal. Tacitus reports of Nero's reign, that the adherence of one's wife to a "foreign superstition" was then adjudged a cause for divorce (Ann. xiii. 31).

[11] See Suetonius, 'Augustus,' on this emperor's abstaining from visiting the sanctuary of Apis, while traveling through Egypt.

[12] Renan, 'Apostles,' remarks: "It was only due to the tolerant spirit of Augustus himself, that no repressive measures were enacted against Judaism and other foreign cults" (from Dio Cass. li. 36).

[13] Graetz' conjecture in his 'Proselytes in the Roman Empire,' that allusion is here made to the conversion of Flavius Clemens, is too visionary to deserve any earnest notice.

[14] Such measures had already been employed in the best days of the Republic. There is a notice of Valerius Maximus preserved (quoted by Schuerer, 'The Jewish People, etc.') which reads: "The same (the prætor Hispalus) compelled the Jews who had attempted to infect the Roman customs with the cult of Jupiter Sabazus, to return to their homes" (own country). This was about B. C. 139. There can be no doubt that some Jews had then made zealous efforts to win Roman polytheists over to their faith. Who those proselytizers were, whether, as Schuerer suggests, the envoys of Simon, the Asmonean prince, sent to Rome to renew the former mutual league (see 1 Macc. xiv. 24; xv. 15-24)—and this is by no means unlikely, considering that in the Asmonean family, at least in the branch starting from Simon, proselytism was a conspicuous, vehement trait; see on John Hyrcanus, Ant. xiii. 9, 1; on his son Aristobulus I. ib. 11, 3; and on his other son, Alexander Janneus, ib. xv. 4.—or some other Jewish enthusiasts making it their mission to acquire proselytes out of paganism, is by far not so important to submit to inquiry, as is their numerical proportion to the generality of the Jewish residents of Rome. We hold, against Schuerer, who would deduce from said notice, that "no Jews dwelt permanently in Rome about B. C. 139," that there was indeed a previously established Jewish settlement there, the Jewish population comprising more than just those banished

thence in that year. That notice, we contend, does not warrant the assumption, that every one of the then Roman Jews was engaged in proselytism, so that the order must have affected each and all of them. There was beyond doubt a considerable number of them in the city, who were not eager at all to meddle with the religion of the pagan inhabitants, being perfectly satisfied to follow their several pursuits and ply their trades inoffensively. We presume that such Jews were not included in the order, and remained unmolested in the city they had chosen for their habitation.

The same view we apply to the state of Jewish propagandism under Tiberius. That it was in his reign carried on rather zealously, we admit. There may have been more missionaries in Rome at that time than merely those four described by Josephus, and to whom he imputes the origin of Tiberius' proscription of the Roman Jews. But, on the other hand, we cannot reconcile in our mind the assumption that more than a limited number out of the whole Jewish population were engaged in proselytism. The Jewish people were neither then, nor at any other period, a nation of proselytizers. Kuenen's judgment is doubtless correct, that "the conversions were rather the result of the zeal of a few, than of general measures concerted in Judea" (Religion of Israel, iii. 274.)

We hold it important to emphasize once more our opinion of an established settlement of Jews having existed already in the year B. C. 139 in Rome, in order to controvert the common notion, (Hausrath, N. T. Times, i. 177, entertains it, too) that the Roman Jews occurring in the extra-Jewish literature of the empire, were none other than descendants of slaves. This notion is mainly founded on Philo's statement, that the Jews of Rome in Augustus' time were "mostly Roman citizens, having been emancipated, etc." (Leg. § 24.) We have to charge Philo with being indeed accountable for that notion. He conveys in truth the idea, that there were at the beginning of the empire no other Jews in Rome, than freedmen and a residue of those still bound in slavery. But such assumption is not only unreasonable, but is, as we will prove, refuted from Cicero's Oration for Flaccus.

There can be no doubt whatever, that the agreeable and friendly relations which had obtained between the two nations since the early Asmonean period (see above Note 9), drew many Jews towards Rome. They cannot but have met with a hospitable spirit at the hands of their new allies, and felt themselves at home and secure under the potent ægis of the all-ruling Rome. They immigrated thither of their own free accord, as free men, and enjoyed the liberties and privileges of citizens. The before-noted incident of the year 139 had not, as already suggested above, affected the entire Jewish settlement of Rome, nor was perhaps the proscription enforced for any length of time. New accessions steadily increased the original stock till, when masses of their unfortunate brethren were carried as prisoners of war from the east and sold as slaves about the middle of the first century B. C., these found in them a respectable, compact community of free and, therefore, very helpful citizens.

We further object against the theory that the Roman Jews of the empire descended from manumitted slaves only, that Cicero, in the named Oration, presumably held B. C. 59, refers to the Jewish people as ".very numerous," and having great "weight in popular assemblies." Is it, we ask, thinkable that he could allude to them as of such quality, had they been no more than emancipated slaves, with a residence in the capital of only four years' duration? For such a short time only had then elapsed since Pompey's conquest of Jerusalem. Moreover, we have to ask, what authority is there for the supposition that Pompey carried masses away as captives from Judea? Josephus at least makes no mention of it. The captivity of the Jews and their slavery in Rome are, in our view, authenticated only for B. C. 53–52, in which time fell the conquest of Crassus, when "about 30,000 of them were carried captives (Ant. xiv. 7, 3). This we assert, though we are aware of the apocryphal book of the Psalms of Solomon presenting in Ps. ii. 6 sq., viii. 24 sq., and xvii. 13, a numerous captivity of Jerusalem's sons and daughters, which three psalms are by Wellhausen, 'The Pharisees and the Sadducees,' put down as alluding to Pompey's invasion. (See also Hausrath, N. T. Times, ii. 183, who, moreover, lets the whole work be composed as an expression of indignation over Pompey's act at that juncture).

We have then to adjudge Philo's statement in question as inaccurate, in so far as he mentions no other Roman Jews as citizens than those coming from enslaved captives. Admitting that the number of these was larger than that of the ancient Jewish community of free citizens of Rome, we yet uphold emphatically our conviction, that the latter existed there since very early days, and formed a respectable and influential part of the entire Roman population, to whom by-the-by the gibes of Roman satirists would most illy apply. A Juvenal and Martial may have been acquainted only with that class of Roman

Jews living in abject poverty, or purposely chosen such as specimens for their depictions of Jewish life and habits, in about the same way as modern scribblers in preponderantly Christian cities are wont to present American Judaism as they find or seek it out in the squalid quarters of wretched immigrants from half-civilized European countries.

As to the gibberish 'Jupiter Sabazus' in the above notice of Valerius Maximus, we will yet adduce Schuerer's suggestion (l. c.), that the name may be a confusion of the Hebrew Sabaoth with (Jupiter) Sabazius, a Phrygian deity; and likewise the peculiar interpretation put on it by Mommsen, Roman History, ii. p. 429, who relates: "The same fate (that befel the Chaldean astrologers) was simultaneously visited on the Jews, who had admitted Italian proselytes to their Sabbaths." He obviously took Sabazus in the sense of Sabbath.

[15] Philo, as contemporary, should, as we would presume at first view, merit the credit of supplying a correct report in assigning the entire persecution to Sejan, and not to Tiberius. That this emperor was no decided enemy of the Jews, we should, farther, in the premises, conclude from the assurances, mentioned in our text, which he gave to the Jews of the various provinces through their governors. That such assurances were given, must, moreover, appear as certain, because Philo who reports the fact could have had the most accurate knowledge of it, as doubtless a communication in behalf of the Egyptian Jews had also come to Alexandria, his home. Indirectly it might also be inferred from Tacitus (Hist. v. 9, and Annals ii. 42), that Tiberius was not unfavorably disposed to the Jews. Yet since the other three writers have not mentioned Sejan in connection with the persecution of the Jews, Philo's single attribution of it to that powerful intriguer will remain subject to serious doubt. The more so, when we hold in view Suetonius' characterization of Tiberius. He asserts regarding the popular notion that Sejan was the author of the cruel acts committed in his reign, that in reality "he was not so much set up by Sejan, as that this councillor only furnished him the occasions when he sought them." Philo may then have labored under the same impression with many other people of that day, judging that crafty councillor to have been the author of the atrocities which in fact Tiberius perpetrated of his own cruel mind.

[16] Both Josephus and Tacitus agree in stating that 4,000 men were in penalty levied out of the Roman Jews and sent to the island of Sardinia, the latter-named author representing them, moreover, as young men of the families

of freedmen who were assigned for the penal labor of putting down the robberies on the island. Suetonius, too, lets the Jewish youth of Rome be enlisted and distributed in provinces of unhealthy climates. This threefold testimony would at once give the lie to Tiberius' assertion, quoted in our text from Philo, that "the punishment was not executed upon all, but only on the guilty ; and they were but few," were it not for the reconciling view, that such enrollment in the army was in the eyes of that cruel emperor no punishment at all. This view could, however, scarcely hold out to account for the penalty decreed, according to the same three historians, on the other Jews. Josephus presents it in the following : * * "but punished (with banishment from the city, as the context shows) a greater number of them who were unwilling to become soldiers on account of keeping the laws of their forefathers." Suetonius gives it : "The rest of that nation, following the like persuasion, he removed from the city (that is, ordered to leave it) on pain of perpetual servitude, if they should not obey (this order)." Tacitus advances : "The rest should have to leave Italy, unless they would before a certain day have renounced their profane rites." However divergent these three accounts are from one another, they agree at least as to the main point that, after the forcible enlistment of the younger Jews designated for Sardinia, the rest of the Roman Jews were punished also. Whether with banishment from the city, as Josephus and Suetonius have it, or with compulsion to renounce their religion, if they wished to remain in Italy, according to Tacitus, there can be no dispute on the proposition that either proscription was a real, heavy penalty. Or should we resort to the extreme view that Tiberius at least esteemed no penal infliction of any sort a real punishment, as long as the head remained on the trunk, capital penalty alone coming to him under that category, in order to square his reassuring assertion to the Jews through the governors, with the opposite reports of those three historians ? We have not the mind to venture such view, although we would gain by it the advantage of accounting for that assertion in this manner, that the "few guilty" ones were those who had actually to suffer with their lives for the accusation laid against them.

[17] We cannot withhold our mistrust of Josephus' account of fraud as the originating cause of the order of banishment of the Roman Jews. Not only have the three other writers not mentioned it, but it appears, moreover, too strange, not to say, suspicious, that the repression decreed alike on the Egyptian and Jewish cults, should have been called

forth almost simultaneously by crimes committed at about one same time in both communities, the one incest, the other, fraud (Ant. l. c. 4, 5). It is our opinion that Josephus got his information on the subject from a tainted, pagan source, and one partial to Tiberius and attempting to free him from the odium of uncalled-for religious persecution. In it the crimes were invented for this purpose. Our own view that the measure was concerted from an invidious and jealous sentiment towards foreign worships, believed to become more and more detrimental to the State religion, will find confirmation in the fact, that Suetonius adds yet the proscription of the Chaldean astrologers, as being then ordered likewise. For it would be preposterous to suppose that this proscription was also caused by a particular criminal act. We have at least no intimation to this effect, either in the work of Suetonius or any other Roman writer. From all indications offered us by that author, we cannot assume any other motive to have actuated the Roman authorities in proceeding against the astrologers than the same puritan one, which made them proscribe the Jewish and Egyptian worships. In their case it was the strong apprehension in the minds of the authorities, that the national institutions of divination would be seriously impaired by being longer indulgent towards their art and practice.

[18]If Tacitus alone were to be consulted as to the banishment of the Jews under Tiberius, it would appear to us as more plausible, that born Jews were not at all affected by his decree, but that it was aimed only at freedmen of pagan descent, partially converted to Judaism, and belonging to the class of the God-fearing or half-proselytes. It is true, the number of several thousand Judaizing freedmen existing in Rome at one time, seems stupendously large. But it can surely not be pronounced impossible, considering the zealous propaganda then made by Jews, and which we prefer to hold as having been chiefly active among people of lower grade, as these could much more easily and with an immeasurably better prospect of prompt success be approached by the missionaries — the Christian missionaries of our day furnish sufficient illustrations of the truth of our opinion —, than the high-born and wealthy persons of Roman society.

Freedmen were only half recognized in Roman society. Their position was a middle one between the free citizen and the slave. It could then not have been such an arduous effort to turn a large number of this class away from the polytheism of their former masters, in whose service they were treated so cruelly and vilely, and gain them for the Jewish worship.

Taking those freedmen of Tacitus for converts from paganism we can, further, much better and readier understand his other statement, "the rest were ordered to leave Italy, unless they would before a certain day have cast off their *unholy rites.*" Not only do these last words convey, in our view, the sense of adopted in contradistinction to hereditary religious rites, as likewise the expression employed in the same context, "*infected* by that superstition," seems unmistakably to point here as in the similar decree of the proscription of B. C. 139 (see above Note 14) in which it is also used, to a propagandist introduction of Jewish rites into Rome ; but we would, if born Jews were to be understood as the subjects in the passage in point, be at a loss to account for it, how a wholesale coercion of them to forsake their own national religion within a certain, short period, on pain of total expulsion from entire Italy, could have been decreed by the Roman authorities. The Jews of Rome were, as Philo reports, mostly citizens and as such, however much prejudice there may have prevailed against them in that city, they were legally guarded and guaranteed against any infringement of their religious liberty. An order of religious ostracism directed against any class of real Roman citizens, seems to have been impossible, as it would positively have been utterly un-Roman. Whereas the order gains a different aspect, when we take the freedmen against whom the proceedings of proscription were enacted, as of pagan extraction, and only partially converted to and leaning on Judaism. They, being yet in a state of semi-dependence, had no legal right, so the Senate may have held, to apostatize from the national religion and embrace a foreign. Or the Senate would, on the whole, not scruple to resort to violent measures against those descended from slaves, their lives and persons being otherwise valued rather low (cp. Tacitus' "vile damnum"). The "rest" of the freedmen who, according to this historian, were by order of the Senate threatened with expulsion if they would not abjure their religious rites, were, we further intrepret agreeably with our proposition, those half-converts to Judaism of older age or otherwise unfit for military service.

Lastly, we contend that, had those freedmen of Tacitus been born Jews, they would we firmly believe have promptly allowed themselves to be expatriated, rather than leave off their paternal worship or religious rites. But we know them to have existed in large numbers in Rome, when Philo visited there in the reign of Tiberius' successor, Caligula. How could this have been, were we to maintain that the penal proceedings were aimed at born Jews? They would in this case without doubt have to one man emigrated from Rome, so that Philo could not possibly have found them there in the way described by him.

Graetz' suggestion that, having really been banished by Tiberius, they were recalled by him twelve years afterwards (Hist. iii. 261), could not offer us any acceptable egress from that dilemma. For it is a mere conjecture, without any historical warrant. Jost, Hist. of Judaism, i. 332, too, objects that it is insupportable.

[19] By Herod's days he meant without doubt the Sabbaths and holidays of the Jews. In the same significance "sabbata," in v. 184, is to be taken. This term was with the Roman writers the generic appellation for all Jewish solemn days, including even the fasts.

We may remark here that Persius' description in vv. 180-81, throws a desirable light on the estimation of the Jewish custom of lighting the rooms and premises on Sabbaths and holidays. The Talmud represents it as a means of cheerful comfort, appropriate for such sacred days. This view seems to us, however, a late interpretation of an old, firmly established usage, reaching perhaps back to obscure antiquity. Be this as it may, we can at all events conclude from Persius' illustration, as also from Josephus (Ag. Ap. ii. 40), who mentions it as adopted by Judaizing Gentiles apart from the abstinence from labor on the Sabbath, that it was held as an obligatory observance of essential religious importance.

That Persius designates the Jewish holidays Herod's days, may be explained by the circumstance that Agrippa I., who passed under the name of Herod (see Acts xii.), was a reputed, high Jewish personage, a representative Jew, as the phrase runs nowadays. His name offered itself consequently very availably to a contemporary Roman writer, for affixing to it customs descriptive of the Jewish people.

[20] The inconsistency of Claudius' persecution of the Roman Jews related by Suetonius, with his published friendly edicts for the Jews in the provinces (see Josephus, Ant. xix. 5, 2, 3), could in itself not make us discredit that biographer's account. It could be reconciled this way, that

the emperor, being truly of a tolerant spirit to the Jews, was yet provoked by some dangerous act of Roman Jews to such a degree, that he could not well help resorting to severe measures against them, which, moreover, were confined to the capital.

Again, it is quite possible that true Jews were not affected at all by the edict of expulsion. Suetonius' attachment of "impulsore Chresto" would render it quite plausible that it was aimed at Christians of the Jewish stock, and not at orthodox Jews. The relative statement in Acts xviii. 2, may mean the same thing, and Aquila and Priscilla, too, can be supposed as having been adherents of the Jewish Christian party already in Rome. (Comp. Baur 'Paul,' i. 328, who suggests so much at least, with reference to that relation of Acts, that "they were by no means entirely unacquainted with the Christian faith"). It is well known that the Christian sect was in those days yet counted among the Jews. The ordinary Roman did then not distinguish between the Jewish believers in the Messiah of Nazareth, and the bulk of the Jews denying the claim of his Messiahship. The imperial order of which Suetonius speaks, may accordingly have been called forth by those sectaries only, and the tumults he mentions as frequently made by them, have been nothing else than disputations they engaged in with orthodox Jews on the merits of the new faith, and quarrels resulting therefrom; or they were, perhaps, merely the self-conscious, loud and open proclamations by those sectaries of their Messiah and of his eagerly awaited second coming, which had to impress the Roman authorities as being plots of political innovation, that were to be met with striking measures of repression.

Baur, l. c. i. 327, too, interprets the "impulsore Chresto" as meaning nothing else than Christianity itself, which was then becoming known in Rome, and gave occasion to disturbances and disputes within the Jewish population. Only that he declares it as natural that the two contending parties, the Jews and the Christians, were both expelled from the city.

While our construction would promptly lift the inconsistency in question, we yet have to object that the expression "impulsore Chresto" does not without violence to the letter warrant the assumption, that the author meant by it a movement or commotion stirred up by or on account of Christian sectaries, but rather demands our supposing one created by a personal Chrestus or temporal Messianic kingly pretender. For it was in the latter capacity only that the Roman authorities were apprehensive of the

Christus's, who rose among the Jews from time to time. This appears not only from Pilate's proceeding against Jesus (see Matt. xxvii. 11, Mark xv. 2 and in especial Luke xxiii. 2, 3), but also from the fate of the subsequent Messiah-pretender, Theudas, who, as Josephus reports (Ant. xx. 5, 1 ; comp. the respective unhistorical notice in Acts v. 36), was put to death by order of the procurator Fadus. Later, under the procurators Felix and Festus, there were other Messianic pretenders likewise punished with death ; see Ant. xx. 8, 5, 6, Wars ii. 13, 5, Acts xxi. 38, Ant. xx. 8, 10.

The severity with which tumultuous concourses, especially under leaders, were viewed and visited by the imperial Roman authorities, is further evidenced by the violent interference of Pilate, in the year 35 or 36, against the Samaritans who, incited by a certain prophetical leader and Messiah (see Hausrath, l. c., who not only represents the movement as a Messianic one, undertaken in rivalry with John's *Jewish* preaching of the Kingdom, but expresses by-the-by what has long been our own firmly maintained opinion, that that leader was none other than the notorious Simon of Gitto, nicknamed the Magician, of Acts viii.), marched in arms to the Mount Gerizim to recover hidden sacred vessels (Ant. xviii. 4, 1). Pilate at once construed this as an attempt at revolt (ib. 2), and made bloody havoc among them.

A short time before, John the Baptist had suffered death at the hands of the tetrarch Herod Antipas, because he had feared a rebellion from him and the crowds that had joined him (ib, 5, 2). No matter how spiritualistic the motives of such Messianic illusionists were, the Roman officials or creatures of the Roman power and favor knew of no pity towards such offenders. (Let us observe here yet in passing that Keim, History of Jesus, ii., insists that the most reasonable account for Antipas' cruel procedure against John was his *political apprehension*, just as Josephus states it. Hausrath, l. c. p. 116, coincides with him in preferring Josephus' account to the Gospel explanations of it.)

We would according to our foregoing suggestions interpret Suetonius' report, that the expelled Jews were the followers of a Messianic pretender, who acted his part in Rome in an aggressive and boisterous way. The indulgence with which Claudius treated the Jews, owing perhaps to the most favorable esteem in which he held the princes Agrippa I. and his brother Herod II., made the Jews of the empire once again breathe the breath of ease and self-confidence. Nay they, or some of them at least, may through that prestige have become proudly elated or, as

Dion gives it, been "again overweaning." The hope of a speedy release from the Roman supremacy may under such circumstances have been fondly and freely cherished by a considerable number of Jews. This temper was possibly improved by a certain pretender who set up for the Messianic deliverer, preaching in the synagogues or other gathering places of the Jews his tidings of the mission to recover the Jewish independence. That person may even have been identical with the Theudas noted above. He may have come to Rome also, where he incited the Jews to co-operate with him in his scheme of a Messianic insurrection. Claudius then cut the movement short by his order.

By way of conjecture we will yet propose, that the "impulsor Chrestus" might have been Paul, to whom it happened later in Palestine, to be mistaken by a Roman chief captain for a Chrestus, or Messiah, see Acts xxi. 38. By his unheard-of pretension of the abrogation of the Mosaic Law and his attempted fusion of Judaism and heathendom by means of his Christian system, it is possible that he brought the Jewish inhabitants, even the Jewish Christians of Rome, to a pitch of rage that sought its vent in loud retorts and, perhaps, even assaults upon him and his retinue. The emperor may have put a stop to such uproarious scenes by his order.

As to the discrepancy between the account of Suetonius and Dion Cassius, we will yet mention that Schuerer, 'The Jewish People, etc.,' attempts to harmonize both by suggesting that the word "expulit" used by the former writer means only, "he contemplated to expel," the same as in the analogous case of the decree of Tiberius against Chaldean astrologers; see Suetonius, on Tiberius, 36.

In conclusion we may be permitted to suggest, that Claudius' proscription of Roman Jews must not at once be considered as prompted by a decided aversion to the Jews as a nation, or to their religious customs We have to bear in mind that imperialism was very sensitive and suspicious of anti-monarchial tendencies coming forward within its domain. When we hold in view the persecutions and banishments which the Roman philosophers, in particular the Stoics, endured from Nero, Vespasian and Domitian, we will be obliged to discard the prepossession that Claudius and other emperors interfering against Jews engaging in tumultuous movements or for other State reasons, were at the same time inspired by national or religious hatred to them. The fate of the Roman Jews under Claudius was surely not any worse than that of all but one of the philosophers who were expelled from Rome in the years 71-75 C. E. Nor was it equal in severity to the persecution visited on this class by Domitian, in 93. The supposed or open republican opposition of the Stoic philosophers to monarchy was mainly the cause of it. Likewise will we have to judge of Claudius' proceeding against the Jews, since it was called forth by some agitation which doubtless appeared dangerous to the government, as having been a measure of political discipline rather than a national-religious proscription.

[21] Suetonius who passed his youth in Rome under Domitian, could have given us the most authentic and explicit account of that imperial act of inquisition. But he has neglected doing so, leaving only a brief notice behind, in which he does not mention at all any penal proceedings against Domitilla and many other Judaizers, touching even on the fate of Flavius Clemens only in the few words, that the emperor "suddenly punished him with death on a very slight (trivial) suspicion" (Domitian, ch. xv.).

The Christian church claims Domitilla as her own. It makes of him a convert to Christianity. Eusebius, using Bruttius' Annals, has fathered this tradition. On the strength of it Christian writers qualify Flavius Clemens as a Christian, too. Both pass in Church history as martyrs. Chandler, History of Persecution, p. 45, argues in favor of the theory that they were Christians, from the view that *atheism* was the common charge laid against the Christians, and that Domitian was not known to have persecuted the Jews for their religion. The same opinion Gibbon propounds; see 'History of the Decline etc.,' ii. p. 25. He contends that the charge of atheism and Jewish manners imputed to the accused, was "a singular association of ideas which cannot with any propriety be applied except to the Christians." We, on our part, cannot however perceive the singularity of that association. Nor is there in Dion's account such an association only. It really exhibits a perfect identification of both the charges of atheism and Jewish customs (not "manners"). By these customs the Jewish worship and religious usuages are doubtless understood.

Dion says (lxvii. 14): "Both were indicted for atheotes"— which, in view of the parallel expression 'asebeia' used by him in connection with the account of Nerva's clemency, can mean nothing else than irreligiousness, that is, a defection from the national worship, by either embracing another religion, or adhering to any one odious philosophy of the age, or being otherwise a freethinking despiser of the country-deities — " of which even many others who had fallen away to the customs of the Jews were convicted."

Can the thinking reader for one moment doubt that he had here perfectly identified the Jewish customs with atheism? It is true, he holds in the account about Nerva ' asebeia ' and ' Jewish life ' apart. He says of this emperor: " He did not permit that any people should be accused of either asebeia (irreligion, godlessness) or a Jewish (mode of) life." But this does not in the least indicate that he had in the former notice not identified both, atheotes and Jewish customs. No. Dion did in the relation about Nerva not in the least think of contrasting both Roman offences. They were in the two accounts identical in his mind. In both of them he used irreligiousness, which he once denoted atheotes and then again asebeia, as a generic atheistic misdemeanor, expressive of every manner of desertion of the country-gods. Only that he conveyed, in the first-named passage, Jewish religious customs as directly included in the term atheotes, whilst in the other he thought it important enough to mention yet expressly Judaism, because this religion had then without doubt been the most widespread and popular of all the alien ones in Rome.

It could readily be expected from Domitian, infuriated as we hold him to have been against any alien worship that had gained ascendency in Rome, that he dealt with cruel decision with Judaizers from the ranks of the Latin stock, who committed the high treason of denying the native tutelar deities, among whom he himself claimed to be ranked as Rome's guardian genius. He could not bear to see his good patricians and withal his superior citizens affected by the astounding ideas of an immaterial God and the adoration due to him alone. His Roman puritanism revolted against it, as it was the case with Tiberius before him.

Baur (Paul, ii. 61) presents also the ordinary Christian conception, that Flavius Clemens was an adherent of Christianity. He grounds it not only on the charge of atheism stated by Dion, but on the " most contemptible sloth " with which he is reproached in Suetonius' account. This sloth he construes into a lack of interest in the politics of Rome, which was so peculiar to the Christians as a class. His misdemeanor then lay, according to Baur, not so much in his contemptible political inactivity as in his profession of Christianity. It must consequently, however, appear very strange that Suetonius should not at once have called the offence by its right name, that is, Christianity!

Graetz, History of the Jews, iv. p. 435 sq., and in his essay, " The Jewish Proselytes in the Roman Empire," has, to the contrary, raised it beyond any doubt, that in Flavius Clemens nothing but a convert to Judaism is to be recognized. He brings to bear on the question some Jewish legends, in particular those of the Midrash Rabb. Deut. ch. ii. f. 255 and of B. Abodah Zarah f. 10, which, while they are far from being directly available for historical use, may yet safely be adduced for the elucidation of the problem, whether Flavius Clemens is to be adjudged a convert to Judaism or Christianity.

In the two before-named places a Roman dignitary figures as a self-devoted Judaizing intercessor to rescue Israel from an impending expulsion (or extermination), once decreed by a Roman emperor and senate. His Judaism had been consummated by the initiatory rite. This description the two relations have in common. In all other points they differ from each other. The Midrash designates that high Roman as a synkletos "senator." The Talmud produces him under the fantastic name Ketia bar Shalom. The former makes him take poison at the urgent request of his wife who was still more attached to Jews and Judaism, which act of the self-destruction of her husband she had devised, that the execution of the imperial decree against the Jews would be stayed and the sentence ultimately nullified. The Talmud makes of him a mere martyr on his own account, and that only in a certain sense. It lets him suffer involuntary death for daring to remonstrate with the emperor about his attempt on the Jews, and to deprecate it. Whilst he succeeded in convincing him alike of its inefficiency and inexpedience, and prevented his carrying it into effect, he yet was guilty of a capital crime, consisting in the confutation of an emperor by a contradicting argument, for which he incurred the penalty of death that was really, as it is alleged there, inflicted on him. The woman figures in this passage also as more devoutly Judaizing than himself.

Now, as to the historical availability of this story or these stories — for both relations differing from each other indeed more than they agree on the points set forth therein, should by right be considered as two separate accounts — we assent to Graetz in so far as to discover a latent kernel of history in the chaff with which it is handed down to us. But we can by no means subscribe to his opinion (History l. c. p. 436), that the Midrashic story has a "sober and historical" stamp. It positively has all but this. It is on the contrary one of the many fantastic pieces of glorification of Israel, gotten up to illustrate the occasional self-sacrificing acts of friendly Gentiles, in which precious little regard is paid to real history.

Let us adduce a Rabbinical counterpart to our story, occurring in B. Taanith f. 29, which the reader will find totally akin to it as to tendency. We are told there of a Roman officer (senator or judge) having given up his life to save that of Rabban Gamaliel in the period of the Hadrianic persecution, when he was by the governor Tinnius Rufus condemned to death. That Roman "lord" proposed to rescue him from his dire fate, if he would promise him under oath to insure him entrance into the 'World to come.' This readily done, the Roman lord killed himself by casting himself down from a wall. Thus Gamaliel's life was saved. For, it is remarked there, further, the rule was, that if one of the judges who had passed a capital sentence died, it at once became void.

The fabulousness of this tale is too obvious and glaring to deserve any earnest attention except from the view of curiosity. The reader will at once conclude from the fabric of its impossibilities and inaccuracies, that it is nothing but a tendency-fiction, devised by a credulous author or, at any rate, for credulous masses, to exhibit another specimen of magnanimous self-devotion of pagan patrons to Jews and Judaism. It is assuredly of the same type as that of the Midrash under discussion.

But yet we cannot altogether reject the latter as bare of every true historical reminiscence. Dion's attestation of the two high Roman personages having leaned on Judaism and the penalty which the cruel emperor had inflicted on them therefor, may safely be held as the original substance of which the legendary web presented in the Midrash and Talmud was woven. The historical fact that Flavius and Domitilla were as devout Judaizers cruelly punished for persisting in the religion they had newly embraced, was doubtless delivered to the fervent memory of succeeding ages in Israel. The inference of their being most friendly to the Jews and showing them many favors, was easily drawn from that traditional circumstance. And as tradition had, further, presumably preserved many an occasion from the reign of the cruel emperor Domitian, on which interference for the sake of Israel was pressingly needed at the hands of Roman men of influence, those two martyrs offered themselves readily for the origination of legends, such as we meet with in the above-cited relations of the Midrash and Talmud.

[22] Josephus, Against Apion, ii. 40, states the Judaizing character of a "multitude of mankind from inclination," and that there is "no nation whatsoever, whither our custom of resting on the seventh day hath not come, and by which our fasts and lighting up lamps (on Sabbaths and festivals comp. ib. 10), and many of our prohibitions as to our food, are not observed."

His representation, dating from the end of the first century of our era, and delineating as it evidently does the practical observance of Jewish rites by Gentile Judaizers along that period, is borne out by Juvenal, Sat. xiv., who mentions about the same religious customs of proselytes to Judaism. He left out the fasts, because they were to him doubtless included in 'Sabbata;' also the lighting of lamps, which is easily thought to have been comprised in the 'fear of the Sabbata.'

Let us remark here in passing, that with Juvenal's "metuentem Sabbata" and Persius' "Sabbata palles," which phrases are expressive of awe-struck reverence felt by proselytes towards the Sabbath, may be compared the Talmudical Emath Shabbath "fear of the Sabbath."

As to Josephus' enumeration of Jewish rites adopted by a multitude of Gentiles, we must not at once conclude that all those heathens who were, according to his testimony, practicing them, had conceived a sincere attachment for Israel and devotion to their God, and that they were if not full, at least half-proselytes. There were without doubt a number of them whose minds had not turned to the true God, but who, loathing the trite ceremonies of their own country-religion, or moved by a certain superstitious preference, chose some Jewish religious rites, whilst they yet remained within the pale and the fetters of polytheism.

We will not, to prove this, refer to Riley's proposition quoted above, that Ovid in speaking of the "seventh holy-day observed by the Jew, etc.," as the day on which ladies were to be met at the synagogues, had before his mind the custom of pagan Roman ladies to visit there from sheer curiosity, who were all but devout worshipers of Israel's God. This explanation would indeed carry with it a decided moment of doubt as to many other cases of supposed Sabbath observance by Gentiles, which might have consisted in nothing else than their attendance, upon some outward motive, at Jewish synagogues, but yet caused the impression that a sincere religious disposition and conviction of the truth of Judaism had drawn them thither. But as that commentator's view lacks every internal evidence, and it is certainly possible that the poet alluded to real God-fearing Roman women of pagan extraction, we must not bring it to bear on our question.

A rather reliable testimony as to the co-existence of polytheism with the practice of Jewish rites, is furnished us, however, from another source. Tertullian, the Montanist church Father who flourished in the latter part of the second century, apologetically argues in his treatise 'On Fasting' (Works, vol. iii. Ante-Nicene Libr. ed.) against the so-called Psychics, who had opposed the few special fasts of the Christians, that the custom of holding fasts was so genuinely adapted to religious minds that it was found even among heathens. Even they, he reasons, recognize every form of "humiliation of spirit." "When the heaven is rigid and the year arid, barefooted processions are enjoined by public proclamation." That here the adopted features of the Jewish communal fasts for rain are brought forward, will at once strike the reader as probable. Tertullian's subsequent exposition renders it the more plausible. He continues: "There are moreover some colonies where, besides, [the inhabitants], by an annual rite, clad in sackcloth and besprent with ashes, present a suppliant importunity to their idols. * * * There is, I believe, a Ninevitan suspension of business! A Jewish fast, at all events, is universally (that is, everywhere in those colonies) celebrated; while, neglecting the temples, throughout all the shore, in every open place, they continue long to send prayer up to heaven." * * *

Who will not at once recognize in this heathen rite an imitation of the Jewish Atonement day? But it was outward only. Those pagans, whoever they were—Tertullian was not explicit enough to describe their nationality and locality—had in some way learned of the great annual Fast of the Jews, and seen fit to adopt it as part of their ritual, whilst they never thought of leaving off their idolatry on this account. The heathen custom of fasts for rain, represented by Tertullian as a rather general one among idolatrous nations, seems likewise to have been borrowed from Judaism. But were they by it any nearer to the real Jewish religion, especially its ground-principle, Monotheism? By no means.

We have accordingly to suggest that the apparent Judaizing with which many an ancient observer met among some pagan people in certain lands, may have misled him to take it for a true and real conversion, or at least for a strong devotion to Judaism, while it was in fact a mere outward imitation of some Jewish ritual observances, alongside of which those pagans may have been addicted to the grossest forms of idolatry. How much Josephus or the authorities upon which he based his above assertion, might have been affected by deceptive impressions of that kind, we have no means of ascertaining.

³ The reason why this rite vexed them, as it seems, most, is doubtless, because it was in their eyes the pitch and therefore formed the criterion of denationalization. That this view prevailed among the pagans, we may infer from the circumstance that Tacitus (Hist. v. 5, 25) lets the contempt of Roman Judaizers for their nationality follow immediately, in the same sentence, after his mention of their practicing the rite of circumcision. This necessarily impresses one that he meant to convey the notion that that contempt was the inevitable result of the initiatory rite, as being the unambiguous symbol of casting off the old and putting on the new nationality—Judaism. He says there: "Those embracing their religion practice the same (namely, circumcision), and they are early impressed with nothing sooner than to contemn the gods, to cast off (the allegiance to) their country, and to despise their parents, children, brothers."

The same local and logical sequence we find in Juvenal, Sat. xiv. Discoursing there on the children of Roman proselytes to Judaism, he declares, "soon they are circumcised, too. But they are used to contemn the Roman laws, and learn, observe and revere the Jewish law, etc." That this juxtaposition and connection is not accidental in either writer, but was intended to insinuate what we suggested, the reader will readily allow.

Our view may be substantiated, further, from Josephus, Ant. xx. 2, 4. He reports that the mother of King Izates of Adiabene objected to his decision of consummating his conversion to Judaism by undergoing the performance of the rite, that "he would thereby bring himself into great odium among his subjects, when they should understand that he was so fond of rites that were to them strange and foreign."

We suggest, by-the-way, that Hadrian's prohibition of circumcision, while it was surely not the only original cause of the tremendous uprising of the Jews, as Spartianus relates, but was perhaps imposed on them in penalty for it after it had been subdued by the Roman forces (see Graetz, History, etc., iv. p. 451), was likely intended by that emperor as a most crushing blow at once at the Jewish religion and nationality, since he knew well that it was the indispensable sign of the religious-national identity of the Jews, and their demarcation from all the other nations of the empire.

That the prohibition might not have had any religious-national bearing, was again and but recently advanced by Mommsen, 'Provinces of the Roman Empire,' ii. His older predecessor in this opinion, Casaubonus, is quoted by Muenter, ' The Jewish war under the emperors Trajan and Hadrian,' p. 36.

[24] The Roman writers Juvenal and Tacitus knew or noticed converts to Judaism only by the mark of the rite of circumcision. This deserves special remark the more, since several modern writers exaggerate the proportions of the so-called God-fearing proselytes, who had connected themselves with Israel without the submission to this rite. Tacitus' direct statement, " Those embracing their religion practice the same," allows of no other construction, than that he had before his mind and knew of no other than such full converts. Had he known of any cases of Judaizing without the acceptance of that rite, he would surely have mentioned them. The same is true of Juvenal, in the satire quoted above. Even if his words "soon they are circumcised too," should have to be taken as expressive of a gradual advance from other Jewish religious usages to circumcision as the final act of their initiation into the Jewish communion, we still contend that he thought of this concluding act as the fixed rule and custom, and these not left optional with the sons of proselyte parents, but obligatory on them. We insist—supposing the perception of progression in time was the only correct one in the context—that he wished to convey in that passage that, as the converted fathers were circumcised, so will the sons be, only that these were in their earlier childhood first being trained to regular Jewish observances, and ultimately, at a later, more convenient period, the initiatory rite was performed on them also. But we can allow that perception only provisionally. There is indeed no cogent evidence, that Juvenal used the word mox " soon " in the strict sense of temporal progression. In poetical works a small word or phrase inserted in the context, often serves only to round off the rythmic form, and its literalness must not be pressed at all. The adverb " soon " may accordingly have suggested itself to the author on going on in his composition as a metric stop-gap at the very point where we find it placed, while his mind was far from expressing the idea of temporal succession.

Be this as it may, thus much appears as most certain at least, that Juvenal's sentence in point allows of no other interpretation than that he reflected on the circumcision of the sons of Roman proselytes, and implicitly on that of the fathers themselves, as the settled rule, knowing of no other mode of admission to the fold of Judaism.

But such view did not alone prevail in the minds of the named Roman writers. We may lay it down as a certainty that the distinguishing mark, by which proselytes were commonly known and judged in the whole Greco-Roman world, alike by Gentiles and Jews, was the acceptance of the initiatory rite and the Mosaic religion in general. As to the Jews, it unmistakably appears from the various relative accounts of Josephus, that they would ordinarily approve of no other conversions than those attended with circumcision. He would himself, while he was tolerant enough to discountenance compulsory circumcision of pagans (see Life, sect. 23), yet recognize a merit of *true piety* only in such voluntary conversions to Judaism, as were accompanied by the self-imposition of that rite (see Ant. xx. 2, 4, end). Nor is there any warrant for that license in the interpretation of the term sebomenoi ton theon "worshiping God," occurring in his works, by which some modern writers attempt to prove their exaggerated view of mere outward Judaizers having formed that large contingent of proselytes, known to have existed in that century almost everywhere in the Greco-Roman world. [On the whole, we have to reproach a number of modern writers with being altogether too boldly conjectural in their view on the so-called God-fearing of the Judaic-Grecian literature. In Voelter's 'The Revelation of John, etc.,' p. 8, we learn of the theologian Harnaek having discovered in those "fearing the name of God" of Rev. xi. 18, proselytes to Judaism. Voelter disputes this and contends for the view, that pagan proselytes to Christianity were there understood. But neither exposition is justified by the text. Those authors are too prepossessed by the notion that a God-fearing must be a proselyte. John has in our opinion merely borrowed in xi. 18, as he did in xix. 5, from Ps. cxv. 13, alluding to no proselytes at all.

Even the conservative Ewald, in his History of Israel, vol. vii., would trace proselytes in the God-fearing of several Psalms. We admit the remote possibility that e. g. in Ps. cxviii. 4, which he also mentions, proselytes were meant. But there is in fact no internal or lingual evidence whatever for such an assumption. The "Yirai"-or "Abhdai

Jehovah" of Scripture are generally — and we prefer to think in all instances — nothing but *Israelites devoutly revering God.* They are identical with the Tsadikim "righteous" or "pious;" comp. Mal. iii. 16, 18.

Some of our ancient Rabbis have already indulged in the exegetical venture of discovering proselytes in the "Yirai Jehovah" of some passages of Scripture, thus setting the example to modern writers to do likewise. But they had no more authority for doing so, than the latter have. In Rabb. Lev. ch. iii., for instance, the God-fearing of Ps. xxii. 24, are explained to mean proselytes. But there is actually no plausible reason, why it should have been so explained. The God-fearing of that verse are, we aver, none other as to national extraction than those of the "seed of Jacob and of Israel," named therein afterwards. The latter two appellations are solely parallels of the first, such as Scripture exhibits in numberless instances. Moreover, the Psalmist can surely not be supposed to have distinguished those "God-fearing" by placing them ahead of "the seed of Jacob and Israel," had they been meant for proselytes. Our objection holds good against the same construction put on the God-fearing of Ps. cxxviii. 1, in Rabb. Numb. ch. viii. A more forced interpretation than this Rabbinical one could not have been ventured!]

Let us observe that the "worshipers of God" reported in Ant. xiv. 7, 2, as having everywhere joined the Jews in sending contributions to the Temple, cannot have been others than full proselytes. Not only is it not conceivable that half-proselytes should universally have taken such fervid interest in the national sanctuary as to help maintaining it, but the analogy of the use of the title 'sebomenoi' in Acts xiii. 43, where it either designates full proselytes or comprises them at least, precludes the supposition that Josephus understood by it only partial converts. When, further, Josephus relates in Wars vii. 3, 3, that the Jews were "continuously gaining over large numbers of Greeks through their religious rites and thus making them, after a sort, a portion of themselves," it would show the most ignorant disregard for the known facts of history to assume, that he meant by these Greek converts none but half-proselytes. The Jews had at no time made converts a "portion of themselves after a sort," unless these were previously consecrated by the rites of initiation and solemnly assumed to conform to the Mosaic religion. Moreover, the privileged and flourishing condition of the Jewish citizens in which he presents them there, can leave no doubt, that they will have made their own uncompromising terms to those who wished to join their community as equal members.

We incline to think that both Josephus and the author of Acts, have in the passages quoted before (comp. Acts, ib. v. 26) employed the appellation sebomenoi "worshiping God" in a generic sense, that is, for all proselytes, whether full or partial, and that in contradistinction from born Jews. This appellation, we further suggest, was commonly preferred in Greek-speaking Jewish communities to the other, foboumenoi "God-fearing," for denoting proselytes, though the latter title corresponded more directly, because literally, to the Scriptural "Yirai Jehovah" (for which latter word the Rabbis were accustomed to use Shamayim "Heaven"). In Acts, at least, where proselytes are so often noted, the word sebomenoi is almost exclusively employed for proselytes. It strikes us as most probable that the Rabbis, who by-the-way make a very sparse use of the term 'Yere Shamayim,' adhering more generally to the Mosaic name 'Ger,' had originally, like Josephus and the author of Acts in said passages, adopted it as the generic designation of proselytes, without regard to the mode of their admission and the range of Mosaic precepts they were to have accepted. It stands at all events in such a generic bearing in Rabb. Numb. ch. viii. In other places of the Rabbinical literature, again, it is used in contrast with Ger Tsedek, a "true (circumcised) proselyte;" so in Rabb. Lev. ch. iii.; Mechilta ch. xviii. The question whether in those passages in which the two terms are opposites, the Yere Shamayim corresponded entirely to the Ger Toshab of the Talmud, is not so easy to solve, considering the indecision of the olden Rabbis concerning the needed qualification of the latter-named proselyte. There are indeed three relative divergent opinions of Rabbis of the second century C. E. reported in B. Abodah Zarah, f. 64. But this much may be taken for certain, that the title Yere Shamayim was by the Rabbis intended to serve as the equivalent of the Greek terms sebomenos "God-worshiping" or foboumenos "God-fearing." It varied in application, we propose, as likewise these Greek terms did with the Greek-speaking or writing Jews or Jewish Christians. It once designates the proselytes as a class, and again, in contrast to the formal converts, the partial ones.

In the latter application Josephus wished without doubt to characterize Poppaea, the wife of the emperor Nero, when he calls her theosebes "God-worshiping" (Ant. xx. 8, 11).

She had, we suggest, turned away from polytheism and professed the Unity of God—as so many women of rank, wealth and superior intelligence appear to have done in the first century of our era in Grecian communities as well (see Acts xiii. 50, xvii. 54), and as many other women, wives of Greeks or Syro-Greeks, are reported to have done (see Wars ii. 20, 2, Acts xvi, 14)—, attending perhaps also at times at Jewish places of worship.

Likewise were the many "Judaizers" in the cities of Syria, from the description Josephus gives of them in Wars ii. 18, 2, in connection with the affairs at the beginning of the Jewish revolutionary war, mere nominal adherents of Judaism by the profession of Monotheism, the attachment for which they may have solely evinced by visiting the synagogues more or less regularly on days of Divine service, on which latter account the Judaizers everywhere may preeminently have received the title sebomenoi "worshipers of God." Their monotheistic leaning on Judaism was possibly, besides, marked by some other Jewish ritual observances, such, that is, as they found congenial to their minds.

To such kind of proselytes Josephus doubtless adverted also in his polemical treatise 'Against Apion' ii. 40, where he attributes to "a multitude of mankind" a "great inclination of a long time to follow our religious observances;" comp., also ib. sect. 11, in which passage, however, formal conversions may have to be understood.

And of such half-proselytes, bearing the name of God-worshiping or God-fearing, there must have been large numbers in Egypt and Cyrene, as Strabo bears witness (cited by Josephus, Ant. xiv. 7, 2), in Syria and the Decapolis, as is attested by Josephus in various places, and in Asia Minor, Macedonia and Greece, as it is evident from many passages in Acts (see besides the before-quoted, xvii. 17, xviii, 4, 6, 7), and certainly in the Jewish land proper.

They were in Palestine as in the other countries of the Greco-Roman world received as welcome additions, although they were reluctant to enter as full members of the Jewish communion by a thorough conversion to Mosaism, as long as they solemnly adopted the monotheistic creed and renounced every vestige of adhesion to polytheism. The Jewish authorities of Palestine may have imposed on such neophites the so-called seven Noachian precepts, although if these alone had been asked, there would, from a Rabbinical view, not have been any difference between them and any other pagans who were unconverted, since they were incumbent on them as well — an objection which is already uttered in the Talmud (B. Ab. Zarah, l. c.) against the opinion, that those seven precepts constituted the obligation of a Ger Toshab "half-proselyte."

In the various countries of the Dispersion a thorough renunciation of every trace of polytheism and a sincere profession of the foundation-principle of Judaism may have sufficed for their limited admission. The acquisition of such converts, it is safe to assert, gave nowhere and at no time that satisfaction to the Jewish proselytism which it expected. But it was provisionally contented with such trophies of Monotheism, in especial since it always held the end in view, that by degrees the new converts would submit to the initiatory rite and become devoted to the entire Mosaic religion. Preliminarily they were accorded a distant fellowship with Israel, and surely they enjoyed all the rights and privileges prescribed for the Ger in the Pentateuch. Perfect fellowship, religious-national equality, however, they could attain only by their formal transition.

Those modern writers therefore, among them Schuerer, 'History of the Jewish People,' and Mommsen, 'Provinces, etc.,' who advance the theory, that those proselytes designated in the Greek-Jewish or Jewish-Christian literature as 'God-fearing' or 'God-worshiping' (both terms are used interchangeably in Acts xiii. 26 and 43), were indiscriminately ranked as equal accessions among the race and nation of Israel, at certain periods and in Grecian communities at least, greatly err and misrepresent the status and standard of the pious, national Israel of the ages of antiquity. This theory would already be refuted by the circumstance, which certainly should not have escaped their notice, that the great sensation and alarm which Paul's and Barnabas' anti-covenant conversions in Antioch, Syria, had created among the Palestinian Jewish Christians, could never have occurred, had it been the rule in the Grecian communities to recognize uncircumcised Judaizers as real Jews. Ewald, History of Israel, vii., has the almost correct perception of those God-fearing proselytes. He lets them be regarded solely as *partial* members of the Jewish communities. We, on our part, differ from him only in that we ask discernment being used in all places in which the title occurs, since it stands sometimes, as set forth above, generically, including both species, the whole and the partial converts, and may in single cases denote as well whole as partial ones.

A few cosmopolitan compositions, such as the pseudograph moral poem of Phocylides (Ewald adjudges this production to the early times of the Ptolemies), or the address to the Gentiles in the fourth book of the Sibylline Oracles (written about 80 C. E., and *probably* of Jewish origin; so Schuerer), in which the worship of the true God attended by righteousness of life is more or less directly put forth as the only requisite for a welcome entrance into Israel's communion, must not be held out as the expression of the religious disposition regarding proselytes, predominant among the body of the true and orthodox Jews of the Dispersion. (Hilgenfeld, 'Judaism and Jewish Christianity,' p. 33, attributes this Sibylline book to an Essene or Essene-like Baptist. In this case the book could the less be referred to as offering a standard by which to measure the disposition of orthodox Judaism.) They were individual sentiments, shared yet at most by a few other philosophically cultured Jews. Yet the generality of the Jewish people would not countenance such liberal ideas, nor permit them being put in practice.

Neither must, in this question, reference be made to Philo's relative reasonings, and the proposition derived from them, as it is done by Schuerer, that Hellenistic Judaism was much more inclined to a free reception of Gentile proselytes, if they but adopted the worship of the true God, because it considered the Abrahamic descent "only as a secondary matter after all." To Philo, we positively object, such descent was by no means only of a secondary concern. It was to him of as primary an importance as it can be imagined to have been to the most devout Rabbi of any school in Palestine. Much as he exalts "the proselyte who has come over to God of his own accord" (On Curses, ch. vi.), he nevertheless would not hold him equal to the born Israelite. And notwithstanding his philosophical universalism in pronouncing virtue as the only preference valued by God, he firmly adhered to the notion of Israel's special choice from all the nations and predilection by God.

"Israel has been selected from all mankind and apportioned to the Creator and Father as a sort of first-fruit." This superiority is inherited by the race from their most righteous and virtuous ancestors — reasons he in 'On the Creation of Magistrates,' ch. vi.

Israel, "the most God-beloved of all the nations," was to him appointed and consecrated to be the "priests and prophets to all mankind" (On Abraham).

The twelve tribes over whom Moses pronounced his entreaties of blessing before his demise, were "of noble descent and noble birth, ranked highest by the Commander, the Maker of all things and Father" (On Humanity, ch. iv). Those blessings, he proposes there, are yet to be fulfilled;

his implicit view being, that even the latest generations of Israel would be titled inheritors of that ancestral nobility and superior rank. He argues there, further, that "Moses alone had from the beginning perceived the closest relationship in which the whole nation of Israel would stand to the Divine, a relationship much more genuine than that of blood." (See on all these and kindred passages, Gfoerer, 'Primitive Christianity' i. p. 486, sq.). It is, from the foregoing, clear enough, that Philo was as fervently national, as any most orthodox Rabbi could ever have been. He emphasized Israel's nobility of descent and superior estimation by God as pointedly, as any orthodox Jew in the heart of the nation's capital could have done. And yet would that author impute to him the universalistic position of accounting 'God-worshiping' converts from paganism, who had not formally passed over to Judaism, as equally privileged members of the Jewish nation!

What passages from Philo could be alluded to as warranting such a position? In 'On Repentance,' ch. i., where he expresses the loftiest religious and humanitarian sentiment, that those who have turned from polytheism to monotheism, should be regarded as "our friends and kinsmen," he has been but an enthusiastic exponent of Lev. xix. 34 and Deut. x. 19. And what else can be justly proved from 'On Monarchy,' ch. vii., but that he reproduced the pith of the various injunctions of justice and benevolence, set forth in the Pentateuch with regard to proselytes? All that he has added there of his own mind is, the figurative paraphrase of Numb. xxxv. 15, and the interpretation, peculiar to himself and at the same time, we own, most tolerant, of the first part of v. 27 in Ex. xxii., namely, that the former gods of the proselytes should not be blasphemed by the Israelites. As to his Fragment on Exodus xxii. 20, it would indeed, were it genuine, show that he held the circumcision of a proselyte not needful, and consequently justify the inference that he regarded such a new convert as equal with a native Israelite. But whoever looks closely at this piece will at once be convinced of its spuriousness. Philo is there, in commenting on said verse, alleged to have remarked the following:

"He shows most evidently that he is a proselyte, (and) not one circumcised in the flesh * * * for in Egypt the Hebrew race was not circumcised, etc."

Now we ask, is it possible to suppose that Philo exposed such ignorance as to state the Mosaic type of a proselyte to be invariably—for this import his assertion has, from the antithesis he employs—uncircumcision? Is it fair to think him unaware of Ex. xii. 48? Again, can he have betrayed such inacquaintance with Scripture as to put forth that the Hebrews were not circumcised in Egypt? Does not Josh. v. 5 attest the contrary?

These objections will we hope convince the reader that the above Fragment is inauthentic, and can therefore not be brought into play in the question before us.

Moreover and mainly we object concerning this, as all the other attempts to make out Philo such a cosmopolitan religionist as to have dispensed a proselyte who had only adopted the worship of the true God, from all the ritual observances of Mosaism, that in the above-cited chapter in 'On Curses,' he incontestably shows his ground-sentiment in our problem to be, that the proselyte was inferior to the born Israelite. Freely dilating on Deut. xxviii. 43, in which passage the proselyte is threatened to gain more and more the ascendancy over the Israelite, if he should fall away from God and his commands, he explains as follows: He who has "come over to God of his own accord" will be up, and the man of "noble descent who has adulterated the coinage of his noble birth, will be dragged down to the lowest depths."

Here he has not only reiterated his innermost view of Israel's inherited and appointed nobility and precedence above other nations, he has also most directly and unmistakably signified his other perception of the normal superiority of the born Israelite over the converted heathen. This condition would, he reasons in accordance with the Scriptural threat, be inverted, however, if the Israelite should apostatize from his faith.

We have then to declare positively and emphatically, that Philo can by no means be accounted as putting forth a universalistic doctrine about proselytes. But even if it could really be proved that he was so liberal in his opinion as Schuerer imputes to him, we could yet not attribute with any semblance of fairness the same cosmopolitan view to the generality of the Hellenistic Jews. It would be the height of frivolous conjecture to assert, that they were in their religious practice guided by the abstract speculations of that Pythagorean-Platonic theosophist and allegorist of Alexandria. They were, we aver, on the contrary as strict in their position regarding the admission of Gentiles as the Palestinian Jews were. They too held the initiatory rite with the body of the Mosaic precepts as incumbent on any Gentile convert, who aspired to be recognized as a full member of the Jewish community.

We have yet to continue our argument, and extend it to Jewish Christianity. We will subsequently see that these sectaries, too, set such a high value on the initiatory rite, that they insisted on its imposition on converts to their creed, who wished to be on a par of immediate spiritual fellowship with them. That none of the primitive apostles ever thought of dispensing formal converts to the Jewish Christian body from it, we hold to be a positive fact. As to the four well-known decrees set forth in Acts xv., we have passed on them at another point. We maintain that, if they are to claim any genuineness at all, it consists at most in their being ordained for half-proselytes to their creed, just as the true Jews had their own so-called seven Noachian precepts for such neophites. But that any of the apostles should have remitted the rite of initiation to those Gentiles passing over to the Christian community as claimants of full membership, is utterly unhistorical. Not in a council meeting, nor even by private transaction — as Baur proposes on the strength of Gal. ii., after positively rejecting the former as inauthentic—can it be supposed that either Peter or James should have approved of Paul's anti-covenant mode of receiving Gentile converts. We, on our part, cannot attribute any more genuineness to Gal. ii. 9, than we can to the liberal speeches of Peter and James in Acts xv. The complete exchange of roles in this tendency-work, in which these two apostles are made Paulinists, is conceded by the foremost critics of our day. They will surely not have deviated from the fixed norm, which they had doubtless carried over to their new relations from their former unmixed Judaism, that Gentile converts were to attain equality with born Israelites only by the initiatory rite and the acceptance of the Mosaic religion (the latter with the Jewish Christians, of course, minus the sacrificial precepts.)

If the apostle James, the head of the Church, deputed an inquisitorial party to investigate Paul's liberty of anti-Law reception of converts in Antioch (Gal. ii. 12, 4), he will surely not have yielded to Paul afterwards, and sanctioned his course. Nor could Peter who, while at Antioch, was "compelling the Gentiles to live as do the Jews" (ib. 14), have given his approbation to Paul's proceedings, as it is stated there (v. 9). It is an incontrovertible fact that not only in the primitive Jewish Christian church, but among its conservative perpetuators, the Nazarenes, as well as the ascetic sect, the Ebionites, circumcision was the indispensable sacred rite of initiation into Israel's and their own communion. It were not only "certain of the sect of the

Pharisees who believed" that insisted on the complete Judaizing of Christian converts, if they wished to be thoroughly united with them, as the Pauline author of Acts (xv. 5) represents, but all the Jewish Christians together with their leaders did so, as it is evident from Acts xxi. 20-22 itself, and in especial from Paul's own Epistle to the Galatians (ch. ii.). And it were not only all the Jerusalemite Jewish Christians who were indignant at Paul's "liberty," that is, the Jewish lawlessness he preached everywhere, but also those of the cities of Asia Minor and other Grecian communities where he held forth as missionary, although the tendency-writer of that work makes out solely the *Jews* of those communities as having been his opponents (xx. 3, 19). The Hellenistic Jewish Christians, all of them, that is, who remained in sympathy with the mother-church—and their number was doubtless much larger than that of the Paulinists of Jewish descent—will have continued to insist on the complete conversion of Gentiles, with the initiatory rite, as they persevered in the strict observance of the latter for themselves.

That they should with Paul's anti-covenant propagandism have gradually left off circumcision among themselves, as Baur ('Paul,' and ' History of the Church,' etc., p. 101) proposed, lacks every historical warrant. The contempt of circumcision in Ep. Barn. and Ep. of Ignatius proves nothing, for both writers were Gentile Christians. And as to his other argument from the Clementine Homilies, there can be deduced from this work neither an evidence of the leaving off of the rite by the Jewish Christian sect of the Ebionites, nor of their renunciation of it for Gentile converts. Baur argues from the circumstance that there is not the least question of circumcision in the Homilies. But since he has to concede himself that in the Contestatio, attached to the Homilies, there is a trace of circumcision being held indispensable by the then Ebionites, its author's silence about it cannot carry much weight. When we further consider that, according to the most reliable testimony of Epiphanius, the Ebionites held yet in his own time the rite of circumcision as all-important—as we will exhibit hereafter—the non-mention of it in the Homilies can certainly not be accounted for by the unconcern entertained for it by their Ebionite author. The omission of circumcision in this pseudo-Clementine work can, we hold, be accounted for, without having recourse to Baur's forced theory.

First of all we have to bear in mind the exalted perception which the Ebionites, as Essenic or Essene-like Christians, had of baptisms. To the Essenes their own lustrations were preferable to sacrifices (Ant. xviii. 1, 5), and the purifications together with the common meals had to them supplanted the need of the sacrificial ritual of the Temple. The same superior estimate of baptism we meet with in John the Baptist. It had to him doubtless a "mysteriously purifying and absolving power" (Strauss, New Life of Jesus, i. p. 254). To John is in the pseudo-Clementine Recognitions attributed the institution of baptism instead of the sacrifices (see Hilgenfeld, 'Judaism and Jewish Christianity,' p. 49). The sentiment that baptism for the remission of sins supplied the place of sacrifice, which latter was to be repudiated, is also expressed by the Essenic or Baptist author of the fourth book of the Sibylline Oracles (Hilgenfeld, l. c. p. 33).

The attribution then of such an invaluable merit to baptism as a ceremonial medium of atonement by the ascetic Jewish and Messianic sects more or less related to the Essenic stock, renders it quite conceivable that the Ebionite Clementine author, too, should have assigned an exceeding merit to and laid particular and intense stress on baptism for the admission of converts from paganism to the Ebionite Jewish Christianity; see Hom. xiii. 9. But as little as the Essenes and John the Baptist and his adherents wished by their ablutions to disparage circumcision as the Jewish initiatory rite, and, further, as little as the Ebionites of the two centuries consecutive on the time of the composition of the Clementine writings, ever thought of neglecting the rite of circumcision — as will later be found indisputably attested —, though they continued to value the baptisms highly, so little must we with Baur assume, that the Ebionite author of the Clementine Homilies intended a disregard for it, because he made no mention of it in the body of his work. (The words "etiamsi non sit circumcisus" in the Clementine Recognitions, v. 36, which work we possess only in the Latin garb, have doubtless been added by a later reviser, since they do not appear in the similar sentence of the Homilies, which is, besides, essentially different in its tenor from that of the Recognitions; see Hilgenf. l. c. p. 102).

Secondly, may the silence of the author of the Homilies be accounted for by the notorious fact, that in his time there rested a dire necessity on Jews and certainly also on Jewish Christians, of keeping conversions of Gentiles attended by circumcision, if any such could be attempted at all, secret, for the edict published by the emperor Antoninus Pius, which strictly interdicted its performance on non-Jews, though it repealed Hadrian's prohibition of it for the Jews themselves; see Muenter, l. c. p 99, and Friedlaender, l. c.

While we provisionally do not agree with the latter author — the relative paragraphs of the imperial Roman law-compends are not presently accessible to the writer in their original complete form, and he has to depend on the abrupt quotations in modern works — that since the publication of that edict formal transitions to Judaism ceased entirely, and converts thence joined to the Jews could only have been of the class of the 'proselytes of the gate,' that is, half-proselytes, we yet hold it quite conceivable that the existence of the edict alone, though it was not penally enacted or, if so, not penally enforced till Severus' time — the first third of the third century C. E.— should have determined a writer, especially one living in the capital of the Empire, such as the author of the Homilies supposably was, to pass circumcision by in silence.

To what end, we ask, should he have mentioned it, if it was then, for its imperial prohibition, not feasible for converts from paganism, or if its performance on them was at any rate fraught with some danger to those executing or encouraging it, though perhaps not subject to prompt, judicial punishment?

As to this, we would propose — whilst we, for the cause stated before, declare ourselves open to correction — that Antoninus Pius merely enacted the prohibition of the circumcision of non-Jews, without at the same time making it a punishable offence. We presume this from the fact that it was apparently the emperor Alexander Severus who first "forbade Gentiles to turn Jews under grave penalty" (Vita 17, cited by Mommsen, as above). Up to this emperor's time the prohibition of Antoninus may have merely lingered on in the letter, without that penalties were awarded against offenders. The Jews and, for aught we can reasonably infer from Justin's Dialogue with Trypho, ch. xlvii., the Jewish Christians also (those whom Justin proposes as not inducing or coercing other (Gentile) Christians to observe circumcision, etc., were doubtless the Jewish Paulinists), may in such condition of abeyance and suspense have, from the exceeding awe of the sacred rite, continued to perform it clandestinely, and with the same caution the Talmud relates of the period of Hadrian's proscription, on proselytes. Yet such attempts were supposably rare, for the fear of imperial intervention must have weighed heavily even with enthusiastic proselytizers.

From Severus' time onwards, when severe penalties had been denounced against such offenders, we own that formal conversions to Judaism or Jewish Christianity were decidedly at an end. That his penal injunction was rigidly executed, even under his several successors, appears from Origen's statement in his treatise 'Against Celsus,' which was written about 250 C. E. In it he mentions that the Sicarians—a nickname which the Romans had then, perhaps already since Hadrian's time, given to every circumcised person, the same that they had, two hundred years before, used in speaking of the wild faction of the zealots—were on the mere evidence of the rite being performed on them put to death. This he testifies of his own time. The Samaritans with whom the rite was also held indispensable as the initiatory one of their nation, were then the chief sufferers, the Jews alone having enjoyed the liberty of practising it among themselves.

On the whole, it may be safe to assume, that formal conversions to Judaism or the apostolic and Ebionite Jewish Christianity, were rare already from Hadrian's proscription forth. The Jews will consequently from the latter period onwards have shown little zeal for gaining additions to their fold from paganism, since the prospect of the final initiation of the converts was so dim and uncertain. With the Jewish Christians it will have been about the same. For we cannot, as far as the Ebionites are concerned—and the Nazarenes were surely as strict, if not stricter than they, with regard to Israel's covenant-rite—accept for one instant the theory that, because they prized baptism so highly, even for the renunciation of paganism, they will have remitted it to new converts to their faith and received them as full members without its performance, even during the period that an imperial injunction was laid upon it. It is impossible to the true historian to coincide in such a theory. For the Ebionites did not only hold the pagans as impure and defiling by touch, which trait Epiphanius relates of them in especial (Haer. xxx. 2, in Hilgenfeld, 'Hist. of the Her. of Prim. Christ.' p. 430), and on account of which they will surely have eschewed all associations with the uncircumcised of pagan descent, might they even have outwardly joined in the profession of their own creed, not to say that they will not have accorded to the latter a complete religious union with themselves. We have, besides, the most authentic testimony of the paramount import ascribed by that sect to the rite of circumcision, which decisively precludes the idea that they should, even during the pressure of its imperial prohibition for Gentiles, have passively connived at its omission and admitted baptized converts to their church as members equal with themselves.

Epiphanius (Haer. xxx. 26, in Hilgenfeld, l. c.) represents them as " boasting of circumcision as being the seal and stamp of the patriarchs and the righteous, who had lived according to the Law, by which they (the Ebionites) believe to become like unto them ;" also as referring the rite to Jesus and putting forth the argument (proverbially), 'Christ was circumcised, so must thou be circumcised.'

Is it then thinkable that a sect attributing such sacred religious-national import to circumcision, will at any time have left it off either for themselves or for converts to their new faith, as long as they could exact it from them without peril to themselves ; or that they, in the epoch of great peril for attempts of formal conversions, recognized uncircumcised, though baptized, new converts as their peers and united with them on equal terms of Jewish and Christian fellowship ? Nevermore.

We can accede to such supposition the less, when we consider that there is unimpeachable testimony, that alike the Ebionites and Nazarenes continued to impose Mosaism on Gentile converts to their faith, at least till towards the end of the fourth century. Can it then be imagined that they were at any time remiss in urging on them circumcision, its chief rite?

Of the Mosaic-Jewish character of almost the entire Christian church up to Hadrian's persecution even the Gentile Christian writer Sulpicius Severus bears witness (Hist. sacr. ii. 31). Likewise asserts the tolerant Jewish Christian annalist Hegesippus, flourishing in the earlier part of the second half of the second century, that he found everywhere, in Greece and in Rome, the " right doctrine as the Law and the prophets and the Lord proclaim," which is conclusive proof that anti-covenant and anti-Law Paulinism was then not the rule, but the exception, even among foreign and Hellenistic Jewish Christians.

The predominance of Mosaism with Jewish Christians, and the imposition by them of circumcision, Sabbath and other Jewish rites on Gentile Christians in the reign of Marcus Aurelius, is attested by the discussion in the before-quoted chapter xlvii. of Justin's Dialogue. It is true, he makes there a division between such Jewish professors of Christianity, who would insist on the acceptance of the Mosaic religious observances by new Gentile converts, without which they refused to hold communion with them, and others who would be indulgent enough not to refuse to live together with them unless they adopted the Jewish rites. And it is sufficiently clear, too, that, although he discusses the subject in the form of a proposition only, he had reference in his mind to the two ways as factually co-existing in his own days. Yet, we cannot, from the other testimonies we possess of the continued imposition of Mosaism at least to the latter part of the fourth century, but suppose, as already indicated above, that the tolerant Jewish Christians, whom he suggests as freely communing with inobservant brethren in the new faith, were none others than Paulinists ; and these were but few.

To about the same period as Justin's writings, belong the complaints in the polemical Epistles of pseudo-Ignatius about the observance of the Mosaic Law among Gentile Christians (see Hilgenfeld, 'Jud. and Jewish Christ.' p. 40).

And that the imposition of the Mosaic religion — minus the recognition of the sacrificial ritual, of course — on Christian converts by both the Jewish sects of the Nazarenes and Ebionites, whatever caution with regard to the initiatory rite they had to observe since the publication of Antoninus Pius' edict, and notwithstanding they had to desist openly from formally exacting the rite at least since Severus' rigid decision, had nevertheless not ceased as late as the latter part of the fourth century, we can derive from the following accounts of Jerome and his contemporary, Augustine.

Of the Ebionites Jerome asserts (in Isa. i. 12, in Hilgenfeld, ' History of the Her., etc.,' p. 441), that they declare the Mosaic Law obligatory upon all, even the Gentile Christians ; and of the "allies" of the Ebionites, that they decide that only the Jews and those of Jewish origin have to observe it.

Who these allies were, is debatable. Hilgenfeld ib. p. 442, admits the possibility of the Nazarenes being understood by them. He yet remarks at the same time, that even in this case "it is not provable that they should have dispensed the Gentile Christians from the observance of the Law generally, and already long before Jerome's time." For even Augustine bears yet witness, he argues further, of the Nazarenes of his time, that they " were compelling the Gentiles to Judaize " (in his treatise against Faustus, the Manichaean). This treatise was written about 400 of our era. And if Augustine adds there, that the Jewish Christians who force Gentiles to Judaize are "those whom Faustus mentions under the name of Symmachians or Nazarenes, who endure to our own times," we have a sufficient testimony for those latter days of Jewish Christianity, as to its vigorous insistance on the Mosaically regulated life of the new converts, who wished to be at one with it. It is immaterial in our argument, whether Augustine employed the title Nazarenes as indiscriminately, as did Faustus himself, namely, with the inclusion of the Ebionites. In any case we gain from his statement the evidence, that the Nazarenes were yet in his days, as it was done by the Jerusalemite apostles in those of Paul, compelling the Gentile converts to adopt the Jewish religious rites. If he included the Ebionites, we would by it have a corroboration of Jerome's assertion as to the same course being pursued by this sect.

We will not any further enlarge on this and correlated points, most important as they are, for fear of wearying the reader. To sum up, we may state it as thus far sufficiently evidenced, that the generality of the Jewish Christians, whether of Palestine or any other country of the Roman empire — the Paulinists surely excepted — would at no time practically depart from the initiatory rite for themselves, nor assume the authority of dispensing Gentile converts from it for a complete union with themselves. If they continued to impose Mosaism on them till the end of the fourth century, as we elicited in the foregoing, they can certainly not be thought as dropping its chief rite, which they so profoundly revered, for the sake of winning Gentiles over the more quickly and promptly, and as being satisfied with baptizing them, in the "conviction that they could never be won over by any other means," as Baur argues. No, neither the Ebionites and Nazarenes of Palestine, nor any of the Hellenistic Jewish Christians, except the followers of Paul, would for any cause surrender the religious bulwark of the Jewish religious nationality, the initiatory rite, nor depart from the inviolable norm, that it be the indispensable condition for a complete union of Gentiles with the Jewish nation.

How they put themselves right with it in the period of its imperial interdiction, with or without annexed penalty, we can indeed not definitely ascertain. Yet we meet everywhere with the surest indications that they have at no time disregarded it, even for the converts from paganism.

And reverting to the initial point of the present discussion we reiterate, that the initiatory rite was in the Greco-Roman world continuously regarded as the indispensable mark of the Jewish religious nationality, by the pagan writers, as well as by the Jews and all the Jewish Christians, except the small number following Paul or his teaching.

[25] Religion is in Cicero, De Nat. Deor. p. 44, defined as "the cult of the country gods."

[26] Sat. xiv. 103. In the sixth satire, v. 544, he speaks of the Jewish laws as the "Solyman laws," alluding perhaps to Jerusalem as the center of Jewish legislation. Or he may have had in mind the fables as to the name of Jerusalem, which Tacitus mentions (Hist. v. 2). The latter reproduces there two opinions, one according to which Hierosolymus was one of the two leaders of the Jews from Egypt, and another, that Jerusalem received the name Hierosolyma from the Solymi of Homer.

[27] From the fact, however, that the account of Sifre quoted in our text, names Usha in Galilee as the place of the Jewish Senate to which the ambassadors were dispatched, we had better suppose that the affair happened in the first years of the accession of Hadrian, who was otherwise a very inquisitive — scoffer. For it does not seem that the removal of the Senate to that town took place earlier than towards the end of Trajan's reign, when it was perhaps necessitated through the destruction of Jamnia by Quietus (see on this, Gastfreund, Biography of R. Akiba, p. 20).

With no less propriety the Rabbinical account of the imperial scrutiny could be taken as referring to the government of Caligula, whose curiosity about Judaism the reader will find well attested in the present work.

[28] Sifre (l. c.) imputes to the emperor the crafty device and request to the ambassadors, that they should first become proselytes — to gain, presumably, free access to the central seat of Jewish learning, and have ample opportunity of listening to the unreserved discussions of points of Law, and catching their freely disclosed inwardness, without that they would in the least arouse the suspicion, that their attendance was inspired by anything but a devout eagerness to enlarge their store of knowledge of the authoritative interpretation of the sacred Law by the lore of the Jewish sages.

[29] Comp. Strabo xvi. 2, in Hausrath l. c. i. 178: "The Jews designate as God what we call heaven and the universe and the nature of things." Juvenal may have gleaned his information from him. But was not Jupiter himself the sky? Ennius at least represents him so: "Aspice hoc sublimen candens quem invocant omnes Jovem" (cited by Cicero, De Nat. Deor. ii. 2).

Juvenal's misrepresentation was possibly original and due to the notice which could broadly be made by all the pagans, that the Jews observed and distinguished by some solemnity the appearance of the new moon for the festivals of their calendar. An analogous instance may be adduced from a passage of a Christian Gnostic work, ' The Preaching of Peter,' quoted in the Stromata of Clement of Alexandria (vi.), in which the author admonishes his brethren to worship God " not as the Greeks, nor as the Jews do, the latter of whom, believing to be the only ones who know God, are not aware that they worship angels and archangels, the month and the moon ; and unless the moon has appeared they do not celebrate the Sabbath which is called the first (Rosh Hashanah ?), nor the New Moon, nor Passover, nor the feast of Passover ('heorten;' cp. Matt. xxv. 5), nor the Great Day" (Day of Atonement). Celsus, flourishing in Marcus Aurelius' time, also reproaches, in his ' True Account,' the Jews with worshiping the heaven and the angels who dwell therein. (Origines, Contra Celsum, v. 6). Origen repels the reproach, and nobly defends the Jews who, he protests, being expressly prohibited to bow down to the sun, moon and stars, and truly fearing this awful injunction, can surely not be supposed to worship the heaven and the angels. This custom would be in violation of Judaism.

[30] Hausrath, l. c. i. 178, remarks: "To worship an invisible Being seemed to the Romans a monstrous superstition and unheard-of credulity. * * * The Jews who had dedicated their whole life to the service of their faith as none other had done, seemed to the Romans to be without any religion at all, because it presented no points of analogy with the religions of the Gentiles. It was possible to endure other gods, indeed, but the disdaining of all gods seemed unendurable."

[31] That Roman writers knew that the Jews observed more fasts than just that of Atonement day, is evident from Tacitus, Hist. v. 4, who speaks of "frequent fasts" of the Jews. Among them he may have also adverted in his thought to the Jewish private fasts for disquieting dreams. Rabbinical Judaism had indeed assigned to them a high rank, in the belief that they were a religious means, by which the ill omens they might chance to betoken, could most effectually be warded off. They were held so important, that one of the ancient theologians is reported to have proposed that they might be kept even on the Sabbath.

This kind of fasts had perhaps in particular elicited the attention of the Romans, who were so much concerned about the ominous presages of dreams: The wisest of them connected them with the Providence of their deities (see Friedlaender, as above, p. 532, sq.).

[32]The reader will we hope not deem it amiss if we insert in this place some sentiments on the Sabbath, the Jewish customs in general, and the Jews as a nation, so very congenial to those of Seneca, though they were uttered several centuries later. Rutilius, a high-bred Roman of the fifth century, originally coming from Gaul, who made a voyage to his native country in the year 418, has left behind an 'Itinerarium,' from which Lardner (Works, vol. viii. pp. 89-90) reproduces the following as to his Jewish experience. At the port of Faleria he went ashore. At the station he found the Gentile people celebrating the feast of Osiris. Ill luck threw him on the mercy of a Jew who had farmed the revenues of the port, and was at the same time keeping an inn or hotel. In it he stopped. Doubly unfortunately for him it happened, that he had to endure the discomforts which the Jewish Sabbath entailed. And what was still worse, his fare consisted of "mashed shrubs and beaten sea-weed,"—a most frugal one indeed. In a furious tone he therefore breaks forth against the Jews, exclaiming: "We despise by right the filthy nation that, itself shameless, observes circumcision. The root of folly it is, however, that to them cold Sabbaths are of great concern; but their heart is still colder than their religion. Every seventh day is (with them) devoted to base inactivity—a weak image, so to speak, of a weary God * * * * Oh, that Judea had never been subdued, in the wars of Pompey and under the command of Titus! The contagion of that exterminated (?) pestilence is spreading wider and wider. The conquered nation is oppressing its victors."

Have we not in this last sentence a close resemblance to Seneca's lament over the wide-spreading influence of Judaism? Rutilius yet differs from him so far that he does not reflect on the Jewish proselytism proper, but rather on the spread of the Jewish people all over the Roman empire, and their acquisition of important official and social positions, by which he exaggeratingly charges they were making the Gentile society dependent on themselves. This gave him deep chagrin. The more so, because he was himself a sufferer from Jewish "oppression," on the Sabbath of his host. That he decries the Sabbath observance of the Jews as the root of folly, is partly accounted for by the sour temper which this same experience had occasioned in him. In the main he has, in the condemnation of the Sabbath for the inactivity of its observers, fallen in with Seneca, Juvenal and Tacitus. New he is only in his blasphemous sarcasm, that the Sabbath was "much like a weak image of a weary God," insinuating thereby without doubt, that the Sabbath with its lack of manifest energy appeared as the type of an exhausted or powerless God, and that the Jews worshiped such a one.

³³ That Juvenal was, for all the slight with which he treats the Sabbath and other Jewish ceremonies, by far not such a vehement antagonist of the Jews as Tacitus, we have already noted above. The latter was the veritable Stœcker of his generation. His attacks were direct bolts of malice and hate. Juvenal, however, exposed the Jewish customs more in the form and tone of an indirect criticism. He wished to set forth, in his 14th satire, the perverse parental influence on the Roman youth. The Jewish mode of life of converted Roman parents, which he held so subversive of the true Roman virtues, offered itself to him as a fit object for such illustration. As to his contempt for the Jewish nation, it surely was not so deep and bitter as that which he cherished against the Greeks—a circumstance already emphasized above with regard to Cicero's onset against the Jews.

Greeks, Syrians and other oriental people with whom Rome seems to have been flooded in Juvenal's time, were, from the language he puts in his friend Umbricius' mouth, hated much more than the Jews, not only by him, but most likely by many other Roman men of letters and common citizens. Against the Greeks he was put out most. They, though the fewest of the "dregs" of society, as the satirist styles those aliens, had yet through their "quick comprehension, desperate impudence, and ever ready and most impetuous talk," succeeded in insinuating themselves into the noble and rich families of Rome, and became their actual "souls and rulers." That the "hungry little Grecians" should by their bland and cunning ways acquire the best houses and crowd out the better citizens, whose "infancy had breathed the air of the Aventine," offended him, as doubtless many other natives, much more sensitively, than did the occasional sight of some poor Jews, we may set down as certain. And it were these exclusively, it seems, whom he at times encountered, or at least had in mind, in writing the passages of those satires, which we will note farther on. The thrifty and wealthy of them—and it will from one of our above discussions appear as very probable, that a good number of this class existed in Rome and belonged to a long settled colony of the times anterior to Pompey's conquest of Judea—he seems not to have known or cared to notice.

In attempting to show, that Juvenal had not despised the Jews in the same degree he did the Greeks, we must not be understood as intending to palliate the odiousness of his reviling remarks on the former, which we meet in his fourteenth satire. For we are well aware from other of his compositions, that he cherished the most decided disregard to the Jews. His intolerant gibe of those wretched Jews whose only property was, to use his own phrase, "a basket and hay" (Sat. iii. 14; vi. 542), proves sufficiently how bigoted he was. He could not brook to see even the pauper Jews, forsaken creatures as they were, because homeless and exiled through the late national catastrophe, and perhaps before doomed to slavery and but recently emancipated, enjoy the scanty shelter and wretched accommodations, which they found in a grove in the eastern outskirts of the city, formerly consecrated to the nimph Egeria, but now let out to them at a fixed rent. Here those destitute Jews, possibly because they had not found room enough in the established quarter of their brethren beyond the Tiber, were encamped, putting up perhaps layers of hay or straw as couches, on which to rest their weary and foot-sore bodies. Here those unfortunate Jews, victims of the disastrous war of the revolution, lived and died. (A cemetery has since been discovered in that vicinity, attesting the separate habitation of some Jews there; Garrucci, in Friedlænder, Darstell. aus der Sittengesch. Rom's, iii. 576). The invidious satirist grudged them even those dingy abodes, because—the Muses were by them forced out of their sacred dwelling-place.

That his knowledge of the Jews was, as we have already observed before, exclusively or at least very largely confined to the poor of them, may be deduced not only from satires iii. 16 and v. 543, but also from iii. 296. And those he at once degrades, too, to the low level of beggars. Possibly he noticed here and there among poor Jews, that their utensils consisted in no more nor better things than "a basket and hay." It may be, too, that he once noticed a poor Jewish woman, following the unenviable profession of a fortune-teller, "beg in the ear" of an inquisitive Roman noblewoman, and offer, for a pittance, to disclose the future to her, for "the Jews were selling any kinds of dreams for the smallest fee." But was all this, if it transpired in fact, sufficient ground for insinuating, as he does in his writings, that the Jews were a sort of shiftless vagrants?

On the other side, we ought not to make such a reproachful account of this disparagement of the Jews, considering that he once, in a manner, allowed himself to be identified with them. In the above-cited third satire he describes how he was once mistaken for a *Jewish beggar*. He introduces there a drunken rowdy who attacked him as he once walked alone of a night along some streets of the city. Drunken ruffians were, as he remarks, in the habit of rudely and abruptly attacking solitary people of mean estates, who would naturally pass the streets without attendants carrying torches before them, in which those of better station could indulge. The assailant suddenly stopped and made him answer the question, What coarse meal he had for supper? and, Where he put up; in what *proseucha* he should look for him?

How shabby must his appearance have been, if he could be mistaken for a Jewish mendicant!

His description makes, furthermore, the inevitable impression, that he had not only himself associated in his mind the Jews with street-beggars, but was prompted by the inglorious design to represent the Jews as a class as being in the low state of mendicancy.

As to the question occurring in said satire, " In what synagogue shall I seek thee?" we may in conclusion add, that it at the same time offers us a bit of valuable information. We infer from it that the custom of beggars and transient poor taking up their nightly abodes in synagogues, either in the apartment adjoining the place of worship proper, which was used as a school-room for children, or in the room of worship itself, had not only existed among oriental Jews (see B. Pesachim, f. 101), but apparently also in Rome.

A sentiment congenial to that of Juvenal, is presented to us by the epigrammatist Martial, his older contemporary and friend. He is notorious for his mercenary, base flattery of the emperor Domitian, as well as a number of courtiers and wealthy patrons among the civilians. His rhymes were sold to the highest bidders. His extreme efforts to magnify the emperor to the sky, met, it is true, with no ready response to his suit for a considerable sum of money. Yet there were others weak enough to be taken in by his fawning encomiums. They paid him well for them. It was perhaps, we suggest, for that refusal by the emperor, that he avenged himself on him after his death by representing him as "the monster of the times, without one virtue to redeem it" (see translator in Bohn's Library). Similarly the case may have been regarding his bitter sentiment against the Jews. It may have been due to the vexatious experience he made with a certain Jewish poet. In epigram 94, book xi., he addresses himself to a rival composer of verses, of the Jewish persuasion, rebuking him sharply for carping at his writings, and for the worse trespass of stealing his verses. But for all this he could pardon him, had he not additionally attempted to seduce the object of his affection. For this most grievous offence he challenges him in these words: "You deny that such is the case, and swear by the temple of Jupiter. I do not believe you; swear, circumcised poet, by Anchialus." That our conjecture is not so far-fetched, will be conceded by all those whose knowledge of Jewish affairs extends below the surface. It is an undeniable fact, that the acrimony of many a Jew-hunter in some European countries, even in modern days, could in some instances be traced to the refusal of a loan or an important favor on the part of a single or several Jewish persons.

Martial may then have identified the Jews with the class of mendicants on account of his ill-will toward his double Jewish rival. Be this as it may, we should at any rate least expect that he, beggar himself — he was constantly asking his patrons for presents, as for a doga, a cloak, etc. (see Friedlaender, Darstell. aus der Sittengesch. Rom's, iii. 398) — would deal so angrily with the poor Jews, as he really does in the seventy-fifth of the xii. book of his epigrams. Replying in it to the interrogation of a friend, why he went so often out of the city and repaired to his small farm at (or near) "arid Nomentum," he states as the reason the unbearable din of city life. A tremendous noise was constantly disturbing him during the day, one kind of which was the endless annoyance (of himself, personally?) by "the Jew taught by his mother to beg" (a matre doctus nec [sc. cessat] rogare Judaeus).

He evidently wished to picture the Jews here as a class of beggars, importuning people on the streets for gifts, and being with their petitions loud enough to disturb him, the musing poet, even in his study, though it was situated as high as the third story of a house on the Quirinal!

The Sabbath in History

BY

Dr. Isaac Schwab,

RABBI

OF

St. Joseph, Mo.

PART II.

The Sabbath in Primitive Christianity:

With Jesus and the Apostles.

St. Joseph, Mo
St Joseph Steam Printing Co
1889

Copyright, December, 1889,
by
Dr. Isaac Schwab.

PREFACE.

Nothing daunted by the great indifference with which the author's Part First published just a year ago was treated at the hands of all but a few of those who were most expected to be devoutly concerned for a literary production of this kind, he now launches out the Second. Neither does he allow any sullenness to come on him and get the better of his temper of mind in the recollection of the many annoying experiences which he underwent in his effort at interesting in his first and, again, in this second book those whom he so safely anticipated to be alive to their importance and become his ready patrons. He is, on the contrary, buoyed up with strong hope that "The Sabbath in History" will gradually make its way into many libraries of both Jews and Christians, and even force recognition as a deserving contribution to religious-historical science from that large class habitually apathetic to serious Jewish literature. He trusts withal that Providence will aid him in carrying through his plan of putting before the world a complete history of the sacred Sabbath.

He contemplates publishing the Third Part which is to close the first volume of his work, next spring. There will follow a second and third volume; the one treating of the Sabbath in olden Rabbinism and in the Middle Ages, the other bringing its history from thence to our own times.

It was mainly economical causes that decided him to narrow the range of the present treatise to the period of Jesus and the Apostles. The Third Part will contain these divisions: The Sabbath with Paul and other Hellenistic Jewish Christians; the Sabbath with the Jewish Christian sects of the Nazarenes and Ebionites; and the Sabbath as regarded by Gentile Christians till the fourth century C. E.

The author confidently expects that every enlightened reader will give him credit for manifesting in the present book a conscientious seriousness as well as scientific honesty. As to its other merits let the book answer for itself. Regarding the various deductions and assertions given forth in it, he submits them to competent and unbiased critics who will, he hopes, accurately and cautiously ponder before pronouncing on them. If that be done, let their verdict come forward frankly. By the friction of critical estimate there may yet more clear light be created to be thrown on the subject-matter of his book. History, being, as Cicero says, " the light of truth," would thus but the more essentially be benefited. But let the judgment of the critics be uttered with due decorum, the same the author himself affirms to have maintained through his entire book.

May it win acceptance and good graces from the intellectual reading public for whom it is intended.

CONTENTS.

CHAPTER V.

The Position of Jesus on the Mosaic Law ... 141

CHAPTER VI.

Jesus' Heterodox Position even on the Decalogue . 146

CHAPTER VII.

Jesus Halts between the Acknowledgment of the Authority of the Mosaic Law and the Problem of its Abrogation 149

CHAPTER VIII.

Ceremonial Religion Recedes in Jesus' Mind and Teaching before his All-absorbing Messiahdom . . 152

CHAPTER IX.

Jesus' Indifference to the Jewish Ceremonial Religion Accountable also by his Prophetical Claim 155

CHAPTER X.

Jesus' Indifferent Treatment of Ceremonial Religion Owing perhaps also to Some Peculiar Messianic Traditions and Popular Notions 158

CHAPTER XI.

Jesus' Position on the Sabbath – His Two Sabbath Controversies 161

CHAPTER XII.

The Other Four Sabbath Controversies in the Gospels 174

CHAPTER XIII.

Retrospect as to Jesus' Position on the Sabbath 182

CHAPTER XIV.

The Sabbath with Jesus' Disciples in his Lifetime 191

CHAPTER XV.

The Sabbath with the Disciples of Jesus after his Death 201

CHAPTER XVI.

The Jewish Christians Ride on Animals on the Sabbath (?) . . 233

PAGES.

Note 34 (marked in the text beside the last word on page 145): The Judicial Persecution of Jesus and of Some Jewish Christians after him for Antinomian Infidelity, By the Statute of Numbers xv. 30, 31 — A New View 241–273

Rest of Notes 273–297

Excursus A 298–301

Excursus B 302–314

Excursus C. 314–318

Excursus D 319–320

THE SABBATH IN PRIMITIVE CHRISTIANITY.

CHAPTER V.

THE POSITION OF JESUS ON THE MOSAIC LAW.

We have in our yet unpublished work "The Mineans of the Rabbinic Writings," of which one division, "The Essenes as Mineans," and again another part, appeared about two years ago in the 'American Israelite,' set forth the point of view thus far entirely left out of sight by both Christian and Jewish writers on early Christianity, that one chief cause of the intense aversion of all classes of orthodox Jews against Jesus was, his heterodox doctrine about the authority of the Mosaic Law. He surely did not hold its Divine authority in all its enactments and enunciations, as was the conception of the faithful Jews. The dogmatic expression for this orthodox belief was, Torah min ha-shamayim, "the Torah is from Heaven" (God). Alike the Sadducees and the Pharisees, and with the latter the large body of the Jewish people, firmly maintained and adhered to it. Only the Essenes with their rejection of sacrifice and defection from the national worship of Israel as established on the basis of the Mosaic ritual, must have contested the truth of that dogma. They will, as we proposed in that disquisition on the Essenes, either have heretically declared the relative Mosaic ordinances interpolated and not forming part of the original law of God, as their later Ebionite kindred, judging from the Clementine Homilies, contended, or treated them in practice with total unconcern, explaining them, at most, figuratively, as types of certain virtues and moral qualities, in the manner of the Alexandrine allegorizers.

That the latter mode of Scripture interpretation subsisted with the Essenes, is testified by Philo, in 'On the virtuous being also free,' ch. xii. Having before credited them with cultivating "most strenuously the *ethical* part of philosophy, in which work they employ as teachers the ancestral laws," he states afterwards, when he relates that the exposition of Scripture followed its public reading on the Sabbath, that "most (Mosaical precepts) are studied with them by the aid of symbols," that is, by that method aiming to discover a hidden ethical meaning in the material letter.

That they were also, on the other hand, eclectic with regard to the Mosaic precepts, may be gathered from Josephus who, in Wars, ii. 8, 6, attests their zealous occupation with the Scriptures of the ancients, in which they chiefly "choose those precepts conducive to the benefit of the soul and the body." This statement does, it is true, not at once imply a rejection of the rest of the Mosaic precepts, which did not afford to them any intellectual or physical benefit. But if we are permitted to trace the Ebionite pretense of the spuriousness of the sacrificial ordinances and many other appointments and utterances of the Pentateuch to their original stock, the Essenes (and why should we not be?), that eclecticism gains the substantial character of a total Essenic repudiation of all those parts of the Mosaic dispensation, contrary to their own philosophico-ascetic doctrines. The above alternative that they may have declared the sacrificial ritual of the Pentateuch as spurious and not coming from the "God-inspired Moses," not to say, from God, will accordingly have a greater likelihood.

That they thus trampled the orthodox dogma of the Divine origin of the entire Torah under foot, and must for this apostasy alone have passed as heretics, will appear to the reader as self-evident. Jesus, having shared with the Essenes the opposition to the sacrificial Temple service,[*] cannot possibly have believed in the Divine authority of the sacrificial ritual as ordained in the Pentateuch, or in the

---

[*] See Excursus A.

Divine command of the manifold ritual institutions laid down in it as pertaining to or connected with the national-religious worship of Israel.

That opposition of Jesus incontrovertibly results from the account of the deposition of the witnesses made at his trial before the Synhedrin (Matt. xxvi. 61, comp. xxiv. 2; Mark xiv. 58); from Matthew xxi. 12, and parallel of Mark xi. 16, 17; from Matthew xii. 6 (we do not refer to xxiv. 2, and parallel in Mark xiii. 2, for these sentiments were added later, after the accomplished fact); from his repeated employment of the phrase adopted from Hosea, "I will have mercy and not sacrifice," and this even on occasions and in connections where there was no logical need of it whatever (see Matt. ix. 13, xii. 7); from his emphasis of the purpose of the Temple to be a house of prayer [only] (Matt. xxi. 13, Mark xi. 17); and further, from the fact that he is not known from the Synoptics—only from the fourth gospel—to have ever made any festival journeys to Jerusalem (so Keim; see also Strauss "A New Life of Jesus," i. 234). His last expedition thither about the Passover season had a mere Messianic object. Even his Paschal supper—the last one of his life—shows no other concern, premeditated or only incidental, than for the exhibiting of his own symbols of bread and wine, and not for the Paschal lamb itself. The latter, while we must not dispute the Synoptical account of its preparation for his immediate circle of adherents, can, at most, be regarded as being prepared out of accommodation to circumstances, but not from a sense of religious obligation on his part. For, if he had indeed laid any value on the Paschal sacrifice, its flesh served at the meal would by all means have offered a much more appropriate object of reflection with regard to remission of sins, than could bread and wine. Moreover, such preparation from the sense of ceremonial obligation, would have conflicted most seriously with his obviously settled opposition to all sacrifice.

And surely is his denial of the Divine authority of the Mosaic Law again proved from his antithetical arraignment, in the Sermon on the Mount, of oaths, which are at any rate sanctioned in the Pentateuch (see Deut. vi. 13,

Numb. xxx. 3); of the judicial laws of retaliation (see Exodus xxi. 22-25, Lev. xxiv. 19, 20, Deut. xix. 16-21); of the law of divorce (see Deut. xxiv. 1); and, above all, from his avowing himself the Lord of the Sabbath (which self-evidently implied also all the Mosaic holy days).

Whether Jesus had adopted the philosophical anti-anthropomorphic view of the Law being given through angels,* a view expressly maintained by the Hellenists Stephen (Acts vii. 38, 53) and Paul (Gal. iii. 19), or the opinion that it had an exclusively human, Mosaic, origin, he had in either case set himself radically at variance with the large body of the orthodox Jews. The second alternative of his attributing to the Mosaic Law a mere human authority, seems more plausible, from his open, and, at times, implied contest against many Mosaic enactments, and in especial from his following utterance.

To defend his attitude towards the institution of divorce expressed in his noted Sermon (Matt. v. 31, 32; comp. Mark x. 3 sq.), he represents Moses, in his reply to the Pharisees questioning him on his pronounced antagonism to it (in the correct form delivered by Mark, x. 2, which Keim, 'History of Jesus,' v. 28, maintains to be the original), as the arbitrary deviser and framer of the respective ordinance (Mark, ib. 5; Matt. xix. 8). On this occasion, it would appear, he has once for all explicitly disclosed his mind on the origin of the Mosaic dispensation. This disclosure was, that he held it as having proceeded—if in its parts, so logically in the whole—from Moses, and was not immediately communicated or even directly inspired by God. Nay, he has by that sharp contrast between an original law of God and its later alteration by Moses, which he put forth at that controversy, laid himself open to the suspicion that he entertained the enormously un-Jewish notion, perhaps already deeply rooted in the Jewish Essenism, but appearing in t e rankest growth in Christian Essenic productions of the second century, C. E., that all parts of the Mosaic ritual not congenial with a self-created religio-philosophical system, were to be adjudged spurious.

---

* See Excursus B.

Even if Jesus could be thought as totally disconnected with Essenism,—what will at all times remain impossible to substantiate, so strong and so manifold are his points of contact with that heterodox sect,—we would at any rate, in consequence of that unqualified antithesis, have to assert, that he had by it paved the way for the generalizing distinction of the later Christian Essenes between the "true things" of the Law, as coming from the God-inspired Moses, and the spurious ones in it, as being written down by some one after the death of Moses (Clem. Hom. iii. 47), who was instigated by the *evil one* to do so (ib. ii. 38). Jesus has, it is true, not extended his contrast farther than between God and Moses. But such a dogmatic digression once made, it was on its authority, as being that of the "true prophet" (Jesus), who was esteemed so supremely by the Ebionites, easily enlarged by this sect. The later Ebionites who distinguished no more between an original law of God and a succeeding one of Moses, but between an unwritten traditional, merely God-inspired law of Moses (their marked abhorrence of every thought of materiality connected with God excluded of itself the assumption of any law being given by God to *man*) and a written law, in which true and false things were mixed (the former alone being "from the tradition of Moses"), and, again, between those true and false things themselves, the latter of which were those not consonant with their peculiar religio-philosophical system (see Clem. Hom.), have doubtless started from the platform, the outlines of which were given by Jesus.

In whatever light the antithesis in point in its re-assertion at that polemical encounter may be viewed by different expounders and readers, no one will be able to dispute, that Jesus has in his outspoken negative position on divorce, and the manner of his antagonism to it, positively disowned the Divine authority of this ordinance, thus deserting the orthodox Jewish belief that all Mosaic ordinances alike have a Divine origin.

CHAPTER VI.

JESUS' HETERODOX POSITION EVEN ON THE DECALOGUE.

In the above-noted unpublished work of ours we maintain, that Jesus has not attributed Divine authority even to the Decalogue. We prove this, first, from the expression he used in the Sermon on the Mount, "it was said by them of old" (Matt. v. 21), instead of giving it, in the ordinary way of the orthodox Jews, "the Torah says," or, to avoid all misconstruction of his intent, "God's word teaches us." The phrase as employed by him, has by all means an evasive character. We can compare it with Philo's "men of old," when he speaks of the rite of circumcision (Bohn's Libr. ed. iii. p. 176). That Jesus has once, in a controversy, referred to the fifth commandment of the Decalogue as "the commandment of God" (Matt. xv. 3), cannot be accounted an offset to the impression which that phrase in his Sermon necessarily makes. It can easily be supposed that the spirit of controversy had elicited that acknowledgment. For he had to bring it out in a direct way and with some emphasis, in order to set forth the contrast which he wished to illustrate with a striking pointedness.

Secondly, Jesus' attempt at correcting and improving upon part of the Decalogue in the Sermon, cannot possibly harmonize with a perception of its immediate revelation by God. God's word, believed to be such, can never be subjected to improvement. If the objection is made, that single reforms of Mosaic ordinances were attempted even in orthodox Judaism, from the earlier age of Ezekiel down to the period of Rabbi Judah, the Patriarch, we have to assert in reply, that no spirit of opposition to them, or denial of their Divine origin, moved the single representative men or collective authorities to decide upon respective alterations. It is provable that the Jewish reforms undertaken at certain periods of antiquity, were due either to such economical conditions as demanded most urgently a suspension of this or that law, or, as was more frequently the case, to the sincere belief and conviction that the best interests of Judaism required a judicious setting aside of a certain ordinance, that the more essential part of the Mosaic ritual and withal the monotheistic principle and practice itself, should suffer no impairment. Furthermore, all or nearly all such alterations made at times by Jewish authorities of old, were intended only as temporary, and not as total abolitions. Even if the latter were occasionally intended, it was done with the direct aim of giving a more solid support to other laws held too essential, and affecting too deeply the very substance of Judaism to be even temporarily neglected. No one of those reforming men and councils ever presumed to question the Divine authority of the body of the Mosaic ritual or any portion of it, or to suggest a human improvement of the purport and bearing of the Law, which all the orthodox truly believed to be Divinely given in its entirety. None of them would presume to place the wisdom of their own 'I' above that of the 'I Am', the Author of that irrevocable Law. It was only Jesus who practically did so.

Thirdly, no true believer of the Divine authority of the Decalogue would ever have dared to explain away any single one commandment of it, as we see that Jesus did with the third, indirectly at least, by his unqualified declaration against all oaths (Matt. v. 33, 34).

Fourthly, we will ask, could he, had he really attributed Divine authority to the Decalogue, have left out, in the enumeration of the commandments, the observance of which insured entrance into the world to come (see Matt. xix. 16 sq.), all the first four commandments? Could he — and this question is more directly to the purpose of our main theme—have eliminated from it the Sabbath observance, if he believed it directly enjoined by God as the fourth commandment? Surely, if the observance of any of the Divine commands conditioned an Israelite's share in the good of the future world, must the Sabbath have been considered of such importance by any orthodox Israelite.

None such would exempt or omit the Sabbath law from the range of those religious obligations, indispensable for acceptance with God for rewards and benefits here and hereafter.

The Sabbath must then have appeared to Jesus as not of Divine origin,—a conclusion which is the more indisputably confirmed by his assertion about himself: "For the Son of man is lord of the Sabbath" (Matt. xii. 8), by which he meant to state that his own authority had superseded that inherent in the Mosaic Sabbath law. This, he pretended, had to yield to his own directions, whenever he saw fit to give them.

CHAPTER VII.

JESUS HALTS BETWEEN THE ACKNOWLEDGMENT OF THE AUTHORITY OF THE MOSAIC LAW AND THE PROBLEM OF ITS ABROGATION.

Our view, also elaborated in our work on the 'Mineans' is, that Jesus, while evidently disavowing the Divine authority of the Mosaic Law, even of the Decalogue, has yet not openly declared the ceremonial religion of Israel as abrogated. But since it cannot be denied that from the negation of the Divine authority of the Law to the negation of its permanent obligation, there was but one step, Jesus must be regarded as the spiritual author of the later growing pretension of its abolition, which men like Stephen, Barnabas and Paul put forth in a decided, radical way. Jesus only dropped the seed of this heterodoxy in the soil of Christianity. The harvest was later reaped by the Hellenistic and Gentile Christians. These did not hesitate, in view of the unquestionable opposition of Jesus to the traditional estimation of the ceremonial Mosaism, to recognize him as endowed with the authority of abolishing it. They interpreted his religion—as they were warranted to do from his delivered speeches and declarations—as being more or less directly a system of natural precepts. In this natural Jesus-religion the Decalogue, or rather Hexalogue, assumed a superior place. [See Irenaeus, Ag. Her. iv. 13, where he dilates on the *natural Law* which Jesus has not annulled, referring to Matt. v. 21 seq. That the Decalogue became to the Christians the real body of the Law, strictly so called, as the synopsis of Mosaism, is evident from the Apostolical Constitutions, vi. 20, et passim, and especially from the Talmud, B. Berachoth f. 12, where we read, that "the Jewish communities outside of Jerusalem wished to follow the Temple usage of reciting, at the morning service in the court-hall, the Decalogue immediately before the Shema, but that the authorities (would not permit them to, as they) had already (even for the service in the Temple) abolished this custom on account of the objection of the Mineans."* By these Mineans were meant heretical folks, prominently the Jewish Christian schismatics. That in very fact not the entire Ten Words formed the Law of Christianity, but only the six which Jesus had named to the inquiring rich young man (instead of the tenth, which is, according to his exposition in Matt. v. 28, already partially included in the seventh, he uses the command of love to the neighbor, ib. xix. 19; Mark x. 19 uses instead, peculiarly enough, "Do not defraud," which restraint does surely not occur in the Decalogue), appears from a most interesting passage of the Tosifta, Shebuoth iii. 6, where the discussion between Rabbi Reuben and a philosopher—doubtless a Gentile Christian—turns on the Hexalogue, beginning with honor to parents and ending with the prohibition of covetousness. From this passage we can easily conclude that the Christian Law was just this selection out of the Decalogue. This is further to be deduced from ch. 12, sect. iv. of the above-quoted work of Irenaeus, where he reproduces the Hexalogue as the Law enjoined by Jesus, in the form in which it occurs in Matt. xix. 16 sq. In the form of a Pentalogue the Law incumbent on the Christians is presented by Paul, in Rom. xiii. 9. Christianity had accordingly only adopted the name of the Decalogue, but not its entire contents, as the Law proper.] It was, we hold, doubtless the precepts of natural religion to which Jesus alluded in the Sermon on the Mount, when he declared: "Think not that I came to destroy the law, etc." (Matt. v. 17, 19). He actually mentioned in the whole Sermon not one of the ceremonial appointments, to which his affirmation might apply. He disserted merely on some ethical laws,[35] together with those of retaliation and divorce. The question of his opponents, silently understood from his protesting words of v. 17, whether he believed in the perpetual obligation of the whole Mosaic Law with all its ceremonial ordinances, he shirked entirely. He

---

* See Excursus B.

made a declaration which was not at all expected by his hearers, or by those for whom the composition was intended. No one had suspected or accused him of an opposition to the ethical part of Mosaism and Judaism in general. By nevertheless dilating on some portions of it, and skipping over the real accusation formed against him, he laid himself open to the criticism that his purpose in digressing from that accusation implied in v. 17, and from his asseveration in vv. 18, 19 (if this be genuine),[36] to his ethical expositions, was that of evasion. This the inquirer of our own day will readily discover. That he should, in any part of his affirmation, have adverted to the body of Mosaic enactments, is impossible, considering his vehement antagonism to the Temple ritual, round which clustered, besides, such a vast range of other ordinances, as well as his opposition to the divorce law, and especially his utterance on the Sabbath, Matt. xii. 8. Indeed would an avowal of that orthodox nature, were it even to be construed from his affirmation, have been most inconsistent in him and contradictory to his entire position, which we learn him to have held from various passages of the relative extant literature. No, it is beyond any doubt that the Mosaic precepts which he avowed to be perpetual, were the moral ones, those of the natural religion. As to the ceremonial enactments of Mosaism, he may yet, for all the derogation of a large part of them, be credited with not having come to destroy or abrogate them. For we positively hold that the main and direct object of his public activity lay outside of them. They were indifferent to him, compared with the exclusive aim that possessed him from the beginning of his career, to assert his Messianic dignity.

CHAPTER VIII.

CEREMONIAL RELIGION RECEDES IN JESUS' MIND AND TEACHING BEFORE HIS ALL-ABSORBING MESSIAHDOM.

The standpoint we assume in our work on the Mineans is, that the pretension of being the Messiah was uppermost in Jesus' mind, and that to it all other concerns had to be made subservient. Claiming as he did to be the inaugurator of the Messianic kingdom, and especially to reappear again in the divine-like capacity of Israel's Messiah for its completion (Matt. xxiv. 30), religious rites, even those of superior sanctity, were to him only of a subordinate and secondary value. They were to him indifferent compared to the object he pursued, and he wished, too, that they became so to his adherents. The chief care of his disciples and followers should be, to prepare themselves for the impending event of the world's renovation under his Messiahdom, by *repentance*, which he, like his predecessor, John the Baptist, was preaching from the commencement of his public course. It was his watchword (so Keim). To the cry of repentance he added later certain precepts of moral righteousness, conditioning the participation in the world and life to come. These precepts were joined by admonitions to acts of love and charity, by which treasures and fair claims of reward in heaven[37] would be secured; see Matt. vi. 20, xix. 21. When we compare with these passages the account in Jer. Peah f. 15, of Monobazus, king of Adiabene, disposing of all(?) his property to the poor, which act of charitable self-dispossession he related as being inspired by the motive of "garnering treasures for the world to come," we cannot help noticing the actual prevalence, in the century of Jesus, of associating the merit of charity with the hope of the future world. Charitable deeds were not only held as means of securing God's favor, but also as advocating agencies in turning his wrath of judgment for sins, alike individual and communal, the commission of which was feared as forming the cause for accusation and prosecution before the Divine tribunal, and at the same time as delaying the realization of the Messianic kingdom.

The combination of teshubah, "repentance," with maasim tobhim, "good works," that is, works of charity, is often found in the Rabbinical literature. They are in Pirke Aboth iv. 13, declared to be "like a shield against Divine visitations." As interceding agencies for Divine pardon they are named together in B. Yoma f. 87. That charity was held effective in expiating sin is evident from B. Berach. f. 5; it is there derived from Prov. xvi. 6. That it saves from the chastisement of hell subsequent to the judgment in the Hereafter, was without great violence to the letter deduced from Prov. xi. 4, in B. Baba Bathra f. 10. Its atoning quality is once even set above that of sacrifice; see B. Yebamoth f. 105.

The high estimation of charity for propitiating the Deity was rather a ground-sentiment in Judaism of old. It occurs also in Dan. iv. 24, and in Ecclesiasticus iii. 30. That Jesus added beneficence to the poor to his cry of repentance, would then easily have resulted from a mere Jewish standpoint. Even for a direct Messianic purpose, that combination has an analogy in the Talmudic literature. In B. Synhedrin f. 97, it is related that Rabh, the renowned scholarch of Sura, Babylonia, in the first half of the third century, C. E., uttered the view, that "the farthest term computable from Scriptural prophecies for the arrival of the Messiah was now reached: his coming depends yet on our repentance and good works." The same view as to repentance is expressed in Jer. Taanith f. 64: "The relief from the night of the Roman power over Israel and the arrival of the Messiah, the son of David, are kept back solely by the lack of true repentance." Such sentiments were indeed typical in old Israel. We may safely lay them down as having existed and pervaded the religious conscience of the thoughtful and pious Israelites in the times of the Roman rule, no less than in the former Persian period; see on the latter, Ezra v. 12; ix. 7. Every grievous sin adhering to individuals or the community, was in times of oppressive rule and national suffering considered an impediment to the restoration by God of a state of independence and prosperity. It had to be repented of and atoned for, in order to conciliate the Deity and dispose Him toward a cessation of such suffering, and the approximation of the glorious era so vividly hoped for.

The notion of sin interfering with the enjoyment of Messiahism had so thoroughly worked itself into the minds of scrupulous Rabbis mentioned in the Talmud, that they were haunted by the apprehension lest all their merits of the study of the Torah and practice of charity would not suffice to be held worthy by the Deity of surviving the throes of the Messianic days and witnessing the advent of the Messiah, because they might have committed sins which remained unpardoned; see B. Synh. f. 98, and compare the similar sentiment in B. Berachoth f. 4, that "some sin may frustrate the bliss of futurity." The relative phrase current among the pious Rabbis was, shema yigrom hachet, "sin may cause" (namely, the forfeiture of future good). Can we then wonder that the Baptist and after him Jesus, laid, in their preaching of the Messianic kingdom, such mighty stress on repentance?[38] They only echoed a sentiment predominant in Judaism, that the prerequisite for God's favorable interference against heathen oppression and for the commencement of his kingdom represented by the son of David (or David the second; see B. Synh. f. 98) was, repentance. Meritorious works of humanity, too, were, as we have seen above, held as decided expedients for winning God's favor and accelerating the Messianic kingdom. Jesus naturally urged them in sympathy with other Messianic aspirers and inquirers, in connection with repentance. And as to religion proper, all that he taught, in the suspense of what was by him presented as the transition to the kingdom of Heaven, to be indispensable for sharing in the benefits of his Messiahdom was, to observe the precepts of natural religion.

CHAPTER IX.

JESUS' INDIFFERENCE TO THE JEWISH CEREMONIAL RELIGION ACCOUNTABLE ALSO BY HIS PROPHETICAL CLAIM.

We have in the foregoing exposition aimed to establish that Jesus treated ceremonial observances as insignificant because of his Messianic pretension, which had engrossed his mind and pushed aside all other spiritual cares. We will in this chapter go some further and show that he has, more or less overtly, passed himself as the prophet empowered to suspend or change the Mosaic ritual. That he actually put forth the claim to be the prophet predicted in Deut. xviii. 15 sq., we have no doubt. It is not only testified in the fourth gospel (v. 46), but the fluent application of that Deuteronomical prediction to Jesus in the speech of Peter (Acts iii. 22), as well as its quotation by Stephen in his harangue of apology (ib. vii. 37), which can evidently have had no other object than to convey to the hearers that reference is had to Jesus, leave no doubt that within both the Judean and Hellenistic Christianity it was interpreted as positively bearing on the coming of Jesus. That both those relations of Acts are not purposely fabricated by its author, but are genuine expressions of Jewish Christianity, which originally received that notion directly from the mouth of Jesus himself, may be further proved from the Clementine Homilies, iii. 53. There the declaration is imputed to Jesus: "I am he of whom Moses prophesied saying, 'A prophet, etc.'" These are traces indisputably pointing back to Jesus as the author of the claim, that Moses had in that passage foretold his coming as 'the prophet,' that is, as his only real, spiritual successor. As 'the prophet' Jesus would naturally apply to himself the direction given in Deut. ib. vv. 15, 19, that the people have on pain of Divine punishment, to listen to his announcements and dispositions. It is worthy of notice that Rabbinism had, in its comment upon this Mosaical injunction, advanced the proposition, that a truly accredited prophet of the future must find a ready hearing, even if he should demand of the people a direct transgression of any of the Mosaic ordinances, idolatry only excepted; see Sifre, Deut., sect. 175, and B. Synhedrin f. 90. Whether this construction was already in Jesus' time Rabbinically put on that Scriptural injunction, we do not know. But it is certainly very likely that Jesus, having once fairly asserted the distinction of being the predicted prophet, will of his own mind have interpreted it in that sense. In connection with it he may also have claimed the power, as emanating to him from the Deity, of changing Mosaic laws.

We suggest that he gradually progressed from the pretension of being a prophet to that of himself representing the prophet proper. The Jewish people at large must, from various indications, have in the century of Jesus been much disposed to recognize miracle-workers as prophets. We know that the olden Rabbis would frown down any attempt of individuals pretending the gift of prophecy or the possession of the holy spirit. They firmly held that with Malachi prophecy had ceased, and was never afterwards Divinely re-instituted. This view was evidently maintained also by the author of the first book of Maccabees, who wrote in John Hyrcanus' time; see ib. ix. 27, also iv. 46, and xiv. 41, and Grimm's commentary in loco. But different it was with the common people, especially the credulous part of them. Miracles were in the consciousness of the Jewish people regarded as a prominent signature of a prophet. Scripture itself had variously produced and confirmed such perception. Whatever the mediaeval religious philosopher, Maimoni, has to argue against the supposition that mere wonder-working and the realization of predictions mark the faculty and calling of a prophet (Introduction to Zeraim), it cannot be denied that practically the common Israelites of old, and those of the century of Jesus in particular, found in miracle-working of a Jewish monotheist the chief mark of a prophet. Apparently had thaumaturgy largely flourished, and prophetic claimants had found easy credence, in that century. Josephus was most lavish in awarding the degree of prophet to prominent persons. He credited John Hyrcanus with the prophetic gift; Wars. i. 2, 8, comp. Ant. xiii. 10, 7. Even of the Pharisees as a class he asserts that "they were believed to have the foreknowledge of things to come by Divine inspiration; l. c. xvii, 2, 4. That in the mystic circle of the Essenes and kindred ascetics, with which class John the Baptist and Jesus had at all events some connection, prophecy played an integrant part, is well known; see Wars. i. 3, 5, Ant. xv. 10, 5.

It was mainly miracle-working that readily won for those saints the title of prophets. John the Baptist secured it from his followers (Matt. xvi. 14), from other Jewish people (ib. xiv. 5; xxi. 26), as also in a prominent degree from Jesus himself (ib. xi. 9). And this for no other cause than the performance of "mighty works" (see ib. xiv. 2). Jesus, too, aimed to signalize himself by miraculous exploits as possessed of the prophetical holy spirit. His Galilean adherents were drawn to him by the fame of his miraculous power (Matt. xi. 8, 26, 31, 33), a fame that had spread even far beyond Galilee, in all directions (ib. iv. 23-25). People would give him the designation of prophet, or of one of the olden prophets revived (ib. xvi. 14). As the prophet of Nazareth he was yet distinguished by the multitude toward the end of his life (ib. xxi. 11). And the immediately subsequent Christianity glorified him as "a man approved of God by miracles and wonders and signs" (Acts ii. 22).

That it was not difficult for Jesus to promote himself from the once acknowledged distinction of prophet to the highest rank of the Mosaically predicted prophet, can easily be perceived. We suggest that he resorted to this superior claim mainly, to assuage the consciences of those who, while they were inclined to accept his Messiahdom, were yet too much absorbed by the attendance to the multifarious ceremonial rites of Judaism, such as the written Law had prescribed and tradition established, to give the Messianic questions that undivided solicitous devotion, which he demanded as so needful in the face of the kingdom of Heaven. He had to reassure their scrupling minds, that ritual observances were not all-important, as they believed, but were only secondary, in view of the necessity to attend to matters pertaining to that kingdom. He, as 'the prophet,' had, moreover—so he may have argued—the inspired authority to change the Mosaic Law and introduce modified and partly new rules of conscientious life, fitted for the Messianic period. He was doubtless cautious in advancing this transcendent claim, uttering it perhaps only to his most intimate disciples, Peter, James, and John, or yet, besides, to the rest of the twelve select apostles.

CHAPTER X.

JESUS' INDIFFERENT TREATMENT OF CEREMONIAL RELIGION OWING PERHAPS ALSO TO SOME PECULIAR MESSIANIC TRADITIONS AND POPULAR NOTIONS.

More openly he may have reflected upon the topic, that the Mosaic Law would of itself cease in the times of Messiah,—his own times, as he pretended. It is not at all unlikely that in mystical circles some such notion had gained ground. How it did, is not easy to ascertain. Perhaps that it was worked out from Jer. xxxi. 31, where a new covenant is spoken of by the prophet, although there was not the least warrant for the construction of this verse in the sense of the abrogation of the anciently given Law.

That no alteration of the Torah was implied in those words of Jeremiah, is surely evident enough from the subsequent verse 33. Yet whoever has noticed the loose method of Scripture exposition in N. T. passages, will not find it strange that the true literal sense of that announcement was not consulted by Messiah-enthusiasts. However remote the relation of an agreeable theory might be to a Scripture text, it was yet without any scruple accommodated to it, and made to indicate, or at any rate intimate, that theory. Moreover, it has to be mentioned that even in orthodox Jewish spheres the presumption that in the Messianic era the Mosaic ordinances would be invalidated, had some adherents. The proposition that "in the Messianic future the commands of the Pentateuch would no more be valid," is, it is true, only made as a premise, in B. Niddah f. 61. But the very attempt at premising it shows, that there was some relative tradition back of it. Possibly this tradition had its origin in the same interpretation of the before-quoted verse of Jeremiah, which, it may be, was put on it also by Jesus.

There is another passage, occurring in the Yalkut on Isa., sect. 296, that comes under this category: "God sits in Paradise, meditating on a new Torah, which He will reveal through the Messiah." Such remarks, perhaps never earnestly meant by those uttering them, may nevertheless have passed into the phraseology of the common people, and this in centuries much anterior to that collection. They may in particular have been ventilated in the Herodian period, in which the Messianic expectations were aroused to the highest pitch. Is it, therefore, not plausible, that Jesus, even without emphasizing his prophetic authority against the further obligation of the Mosaic ritual, improved those vague and stray views, to the end that his followers might be relieved of the anxiety of conscience for a periodical neglect of various religious observances?

We have even some direct evidence that he limited the obligation of the Law to the Messianic term. The phrase "Till heaven and earth pass away," expressive of the duration of the Law (Matt. v. 18), we can fairly construe as chosen by him to indicate his own conception of its limited permanence, a limitation which was by his own Messiah-pretension implicitly given out to be then imminent.[39] We might also pertinently adduce Luke xvi. 16: "The law and the prophets (were) until John," to prove that Jesus believed and declared the validity of the Mosaic Law as expired with the inauguration of the Messianic kingdom, in which John was the first and he the second factor, had we not the following objections to the authenticity of this passage. First, the sentence excites our doubt on account of the Pauline, and, therefore, anti-Law authorship, of that gospel. Secondly, the subsequent verse, 17, so flagrantly contradicts the sentiment of the temporal limitation of the Law to John's preaching, expressed in the preceding, that we have necessarily to assume a garbling process to have got hold of the entire context, a process sufficiently evidenced, besides, by the vv. 17 and 18, when we compare them with Matt. v. 18, 32. The supposition that garbling occurred in this context becomes, thirdly, rather imperative, when we hold over against Luke's assertion in v. 16, the parallel in Matt. xi. 13, which the Pauline author unquestionably left incomplete in copying from his source, by dropping the verb "prophesied."[40]

CHAPTER XI

JESUS' POSITION ON THE SABBATH—HIS TWO SABBATH CONTROVERSIES.

The reader will, we hope, pardon us for making him follow us through the length of all the foregoing discussions, in which our main subject had partly to retreat before the general question of Jesus' estimation of ceremonial Mosaism. But they had in our opinion to be premised, in order to afford a better understanding of his particular position on the Sabbath. This we will now proceed to discuss in detail.

There are some Sabbath controversies[41] which he is reported to have had with the Pharisees,[42] only two of which are related in the most reliable gospel, that of Matthew. Keim notes only these two as historical. They are those about the plucking of ears of corn by his apostles, and the healing of the man with a withered hand, on the Sabbath. Whether the two events occurred on one Sabbath, and directly after each other, as Matt. xii. represents it (it is uncertain whether Mark intended to connect both cases as to time, the word "again" in iii. 1, making it doubtful whether immediate succession was meant by the writer), or on two different Sabbaths, as Luke vi. 1, 6 produces it (Keim approves the latter; see his Introduction to vol. III.), will forever remain doubtful. Keim in preferring Luke's relation surely knew no more about it than any other reader of the extant gospels.[43]

We will follow the order in which the gospels introduce the disputes, and start with that on the plucking by the apostles of the ears of corn, when they were once "an hungred" on a Sabbath day. This happened according to Keim (l. c. iii. 358) earlier in time than the other. It occurred, as he further proposes (ib. p. 363), during the first months of his ministry, about Easter (Passover).[44]

To cut (katsats in Hebrew) or tear off (talash) from a tree or plant rooted in the ground on the Sabbath, was by the Rabbinical doctors judged to be a Mosaically prohibited manual occupation; the former was declared a chief labor, the latter its derivate. On this derivative kind of labor, see Mishnah B. Sabb. f. 95 and 103, and the Boraitha there. To invest this prohibition with a more direct Scriptural authority, some later Rabbis attempted to account the Sabbath breaking of the gatherer of sticks (Numb. xv. 32) as having consisted in pulling off limbs or twigs from a tree or shrub. The case of the apostles evidently came, in the mind of the rebuking Pharisees, under this category. According to Luke who adds, that the apostles rubbed the ears in their hands (vi. 1), they would, besides, have made themselves guilty of yet another Sabbath violation. For in the Rabbinical view the husking of grain was a sort of labor derivative from threshing (see Tosaf. B. Sabb. f. 73), which latter was counted among the thirty-nine chief labors. Mark ii. 23 sq., has presented the event with such brevity that one would, without the aid of the other Synoptics, be at a loss to learn from v. 23 alone, whether he laid the stress of the questionable act of the apostles on their making the way in the cornfield by plucking the ears (with the stalks, perhaps), or on their doing the latter for the sake of allaying their hunger.

Jesus, in rebutting the charge of Sabbath breaking by his apostles (Matt. xii. 1-8) proved himself a real Rabbinical dialectician (see Geiger, 'Sadducees and Pharisees,' p. 31). In his plea he points out David's using, in the extremity of hunger, for himself and his men the loaves of shew-bread that had been removed from the sacred table, to be eaten by priests alone (1 Sam. xxi.). By this analogy he aims to give support to the theory, that in a case of distress a layman may presume to do what is ordinarily permitted to priests only. With this theory, unexpressed yet foremost in his mind, he proceeds to draw the final conclusion, applicable to the case in dispute. Priests, he went on to argue (Matt. ib. v. 5), may freely attend to the Sabbath sacrifices, the Law permitting, nay, commanding it. If, then, he meant to urge, priests may carry on manual occupations prohibited to other Israelites on the Sabbath (slaying an animal was accounted one of the thirty-nine chief labors), why should a lay person not be equal to a Temple functionary in so far that he may, in a condition of pinching hunger, do some work otherwise unlawful, but which, from the analogy of David's case who would in a state of starvation presume to be as privileged as a priest, ought to become likewise permissible to every other Israelite, reduced to such extremity? Why, therefore,—this was the implication of his argument,—should my apostles not be as reproachless for their act of necessity as David was in his?

Thus far Jesus himself used a Phariseic-Rabbinical method of arguing. Not only in form he had in that argument not removed himself from Rabbinism, even as to its tenor he had scarcely forsaken its wonted scope. For it, too, had made marked allowances for cases of necessity. Nor even had the sentence attached in Mark ii. 27, "The Sabbath was made for man, and not man for the Sabbath," any direct marks of un-Jewish intent, so that the Pharisees might have become indignant at its use. Phariseism itself —later Rabbinism at least—had formed and employed the identical sentence, though for a different object. It was, to support the old and firmly established rule, that "to save human life and rescue it from danger, the Sabbath has to give way" (see Mechilta ed. Weiss f. 110, and B. Yoma f. 85). The doctors putting it forth in the cited passages did so in consequence of a forced interpretation put on the word lachem "unto you," in the verse, "And ye shall keep the Sabbath, for it is holy unto you" (Ex. xxxi. 14). This word, though it is by no means superfluous or exceptional in the context in which it stands, was yet, in the manner of olden Rabbinical exegesis, pressed to suggest the sentence, "The *Sabbath* is given to *you*, but you are not given to the Sabbath." This sentence was subsequently propounded to furnish a Scriptural support to that rule, which had perhaps since days immemorial entered of itself into practical Judaism, and, for aught we know, never met with the slightest objection, even from the most rigid Sabbath observer.

The difference regarding this sentence between orthodox Judaism and Jesus was, however, that in the former incidents of hunger were never thought of being brought within its scope. It was restricted to instances in which danger to life was feared, if a certain labor prohibited on the Sabbath would be omitted toward the imperilled person. But yet, while the Phariseic opponents of Jesus must have seriously dissented from him as to his license in applying that sentence to cases of hunger as well, they could nevertheless have had some indulgence for it, had he not so flagrantly, and in such an unheard-of manner, aggravated it by adding the assertion: "Therefore the Son of man is Lord also of the Sabbath" (Mark ii. 28; see also Matt. ib. 8, in whose gospel, by the way, the other sentence "The Sabbath was made for man, etc.," is wanting, and Luke vi. 5). That this self-elating assertion is genuine, there can be no doubt. By it he shows himself not only removed from orthodox Phariseic Judaism, but most decidedly cut loose from the cardinal principles of positive Judaism, as professed by each of its sects with deep conviction and unshaken faith. The opponents must have been shocked in their inmost souls on hearing him put forward such an enormous vaunt. Were they to interpose a counter-argument to such a daring claim of divine authority? They must have felt too keen a dismay to reply to him at all any more.

That he should have had no other intention with his self-appellation "Son of man," than to generalize from himself, the typical son of man,—the Messiah,—to all people as sons or children of men, we can not possibly accept with Geiger (as above).[45] No, the impression which the assertion that the Son of man was Lord also of the Sabbath must have made on the expostulating Pharisees, was certainly an entirely different one. It was no other than that he represented himself as the supernaturally endowed Messiah, and, perhaps, 'the prophet,' who could practically, if he had a mind or saw the necessity of it, abolish even the Sabbath.

That he laid the stress of his assertion not, as Geiger proposes, on his human character, in which indeed all his coevals were his equals, but on his pretended divine-like Messiahdom, as adopted from Daniel, Enoch, and some similar mystical books, becomes the more evident as we hold in view the other self-elating utterance which he, according to Matt. ib. v. 6, made on the same occasion. He argues there: "But I say unto you that one (or, something) greater than the Temple is here."[46] He doubtless insinuated thereby that, standing in dignity and sacredness higher than the Temple, he could also, if he so pleased, do away its service. This interpretation is by no means extravagant. It is fully borne out by the trend of his thought, expressed on another occasion with regard to the Temple. When he was, after his violent proceedings in its court, questioned, "by what authority he was doing these things?"—by which things those arbitrary and domineering proceedings were surely meant alongside of his other innovations—he retorted with the counter-question: "The baptism of John whence was it? from heaven or of men? etc." (Matt. xxi. 23-25). In this rejoinder is certainly implied the justification for the assumption of his own authority. He doubtless meant to insinuate that his authority emanated from God, as well as John's. In both the foregoing instances concerning the Temple we, then see Jesus asserting an authority of a divine character, with which he claimed to be vested, in superiority above all other men. We meet with the same self-exaltation in his affirmation, "the Son of man has power on earth to forgive sins" (Matt. ix. 6), which was interconnected with his announcement of his judicial power over all nations, to be exhibited at his second coming, on the Judgment day (ib. xxv. 31 sq.). A divine lordship he surely pretended to as immanent in his Messiahdom. He deduced it rather explicitly from his stock sentence of Ps. cx. 1, in his Messianic controversy with the Pharisees (Matt. xxii. 41-46), on which occasion he gave them also plainly enough to understand that he claimed to be the son of God.

All these instances prove forcibly that Jesus intended to put forth claims of divinity. We have disserted on this subject at large in our work on the Mineans. Here a succinct mention must be sufficient.

As to his assertion to be the Lord of the Sabbath, it could certainly impress those who had called him to account for countenancing its violation by his apostles, not differently from his other pretensions of spiritual magnitude. What else could they judge from it but that he declared the Sabbath, by the bulk of the Jewish nation believed to be Divinely instituted, thrown at his mercy, to be abrogated, or at any rate modified, by his dictate—for those at least who had joined themselves to him and believed in his miracles and mission? Nay, the ultimate inference which the simple Rabbis of Capernaum who questioned him have drawn from it, was possibly no other than that he not only usurped a superior authority over the Sabbath as received from the Deity, but one inherent in himself as God's rival and opposite. For, they may have reasoned, one pretending to a superiority above the Sabbath, must at the same time think himself exalted above Jehovah who had commanded its observance, else he cannot put forward a derogatory sentence like that.

It may not be amiss to quote here the view of Salvador, 'Jesus Christ,' ii. 80-81: "If one placed himself," argues he, "above the institution proper; if, as Jesus did, one proclaimed himself the absolute Lord of the Sabbath, this was an attack upon the Law by overthrowing one of its cornerstones. In fact, this was an elevation of one's self above the God of the Jews, or, at least, a pretension to be His equal." Even Keim who vindicates Jesus throughout his whole work against the presumption of divinity, admits "as early indications of his higher nature the calling himself greater than the temple, a lord of the Sabbath, and one who was authorized to exercise the divine prerogative of forgiving sins" (iii. p. 78). On this last claim of authority by Jesus that author observes (ib. p. 367), that the Pharisees found it to be "his most flagrant breach of the Law. Here he had done violence not only to a divine ordinance, but to the personal majesty, the sovereign prerogative of God. It seemed to dart on them like a light (we can afford to allow for this Gentile Christian sarcastic hit!) that the principle upon which he as transgressor of the Law acted, was contempt of God, blasphemy against God, heathen denial of God." Keim further concedes that "the Son of man (which title he had assumed already in the early part of his ministry) is in the greater number of passages in which he occurs, plainly an exalted being." Let us ask, if a Christian critic of the nineteenth century could not help discovering in those instances of Jesus' self-assertion the claim of a *higher nature* and of an *exalted being*, were the Rabbinical questioners of his own time expected to find less in them? Scarcely so. And if we analyze those veiled phrases, what result will, if we are candid, meet us? None other than that they are high-wrought paraphrases of divinity. We, at least, are unable to discern in the concept of a nature higher than the human, and of a being exalted above all other human beings, anything else than that of divinity. Those Rabbis of Capernaum will then, with their ready comprehension of Jesus' language, have promptly recognized in him a most radical assaulter of the principles of Judaism already at the early period of his public preaching, ere yet he had announced himself, before the Jews of all classes, as the designated judge and ruler of all nations, or openly assumed the additional title "son of God" (on the latter see Matt. xxvi. 64; Mark xiv. 62; John xix. 7), which title he had already before his trial, in his argument against the Pharisees on the descent of the Messiah (Matt. xxii. 41-45), perceptibly enough intimated as belonging to him.

We will now turn to the second controversy on healing on the Sabbath. Jesus is reported to have been asked in the synagogue of Capernaum, "Is it lawful to heal on the Sabbath day?" (Matt. xii. 10.) The interrogators were of course again the Pharisees; see ib. v. 14. This evangelical writer held them, moreover, so strongly in his thoughts that he characterized, though more in passing, even that synagogue as a sectarian one (ib. v. 9), whereas it was surely assigned for the worship of the entire Jewish population. Jesus is said to have rebutted the query by the axiom that "it is lawful to do good on the Sabbath day" (ib. 12; Mark iii. 1 sq. has an entirely different version of the proceedings). This axiom is placed at the end of his argument. It is preceded by an illustration from practical life (vv. 11, 12), to bring it home to them with as deep a sense of confusion as possible. The illustration is of a case in which, as he suggested, themselves would disregard the Sabbatic injunction without any scruple. Now we hold it quite possible that Jesus argued with the questioners from the view of mercy due to the sick and the suffering, as we find it in the gospel account. But the statement with which Matthew winds the story up, that "the Pharisees went out, and took counsel against him, how they might destroy him," we have to pronounce, to give it very mildly, as a bold exaggeration. The Pharisees were positively no such monsters as to try to kill a man or have him killed for making another man's withered hand whole on the Sabbath. That writer evidently calculated on the credulity and ignorance of the generality of his readers. For all his fairly informed Jewish contemporaries knew, as every one else, even slightly versed in Rabbinical legislation, must know, that healing the sick on the Sabbath was among the learned Pharisees held only as a preventive restraint, which no one ever thought of including among the Mosaically prohibited labors, and thus holding a perpetrator legally liable to capital penalty. Healing was only Rabbinically forbidden on the Sabbath, and that with the preventive object, that one might not ultimately go and commit the trespass of crushing medicinal roots or herbs into powder. This would be a real labor, equal to grinding, which, again, was counted among the thirty-nine chief occupations interdicted on the Sabbath.

Secondly, we have to object against that statement that, while the prohibition of healing on the Sabbath was doubtless rigidly heeded in Jesus' time, it is yet incredible that the Pharisees should have taken occasion from the cure performed by him, to even severely persecute, much less to destroy him. We could indeed credit it if the writer had intended to convey, that the Pharisees conspired against him for his pretense of supernatural healing, connected with his Messianic claim,[47] independently of the Sabbath. But this is not the case.

The remonstrance with the Pharisees turns here on the Sabbath-breaking by actual healing, and not on a mysterious Messianic cure by remission of sin, as we find it in Matt. ix. 1-6. But healing on the Sabbath in a desperate case like that of the man with a withered hand, could not make the violator liable even to a severe animadversion from the Phariseic doctors. The Rabbinical prohibition of healing on the Sabbath did not extend to any case of sickness in which danger to life was to be feared, if medical application were omitted. The set rule among the Rabbis was, that no Mosaic command, except the three cardinal restraints of idolatry, incest, and murder, could stand in the way of saving life. The leading view among the learned Jews was, that the Divine commands were not given that life should on their account be sacrificed or jeopardized, but that, on the contrary, it be spared and preserved. They referred this principle to Lev. xviii. 5, in the latter words of which they found a warrant for it. The Sabbath law, sacred and inviolable as it was, should yet not interfere where human life was at stake. There was not one of the representative Rabbis of antiquity who differed from this view. Those of the first and second centuries of our era had received the rule that "saving life vacates the Sabath," from former ages, and were all agreed that it was fair and perfectly in accord with the spirit of Judaism; see Mechilta f. 110, ed. Weiss; B. Sabb. f. 132;

Tosifta Sabb. p. 134. It was as firmly established in orthodox Judaism as that circumcision and Temple service should put aside the Sabbath obligation (this appears from Tosifta l. c.).

It seems to us, further, that the Rabbis had not at all an extreme conception of what was to be called "saving life." Not only was it generally understood that the fear of immediate danger was sufficient cause for setting aside the Sabbath law in any case of sickness or serious accident, but there is all likelihood that even where the danger was only indirect or remote, its fear was by the Rabbis considered a justifiable cause for breaking the Sabbath; see B. Sabbath f. 128, 129. Nay, since opinions must have differed then on what was a real dangerous condition (sakkana), as they necessarily differ at all times; and, further, since we know from the Talmud that the term mesukkan "endangered" was applied even to him who was only sickly (see B. Sabb. f. 37), we have to declare that the scope of dangerousness, on the ground of which medical assistance and relief was allowed to be administered to the sick, was rather wide with the pious doctors of old. Now that a man with a withered hand fairly came under the head of "dangerous," will from the foregoing appear very probable. To treat such a man with the grounded prospect of cure, the learned Jews of Jesus' time are not likely to have held a violation of the traditional restraint of healing on the Sabbath.

Thirdly, we have to object that, since his pretended miraculous cures, whether of the sick or the possessed, were of a magical or, to give it more euphemistically, a psychical nature, produced by the "holy ghost and power" within him (Acts x. 38), and resulting from his mere word of mouth (see Matt. viii. 8, 13, 16; ix. 6, 7, et alias), which was often preceded or attended by his hand touching the sufferer or the sufferer touching him (ib. viii. 3, 15; ix. 29; xiv. 36, et alias),—and surely was the case of the man with a withered hand not intended by the evangelist to pass as other than a spiritual cure,—the expostulation of the Pharisees with Jesus for a cure of this kind performed on the Sabbath is very problematic. We know that the olden Rabbis did not in the least object to wearing magical charms, inscribed with Scripture verses, on the Sabbath, although they were immediately intended as a panacea for bodily ailments and infirmities; see Mishnah B. Sabb. f. 60. They did evidently not attach to any mode of spiritual healing the apprehension that such sanitary process might lead to crushing medicinal substances. The Phariseic doctors of Jesus' time had, we may fairly suppose, no different view. It is therefore very questionable that they should, on finding him about to execute a psychical cure on the Sabbath, have called him to account for its violation by it.

Fourthly, we have to impugn the correctness of the relative account given by Mark iii. 4. (It is, we believe, excusable to note in the question before us, this evangelist, though he can by no means be held as reliable as Matthew.) He adds: "But they held their peace." This assuredly means that the Pharisees were disabled by the point-blank shot of argument hurled at them by Jesus. The questioners, the implication is, were so dumbfounded that they could not reply to Jesus' query: "Is it lawful on the Sabbath day to do good, or to do harm?" We, however, able to judge of the Phariseic temper and skill in debating by many examples of the later consentient Rabbis, would oppose that it is not at all likely that the learned remonstrators felt themselves so badly discomfited by the question of Jesus, that they held it useless to argue with him any further. We have to insist that, if the gospel account of Jesus using that plea in the above questioning form of an aphorism is in the main authentic, they were not at all argued down by it, but had enough courage and presence of mind left to meet him in his argument in this wise: "Yes, indeed. We too allow doing good on the Sabbath. It is with us a dispensatory rule to remove on the Sabbath cases and boxes filled with any articles set apart for use on working days, if they obstruct a place where traveling poor are to be accommodated. We permit this freely, though we otherwise hold burdensome exertions unlawful on the sacred day of rest (see B. Sabb. f. 126). For charity stands with us as high as you claim it valued by yourself. Furthermore, though we are ordinarily very strict in following out Isaiah's admonition (Isa. lviii. 13), to 'honor the Sabbath by not following our own business, etc.,' allowing no talking or figuring about any of our secular affairs, we yet make an exception with objects of charity. We declare it quite proper to apportion amounts of benevolent gifts for the poor, the orphans, and such like wretched creatures of society (see B. Sabb. f. 150; comp. however the observation of Tosaf. ib. on the division of opinions as to some objects of charity). We also permit several things needful for a dead person to be done on the Sabbath, which are otherwise prohibited (see ib. f. 150, 151), for we value charity so highly that we extend it even to the dead (comp. Jer. Peah, f. 15)." It is true, the foregoing statutory rules occur in the Rabbinical literature of an epoch much ulterior to the lifetime of Jesus. Yet we can entertain no doubt that the Phariseic doctors in the latter's time thought and decreed congenially with the Rabbinical sages of the second century, and that the above dispensations passed current already with them.

Such and the like rejoinders, we should think, were readily at the command of the Phariseic opponents of Jesus, so that Mark's allegation, "But they held their peace," must appear most doubtful. Nor does this imputed silence become more plausible by suggesting, that Mark may in his mind have adverted to Jesus' proposition of an only sheep having fallen into a pit on the Sabbath which, while he has, in his effort at brevity (that Mark had, in composing his gospel, the object of abbreviation, is set forth at length by Strauss l. c. i. 169, seq.), not mentioned it in his version, is yet possible to have been in his thoughts, being impressed on them from the original of Matthew's gospel, out of which he supposably gathered his own relative account. According to Matthew, Jesus used this homely illustration to substantiate his argument that doing good was lawful on the Sabbath. If it could be supposed that Mark silently adverted to it when he made the assertion, that the Pharisees held their peace, we would have to oppose our doubt of it for the reason, that it appears from the Talmud that the learned Rabbis—and the Pharisees of Jesus' time presumably as well—had not at all held it as such a matter of course, that the animal was permitted to be drawn out of the pit. It is to be inferred from B. Sabbath f. 124, that they would only hold it permissible, if it could not be fed from the top, so that it might be kept from the pangs of starvation for the rest of the day. Yet whenever this was possible, they will have insisted that the owner must wait with drawing it out till the Sabbath was over. The Phariseic opponents could accordingly have been prompted to parry the stroke aimed at them by Jesus' illustration by replying: "No, we do not admit that your illustration is to the point. We firmly maintain that our prohibition of needlessly assuming any laborious exertion on the Sabbath, applies even to the case of an only sheep that has fallen into a pit. Only that our pity for the suffering brutes—we regard even the prevention of cruelty to and suffering of them as a Mosaical and Divine command—bids us set aside the consideration of laborious exertion on the Sabbath. When, therefore, the animal would have to starve by our neglect of drawing it out, we allow the latter to be done. But when there is a chance of feeding it from the top, we urge that it be left in its place till after the Sabbath."

We will not carry our criticism any further. The reader will at this point have sufficiently recognized the tendency of the evangelists to represent the Pharisees who had polemical encounters with their hero, as so much inferior to him in the power of argument, and as unable to cope with him in any controversy. They must in any case have been crushed beneath the weight of his argument, and he must every time have been gloriously triumphant—is the uniform verdict of the gospel writers, bent on wreaking their vengeance on the antagonists of their Master.

CHAPTER XII.

THE OTHER FOUR SABBATH CONTROVERSIES IN THE GOSPELS.

There are four more Sabbath disputes delivered as having been carried on between Jesus and his Jewish opponents. Two of them, belonging to the author of the fourth gospel, seem to us, however, to be of one same body of narrative, having by some chance been disjointed. Accordingly there would in fact be but one Johannine Sabbath controversy to notice. As to the spittle and clay story in ch. ix. of the fourth gospel, it can of course not be accounted a controversy, and, therefore, not be ranged under the above head.

Our view on the authenticity of these controversies will be stated severally as we go on in our discussion. Two of them occur in Luke xiii. 10-17 and xiv. 1-6. In the latter place the Pauline author puts in the mouth of Jesus the identical argument which Matthew imputes to him in the case previously surveyed; with this difference only, that he changed the sheep to an ass or ox, and the patient treated by Jesus to one sick with the dropsy.

It seems to us that Luke having met with Jesus' illustration of the animal fallen into a pit either in Matthew or in the original copy common to both evangelists, liked it so well and found it of such a prolific nature, that he concluded on weaving it into two separate stories, inventing a new one,—the one in question,—in which another instance alike of a miraculous cure by Jesus and of the discomfiture of the Scribes and Pharisees by his cogent reasoning, could be given to the believing public.

In Luke's other case of Sabbath healing, that of a woman with "the spirit of infirmity" of eight years' standing (xiii. 10-17), Jesus is introduced with an argument of defence, also taken from ordinary experience, but of a different nature from the above. It is to be inferred from its representation that the dispute was a heated one. For the ruler of the synagogue who had taken decided exception to the process of healing going on on the Sabbath, was addressed by Jesus with the collective taunt: "Ye hypocrites." It goes without saying that "the adversaries were put to shame" (v. 17) in this encounter as well! The Pharisees were a set of antagonists to be worsted and cowed, and consequently the uniform verdict of the evangelists was, that they were shamefully beaten, whenever they dared to remonstrate with the Master.

Now we presume to doubt the truth of the account that the adversaries were put to shame by the illustration held out to them by Jesus. We can not accept it as reasonable that they were totally confounded by the retort, that he might as well perform his cures, as that they habitually "loose their domestic animals from the stall and lead them away to watering" on the Sabbath.

The divergence between both propositions was doubtless so great in their mind, that they were most apt to promptly rejoin: "We do lead our animals to watering on the Sabbath (comp. Tosifta Sabb. iv. 1.). What of that? It is not a labor or an act seductive to any kind of it, if proper provision is made with the view to the prohibition of carrying from private precincts to public places (see Mishnah, Erubin ii. 1). Whereas we believe that if healing is permitted to go on on the Sabbath, the apprehension that real labor may ensue from it in the agitation and anxiety of the mind of both the curer and the patient, is near enough. We therefore hold it forbidden. To you, of course, the apprehension that one might heedlessly come to commit the labor of crushing medicinal roots on the Sabbath, may appear as a capricious stickling. For even if he should trespass that way, he would in your view at most violate an *angelic* or *humanly* Mosaic command. To us, however, who are convinced of the Divine authority of the Sabbath law, as well as of the Divine denunciation of kareth "extermination" against its violators, it must be of vital concern to guard ourselves and others from its breach by all possible ramparts of prevention."

We will now proceed to the accounts of the fourth gospel. This half-Gnostic Gentile Christian writer, who, by the way, expressed himself as frivolously about the Mosaic Law as he alluded insolently to the Jews, has in ch. v. 17, after the mention of Jesus' curing an "infirm" man on a Sabbath at the pool of Bethesda (probably situated south of Jerusalem), imputed to him as argument of apology: "My Father worketh until now and I work too." There is surely no intrinsic evidence against the authenticity of this argument, either in its language or contents. Jesus was, we should think, quite as able to resort to this kind of reasoning as he was to the other related by Matthew. But since the genuineness of John's narrative is, on the whole, as will be seen immediately, subject to serious doubt, and the substance of the argument itself bears in our view a native Gentile stamp, we will not be amiss in attributing the quoted sentence to this author as his own free composition, rather than to Jesus. Keim (l. c. iii. p. 215) has already critically noted the circumstance, that John has in the narrative in point totally transposed a certain cure by Jesus of a paralytic in Capernaum, reported by the Synoptics (Matt. ix. 1-8; Mark ii. 1-12; Luke v. 16 transfers the scene to the wilderness, however), to Jerusalem, making, moreover, of the sick a chronic sufferer of thirty-eight years' standing, and fixing the cure on the Sabbath. That the author of the fourth gospel used that Synoptical account and spun out his own story from it, making of it a Sabbath and Sonship controversy, appears to us very probable. Aside from this we have the following momentous objection to the claim of the authenticity of the narrative. The argument itself imputed to Jesus has to us the signature of Gentile reflection. Not that Jesus, having elsewhere made the declaration that "the Son of man is lord of the Sabbath," which was certainly the most sweeping he could utter regarding the Sabbath, was not capable, too, of giving vent to the idea of work being free to him, because God his Father works also on the Sabbath. But we have from several analogies of Gentile Christianity the strongest warrant for our opinion, that such argument was exclusively employed by this class. We hold it to have been the stable one with Gentile Christians in their polemics with Jews on the obligation of the Sabbath.

Justin Martyr, in his Dialogue with Trypho, the Jew, ch. xxiii., holds out to him, whom he wishes to turn to his anti-Mosaic Christianity, the point of consideration, alleged to have been used by the old man through whom he himself had been converted to Christianity,—that "the elements (or stars) are neither idle nor do they sabbatize." He aimed thereby to impress on Trypho, that the Sabbath command cannot be from God, because he continues to put forth his providential energy on the Sabbath as well. (In connection with this point he urges another, namely, that, since the Sabbath was not commanded before Moses, and was then introduced only because of Israel's sins, neither can it be obligatory now, since Jesus Christ, the virgin-born of Abraham's seed, had been sent on account of sin.) In the same Dialogue, ch. xxix., where Justin had previously scornfully remarked that the Jews do not understand the sense of Scripture, he reflects on the non-observance by the (Gentile) Christians of the Sabbath, saying: "Nor must you (the Jews) think it something fearful that we drink warm water on the Sabbath (that is, heat the water to drink or use it), since God administers the world on this day in just the same way as on all the others." He adds there yet in apology of his Christian standpoint the ground of objection advanced in Matthew xii. 5; and further, that so many just men who lived before Moses, had been approved by God, though they observed none of the ritualistic laws of Mosaism.

To strengthen our opinion, that the argument of God's providential working on the Sabbath was peculiar to Gentile Christianity for its opposition to the observance of the day by Jews, we will yet adduce a pertinent instance from the Rabbinical literature. It is a relation of the Midrash which, while it is of a legendary composition, shows yet the settled existence of that argument with the Gentile professors of Christianity. "A Minean," it is said there, "overheard the four Palestinian Rabbis (Gamaliel, Elazar, Josua and Akiba, supposed to have been in Rome about 96 C. E.; see Graetz, History of the Jews) preach in the city of Rome on the topic, that God not only commands, but himself observes what he asks men to do; herein (as in other things) he is exalted above human rulers, who give orders, but do not obey them themselves. (This was, by the way, a favorite theme with the older Rabbis ; comp. Jer. Rosh. Hash. f. 57). When they left after they had done preaching, a Minean questioned them : 'If your affirmation were true, why is it, then, that God does not himself keep the Sabbath ?' etc." (Rabb. Ex. ch. xxx.) We refrain from reproducing the sequel of the controversy. It turns on a scholastic problem in which, we presume, the non-theological reader cannot be interested. That entire Midrash relation is indeed an unreal expository web, which could have been of value only to Israelites in the earlier stage of culture. But yet it contains this historical thread at least, that Mineans were wont to argue against the Sabbath from the point of view of God's providential activity on it. The Minean of the Midrash was, as we prefer to hold from the analogy of Justin's identical argument, a Gentile Christian.

But even if he had been meant for a pagan Roman,—this class were also in the Rabbinical literature denominated Mineans,—our view would not the less gain a very substantial support from that Midrashic relation. In so far at least, as we learn from it that the objection to the Sabbath on the ground of God's exercising his providential energy on it, had a Gentile origin. And this we essentially aimed at when we proposed, that it issued from Gentile Christianity, and was habitual with this party, in contrast with Jewish Christianity.

That the before-mentioned Minean might have been intended for a pagan Roman, is manifest from the following notice in another place of the Midrash. In the continuation of the dialogue between Rabbi Akiba and Tinnius Rufus which we presented above (p. 82), the latter asked the Rabbi : "If indeed it be so as you pretend, that God honors the Sabbath, why does he on it make the wind blow, the rain fall, and the grass grow?" The Rabbi's reply does not concern us now. We only wished here to refer to that dialogue for the purpose of corroborating our supposition, that that Minean could well have been a heathen Roman.[48] The same point of argument having been attributed to both the Minean and the governor Tinnius Rufus, it is surely not far from possible, that the two relations entered the Midrash from the actual experience of disputes on the Sabbath held between Jews and Romans, especially imperial officers stationed in Palestine with whom Rabbis and other Jewish people frequently met and had encounters on points of Jewish religious law. This does yet not exclude the same argument being often used by Gentile converts to Christianity who fanatically opposed Jewish rites in general, and especially contended that they were not liable to the observance of the Sabbath,—all in accordance with the license promulgated by the apostle of the Gentiles, Paul. We have practically shown it used by Justin. And we maintain, too, that it proceeded from unconsecrated Gentile thought, but not from the minds of the Jewish-born devotees of the new sect. (It is yet possible that a few fanatical Hellenistic Christians of the type of Stephen were essentially in accord with the Christian converts from paganism.) Our view therefore is, that the author of the fourth gospel imputed to Jesus the above noted argument from his own mind.

This view, in passing, furnishes at the same time an evidence, indirectly at least,—if any additional one were yet needed,—that that gospel was not written by the Jewish Christian apostle, John, but by a Gentile who had assumed this name. As to the Sabbath controversy in point it remains yet to be noted, that John has given it a twofold bearing. Not only is Jesus rebuked for healing on the Sabbath, but also the cured man is rigidly questioned about his license in taking up his bed and walking away with it, it being the Sabbath (v. 10). The implication is, that the Jews (it is mainly the Jews in general who are brought forward in the fourth gospel as Jesus' antagonists, not the Pharisees, as in the Synoptics; the change was without doubt made from the anti-Jewish sentiment of its author) were indignant at his carrying away his couch on which he lay prostrate in one of the porches of the pool. We have to interpret the accusation, if it is to have any sense at all, that the Jews were exasperated at his breaking the Sabbath law of carrying things from a private precinct to a public place, or, as it might have been, the reverse, which was indeed a grave offence with them, and one prominently included in the thirty-nine chief labors prohibited on the Sabbath. The removing of the bed itself, however, that is, its handling, was surely not thought unlawful by any one of the orthodox Jews. Whether Jesus was also charged with that offence, because he had occasioned it by his address to the impotent man (v. 8), is not directly clear from v. 16.

John's other altercation between the Jews and Jesus about his Sabbatic healing reported in ch. vii., is so hopelessly entangled in the context in which it is placed, that it can yield no satisfactory decision, whether he intended it for an independent controversy or only as supplemental to the previous one hereto discussed. We cannot be expected to try to throw light on the confused matter of the vv. 14-25, in which that altercation is produced. This is a task for Christian expounders. On the whole we have the impression that it logically and locally belongs to the controversy of ch. v. Why it was left out there and came to be placed here, is inexplicable to us.

Now the new argument with which Jesus is introduced here in v. 23 in repelling the charge of Sabbath breaking by "making a man whole" was, that the Jews themselves allow circumcision to take place on the Sabbath. The "ruler" who had called him to account for it, then "said nothing unto him" (v. 26). John insinuates by this statement that they were too much astounded at the overwhelming intelligence of "the Christ" to come forward with an answer.

What is the pith of the argument imputed here to Jesus? This is indeed very difficult to decide. From its external tone and aspect we should judge that it is substantially similar to Jesus' objection of the Temple sacrifice vacating the Sabbath (see Matt. xii. 5). Both sacrifice and circumcision on the legal eighth day, had indeed vacated the Sabbath obligation according to Jewish custom. A solid warrant for the latter is variously attempted to be obtained in B. Sabb. f. 132. The argument attributed to Jesus may have been meant to be: "If out of regard to the Mosaic Law commanding the rite of circumcision for the eighth day, the Sabbath has to recede before it in the instance that both collide, because you hold that without its performance on the proper day the Jew is not *perfect* before God, how can you be angry at me for making a sick man entirely whole or *perfect* (though only physically)?" Possibly—as it has been suggested already by others, see Bloomfield's commentary, in loco—the following antithesis was here aimed at: "If the Sabbath has to yield to a rite performed only on a single part of the body, how can it be wrong to attend to a whole (suffering) human being and completely restore him?" In the same strain a Rabbi of old is reported to have argued to defend and support the rule that "saving life vacates the Sabbath." "If circumcision," the Rabbi reasons, "which is done on only one member of the body, puts the Sabbath aside, how much the more must the entire human body (when endangered) have the force of temporarily vacating it?" (Mechilta p. 110). We venture yet another possible interpretation of the argument as set forth by the author of the fourth gospel. It has to be borne in mind that Jesus passes with this evangelist as the pre-existent Logos that became flesh in him. The Mosaic Law and the dogma on Jesus as worked out by this writer, were utter opposites (see i. 17; and comp. v. 8, 9; iii. 36). The antithesis he imputed to Jesus in vii. 23, may accordingly have been intended to have this force: "If a Jew may be circumcised on the Sabbath, that the law of (your) Moses may not be broken, are you wroth with me because I, viz., the only begotten God (see i. 18), nay, identical with God as the personified Logos (see i. 1), made (by my divine, miraculous power) a human being entirely well again? If the authority of Moses who has commanded you all those laws, is to be respected to such a degree that even the Sabbath has temporarily to yield to another paramount command of his, how much the more authority must I have for my own acts who, in my capacity as the Word incarnate, am surely so much superior to him!"

Putting this construction on the argument, we find it to have about the same motive as the antithesis which Jesus is by Matthew reported to have employed in the Sabbath controversy recorded there. There the superiority of Jesus above the Temple is affirmed; here that above Moses.

CHAPTER XIII.

RETROSPECT AS TO JESUS' POSITION ON THE SABBATH.

The Sabbath disputes brought forward and discussed in the two foregoing chapters, whatever may have to be objected to the genuineness of the one or the other of them, and whether or not only those of Matthew have a claim to historical recognition, show at least this solid kernel of authenticity that Jesus, as Keim remarks in vol. iii. p. 326 of his work, "set himself in conflict with the law of the Sabbath, as he most decidedly did with the Mosaic divorce ordinance." We will, besides, reproduce this author's reflection on the page following there: "No instance of neglect of the Law on the part of Jesus can, it is true, be formally established. But his self-dispensations from the severe rule of the Sabbath, etc., point in that direction."

These concessions we have to put up with, considering that they come from an author who, on the one hand, strenuously exerts himself to defend the Law-abiding position of Jesus, and on the other, can, as a Christian writer, trained in the Pauline faith-religion and consequently imbued with a Gentile anti-Mosaic bias, if not an anti-Jewish disdain, not well be expected to enter with any sympathetic estimation of Jewish religious sentiment into the survey of Jesus' speeches and activity, antagonistic to orthodox Judaism.

We have yet to state that he has ultimately not left those concessions unaltered. In his attempt at championing Jesus as an upholder of the Law, he afterwards modifies them again. The fact is, his view on Jesus' regard for the Law is so unsettled and wavering (we have touched on this already above), that we are at our wits' end in attempting to ascertain which one of his manifold sentiments we shall choose as the standard for accurately judging of it. We can indulge his inconsistency only in view of that of the gospel accounts themselves. The modification of his judgment occurring on page 327, he gives forth on pp. 362-63, where he does not objectively admit Jesus' disregard of the Law, but does so only subjectively, that is, as to the perception and purpose of the Phariseic opponents. "But it was easy for them," he says there, "to establish, in a number of points, his disregard of the Law, etc." His other observation on the conflict of Jesus with the law of the Sabbath on p. 326, he subsequently qualifies in so much, that Jesus "decided, on his own authority, that the law of the Sabbath must be limited by the moral law, which allowed the doing what was necessary to the maintenance of life, and commanded the saving of one's neighbor."

This sweeping qualification has, we own, a very luring sound; but only to the Gentile Christian who swears on the words of the teacher Paul, that with and through Jesus the Mosaic ritual was abolished, and who regards the ethical Jesus-religion as the legal system that was, by a Divine arrangement, to supplant Mosaism. Different it was, however, with the representatives of orthodox Judaism in Jesus' time. They would not only not own any contrast between the ritual and moral law, but would denounce any attempt at putting up such a contrast as a rank heresy. For to them there was, nay, there could be, no moral law *without*, not to say, *above* the Mosaic code. It was fully contained therein, partly expressly and partly by implication. Both the ritualistic ordinances and the moral rules of life were to them equally enunciated by God through Moses. They were to them coming from one source, were of one mould, and most congruous with one another. In their judgment and belief, therefore, the plea that there is an extraneous moral law which is to serve as the regulator of the Sabbath observance, as Keim formulates it, must have been as subversive of true Judaism, as any other radically irreligious assault upon it.

But Keim's qualification is defective and incorrect from still another view. He evidently meant to suggest that the plucking by the hungry apostles of a few ears of corn on the Sabbath, was a thing "necessary to the maintenance of life," which cause decided Jesus to interpose with the dispensation urged by the moral law. But where in the world did that author gather the information that the maintenance of life depended on those few ears of corn? How does he know that the apostles' craving was mortal, or would at least have proved injurious, had they not gratified it on the spot? How does he know that they could not have succeeded to get victuals for satisfying their hunger in many another way, if they were only willing to make some exertion, have a little patience, and impose on themselves a momentary self-abnegation? The text does, indeed, not say that they were famished or pinched with hunger, so that waiting any longer could have been fraught with a dangerous collapse. They were only "an hungred." And since we justly infer from the observation by the Pharisees of the apostles' act, that the latter were then only taking a walk along the near outskirts of the town of Capernaum, we may further fairly conclude that, if they had felt the commonly prevailing reverence for the Sabbath, they could without any real suffering and fear of ill result from their hungry sensations, have wended their way back and got all they wanted to eat in a lawful manner, among the coreligionists in town. As to Keim's other point in that qualifying sentence, that " the moral law commanded the saving of one's neighbor," we indeed agree, as we are positive that the Pharisees of old did agree (see above), that this principle is alike reasonable and coercive. Yet that author's bringing it to bear on the issue of Jesus' miraculous healing of the man with a withered hand on the Sabbath, is impertinent, because he presents that moral law as an extraneous abstract power, demanding that the Sabbath give way to such kind of saving one's neighbor. He ought to have known from the relative passages of the Rabbinical literature accessible to non-Jewish inquirers as well. that orthodox Judaism itself found it totally congruous with the Mosaic dispensation, that "saving life should vacate the Sabbath," without even faintly looking for any external standard that would in such cases urge to interfere on behalf of suffering humanity, viz., the moral law! Lastly, we have to object to Keim's qualifying sentence that, whatever moral considerations may have prevailed with Jesus in defending those anti-Sabbatic acts recorded in Matt. xii., yet as the most weighty and paramount argument stands forth indisputably his assertion of a personal, divine-like authority over the Sabbath, in the words: "For the Son of man is lord of the Sabbath." Here it is no more an abstract ethical criterion urging on to interference with the Sabbath, but a pretended divinity of some sort, personified in himself. What this affirmation must have implied to the orthodox opponents of Jesus, we have already suggested before. Christian writers who propose to themselves the task of exalting, in behalf of Jesus, the moral law that was to repel, in accordance with his precepts, the Sabbath observance, ought at the same time not to overlook or lightly pass over the fact of that affirmation, which by far outweighs in significance the emphasis of humane points of view attributed to Jesus in the record of that Sabbath controversy. They ought to consider, further, that if Jesus had held those moral considerations a sufficiently valid apology for the act construed as a breach of the Sabbath by his opponents, he would not have had to add the argument of his own supernatural authority over it.

If Christian writers made proper account of this, they would not inveigh against the orthodox antagonists of Jesus with such endless volleys of revilement as we find that most of them do, from the relentless Canon Farrar (see his 'The Life of Christ') to the more moderate Keim, who vents the following (l. c.) : " It is well known how scrupulously, how sternly, the Jews, especially the Pharisees (the latter is not true, for the common Jewish people— the Am-ha-arets—were provably, as far as they knew how to be so, every whit as conscientious in the observance of the Sabbath as the learned, pious extremists; and as to the Sadducees and Essenes, their Sabbath strictness was surely without any flaw, though it had, according to their respective sectarian tenets, a somewhat different aspect from the Phariseic ; see our Note 42), upheld the honor of the day which was said to have been solemnized by Adam, although they expressly elevated it into the weekly day of enjoyment (this is the height of insolent perversion of truth, and betrays the author's ignorance of the history of the Sabbath, which exhibits in numberless instances the keenest conception by the pious Jews of the day as one of self-sanctification, while all the enjoyment by which they distinguished it—and they did distinguish it so solely because "delight" was, according to Isa. lviii. 13, one of its signatures—was limited to innocent comforts which were sufficiently tempered, if by nothing else, surely by the many minute restrictions as to acts and movements with which the Sabbath law was traditionally and continuously hedged in) ; how, under the ridicule of the Gentiles they lost battles and repeatedly lost Jerusalem when besieged, through their Sabbath rest, etc." (The ridicule, it need not be said, Keim has surely not witnessed himself, nor is it likely that the hostile forces and their leaders had in the hot pursuit of warfare leisure enough to indulge in it. He has no historical witnesses for it, either, for what he evidently alludes to, was uttered by some pagan writers long after the respective events, but not by the pagan combatants themselves; see above p. 13).

It is, indeed, easy for the Christian biographers of Jesus to follow the contemptuous tone of the gospels towards his orthodox opponents of old, and level against them all the taunt their vocabulary supplies, for their minute ritualistic peculiarities on the one hand, and, on the other, for having had the susceptibility of being scandalized by the various innovations of him, who was one of their own nation, and concerning whom their judgment, but not that of Gentiles, whether of antiquity or of modern days, was the only competent criterion. For, as Hartmann, 'The Self-Decomposition of Christianity,' says, "Jesus was a Jew from head to toe; his culture was a national Jewish one;" and again, "Jesus is Jew and nothing but Jew." Jesus truly belonged to the jurisdiction of the authorities of his own, the Jewish, people. His continuous contact and, as we also know, frequent contentions, were with Jewish people. *And it is the Jews only who have the indefeasible right of submitting his acts and speeches to the critical judgment, which the sameness of racial ties and the common native religion, as well as the common patrimony of one record of ancestral history, alone authorize.*

Again, it is easy for those biographers to pour out every imaginable epithet of abuse and scorn upon the Scribes and Pharisees whose ceremonial austerity, while it was exacting towards others, was at the same time of a most self-denying character, because they stand at the safe distance of nearly nineteen hundred years from them. They have surely not to fear their rising from the grave to avenge the rancorous and derisive language which they employ against them. No Christian writer of our times who, like Canon Farrar, for instance, standing on the proud pedestal of monumental Gentile presumption, looks contemptuously down and vents his biting sarcasm on them, runs any risk on that head. And as to the offence given by such scornful derogation and heartless criticism of the opponents of Jesus to those who are of all others sensitively affected by it, the Jews of every age, there is no scruple about that, either. Do not the Jews for their small numbers stand in vanishing proportion to the multitude of Gentile Christians? These have on their side at once the impunity and the immunities which are, as this world goes, peculiar to the majority and to might. The Christian Gentiles, at least many of them, while they claim to be the spiritual heirs of old Israel,—with an egregious improvement on the heritage to boot,—yet think themselves warranted in haughtily dissociating themselves from the Jews in the inmost range of their feeling, as well as in their turn of mind. They eye them askance with a sort of scornful pity, and in the vain sense of a fancied superiority, which the mingled Pauline and Johannine spirit has, in written and in spoken words, been producing and nurturing all through these past eighteen centuries. There is no denying this to be true. The writer giving unreserved utterance to this deplorable circumstance,—he does it though with resentment and malice towards none,—regards himself entitled to the claim of an accurate notice of it. Close observations running through a period of nearly four decades of his own life, and, besides, a fair proportion of literary information, confirm him in the assumption of its positive existence.

Now if non-Jewish biographers of Jesus cannot help admitting his *conflict* with the law of the Sabbath and its apparent *neglect* by him (Farrar gives it thus in his most amiable style: "Jesus laid his axe at the root of their proud and ignorant Sabbatarianism;" as above, ii. 118), what has the Jewish investigator to say? He will, as the writer does, concede that Jesus observed the Sabbath (comp. also Matt. xxiv. 20), that he did not directly disown its inviolability by common labor, not to say, that he did not decree its abolition, or much the less propose that another day be substituted in its place.

Yet we learn from the gospels, on the other hand, that he opposed the traditional mode of its observance, as it was conceived and practiced by the generality of the Jewish people of his day. We have, further, above essayed to show convincingly that he cannot have believed in the Divine authority of the Law, even of the Decalogue, in which the institution of the Sabbath was so eminently enjoined. As another additional, though only indirect, evidence that he disbelieved the Divine authority of the Sabbath, we have produced above, p. 147, his eliminating its observance from the number of obligations indispensable for entrance into the world to come.

Should there even be a possibility of refuting our relative proofs, yet no one will be able or have the hardihood to deny the authenticity of the sentence, appearing in all the three Synoptics, that "the Son of man (himself) is lord of the Sabbath." This alone would show his denial of the Divine institution of the Sabbath. That sentence unquestionably bears the sense, that Jesus claimed, in his pretended divine-like Messianic capacity, to have the power of annulling the Sabbath at will, or at any rate to order it to yield to his own option.

What of it, then, that he has not directly declared the Sabbath abolished? Did it not practically, as far as the awe of the Sabbath for himself and his followers was concerned, come to the same thing, whether he spoke the final word of its abolition, or withheld it, either for prudential reasons, or because he held all ceremonial religion as weighing too lightly against the main, Messianic question that exclusively agitated and absorbed his thought and should do so with all his believers, for him to set himself to the task of doctrinally expatiating on the merits of the Sabbath, or yet, perhaps, from some scruple restraining him from putting forth that decisive word,—as long as he openly and directly pronounced himself "lord of the Sabbath?"

Has he by this affirmation not substantially laid the axe on the Sabbath of the Decalogue? Has he by it not seriously shaken the sense of its obligation with his disciples and his other votaries, who were in the main guided by his words? If the Messiah called in question the absolute inviolability of the Sabbath, was it to be expected that they should persevere in the traditional awful reverence towards it?

It is a known or, at least, very noticeable fact, that the devotees of Jesus had implicit, indestructible reliance in their Master's Messiahship, and also in the sure fulfillment of the prediction by him of his second coming. He himself having, as we are seriously inclined to maintain, laid the chief stress of his Messianic mission on his second Advent, his votaries have naturally done likewise. And there is abundant proof in the N. T. literature that they were looking forward to that Advent with intense, never faltering confidence. Now since there is no reasonable doubt that those of his followers who overheard him speak that momentous sentence of his being the "lord of the Sabbath," took him actually by his word and interpreted it in the plain sense which it was to convey, viz., that they could, by his arbitration, be dispensed from its observance: may we not justly suppose, too, that this word continued to resound in their consciousness ever after his death, so long as the paroxysm of their feverish hope of his second Advent lasted, which was, indeed, during the whole lifetime of each one of them, deciding them in their attitude towards the Sabbath in the same way that his living word did? And, further, must they not all through their own lives have expected, for the glorious period of his real second presence, a dispensation from the accepted Jewish Sabbath observance all the more authoritative, as then he would arrive "in glory, with angels, and as Judge of all" (see Matt. xvi. 27, xxv. 31 sq.)?

CHAPTER XIV.

THE SABBATH WITH JESUS' DISCIPLES IN HIS LIFETIME.

Our above expressed view of Jesus' indifference to all ceremonial religion over against the concerns of his Messiahdom, will find a manifest support in the recorded conduct of his disciples as to Jewish religious observances. That they were nurtured in his opinion of the comparative insignificance of ceremonial religion at the then fancied juncture of the partially inaugurated and soon fully to be accomplished kingdom of Heaven, with himself as the central figure, we have no doubt. For how else could their various slights of Jewish observances, some of them Mosaic, be accounted for? Wherefrom should it have come to them that they deliberately made light of, or wholly put aside, the one or the other ritualistic observance, if not from the Master himself, and that in consequence of his all-absorbing Messianic object? They had, for example, broken the Sabbath by plucking ears, ere yet he had brought forward the intricate points of argument in defence of their action. From what motive or on what pretext can they, belonging to observant families as they doubtless were, be supposed to have treated the Sabbath so laxly, if not from that Messianic, instilled on their minds in the daily commerce with the Master? It is too evident that the whole immediate environment of Jesus was pervaded by his Messianic spirit and design, as well as by the opinion that no serious concern must be had for anything but for the Messianic kingdom and the narrow scope of the natural religion of Messiahism. In this neither the Sabbath, nor the festivals, nor the fasts, nor surely the sacrificial ritual, nor any outward ceremonial rite of Judaism were included as obligatory, not to say, any observance of the so-called oral Law, whether anciently traditional, or later and periodically instituted by councils of schoolmen. The Mosaic ritual was at the same time not explicitly and openly excluded from the line of religious practice. It was only treated with the laxity which a sense of non-obligation engenders. As with Jesus, to use Keim's words who infers from the necessity of his making the protest that he did not come to abrogate but to fulfil (Matt. v. 17), "the Law had in his daily practical life retreated to the background" (l. c. iii. 324), so it had with the apostles. Or, let us say with reference to another modern writer, Hausrath, who agrees more directly with us as to laying the main stress on Jesus' Messianic design having engrossed his whole mind: As Jesus, "from the first, in accordance with his preaching of the kingdom of God, put aside those Jewish ordinances (the Sabbath observance, fasting, and conversing with publicans and sinners [49]) as things indifferent" (l. c. ii. p. 180), so did the apostles. These men, unlettered though most of them were, had yet a clear enough comprehension to be susceptible to the insinuation of being emancipated, by ardent and sincere adherence to the concerns of Messiahism, from the bulk and burden of religious practices. Surely experience shows at all times that it requires very little sagacity or learning to catch the sense of those preachings, dispensing people from ceremonial observances attended with exertion or self-denial. When Keim, therefore, proposes that the apostles "did not see this," namely, that "Jesus had in his innermost genius overstepped the limits of Judaism," and that "it was left to Paul and John to fully develop the spirit of the teaching of Jesus" (l. c. iii. 327-28), he is right as to the latter assertion, and that so far, that none of the apostles before Paul had decidedly renounced allegiance to the body of Mosaism or dared to declare it abrogated. But he is surely in error as to the apostles' inability of perceiving that Jesus had overstepped the limits of Judaism. A child of sufficiently matured mind noticing the contrast between the religious precepts and practice that prevailed in the average Jewish family, and the attitude regarding them assumed by Jesus, could have promptly realized that circumstance. Keim corrects himself, though, in the same volume (p. 343), when he says: "How early the disciples of Jesus learned from intercourse with him free principles and free practices, is shown by the complaints....(Matt. ix. 14; xii. 2; xv. 1, 2, Luke v. 33). In fact, the general appearance, demeanor, style of life and habits, were such as had never been heard of in Israel for a teacher or a school."

All Jesus' concern was, indeed, his own Messianic kingdom of Heaven, from his initial utterance (Matt. v. 17 sq.), through the Sermon on the Mount (ib. vi. 33) and his entire subsequent course, till his final ostentatious entry into Jerusalem. Were the apostles not naturally infiltered with the same uppermost notion and engrossed with the same concern, subordinating to it not only all worldly care (comp. Matt. vi. 25-34), but also all observance of practical Judaism? It is, indeed, only their minds' absorption by the confident expectation of Jesus bringing about the much longed-for kingdom of Heaven with all its privileges and advantages, that can account for their now putting a lax sense on this ceremonial rite, now on that, and for their now entirely setting at naught another. To what degree they were indoctrinated with Jesus' denial of the Divine authority of the Mosaic Law, as well as, perhaps, with his other prophetical and Messianic dispensatory notions which we proposed above, we would not presume to decide. There is in any case sufficient testimony of their religious ceremonial libertinism.

That Jesus' systematic opposition to the existing Temple service with the vast range of other ceremonial obligations directly or indirectly connected with and concentring in the Temple, passed to his immediate disciples, there can be no doubt. Not only does this antagonism run through the whole of Jewish Christianity, but there is actually not the slightest trace of the apostles having ever attended to any rite pertaining to the Temple or to sacrifice, save the Paschal ceremonial on the eve before Jesus' death, which is, however, above p. 143, accounted for by his Messianic purpose, but not by the ordinary sense of religiously legal obligation. That they made no scruple to break the Sabbath in the way stated in the gospels, is certainly a weighty enough evidence of their religious libertinism. We may justly infer that they made light of the festivals in the same manner.

That they neglected the fasts is also authentically attested; Matt. ix. 14. Their defense by Jesus bears all the features of genuineness. How they came to put them aside is as easily explained as that they slighted the Sabbath. We propose that the slight rested in both cases on grounds of his Messianic claim. Although it was only Jesus who, in both instances, argued with Messianic references, and, besides, even he urged, in that of the Sabbath neglect, the dispensatory virtue of his Messiahdom only in conjunction with other points of argument, and that after the apostles had done the act for which they were reproached by the opponents, it may yet justly be supposed that in both they acted on opinions previously gathered from the Master's instruction, and which they had adopted in their own conscience. We hold that alike their slight of the Sabbath and neglect of the fasts were owing to the very same Messianic motives, which Jesus gave forth in his arguments, that he as the Son of man was lord of the Sabbath, and the other, that fasting was not befitting in the presence of the Messianic bridegroom. These motives, we maintain, they had assimilated in their minds a considerable time before they plucked the ears on the Sabbath, or were found to neglect the fasts and questioned by John's disciples concerning it. For there can be no doubt that Jesus primarily and repeatedly made all things relating to his pretended Messiahdom, or which could be brought to bear on it, subjects of discussions with his disciples. And it is consequently but reasonable to suppose that he had at some time previous to that Sabbath morning when the dispute with the Pharisees occurred, reasoned with his disciples about his Messianic lordship, in order to relieve their scruple on various things known to be forbidden on the Sabbath; and also that he held out to them, already before that inquiry of John's disciples, the consideration of the all-ingulfing ecstasy which the presence of the bridegroom-Messiah must inspire, so as to shut out the gloom and mournfulness of the fast. [50]

The fasts were many in Israel. Not only was there the great Fast of the Atonement day, Mosaically enjoined, and that with the threat of "kareth" extermination for its violation, but there were four other Scriptural fast days, which were surely by common consent generally observed during the period of the second Commonwealth, viz., those of the fourth, fifth, seventh and tenth month respectively, named by the prophet Zechariah, viii. 19. They were commemorative of dire national calamities. What dates were in Jesus' time fixed for the one or the other of them, can here not be investigated. Suffice it to say that it admits of no doubt, that the Israelites everywhere in Palestine then kept them, as well as those of the pro-restoration belief of our own times still observe them. That the apostles neglected these and all other fasts, though perhaps not that of the Atonement day, which may have had as awful a hold of their conscience as of that of every other coreligionist, appears from the expression of the question, "but thy disciples fast not" (ib. 14).

By such neglect they had practically seceded from the religious conception prevailing in Israel since antiquity, that fasts (with prayer) are an efficient means of expiation and atonement. We cannot here enlarge on this subject, but will summarily state that from the many notices in the Bible and the Apocrypha, as also from the Rabbinical literature, fasts were a fixed religious institution in memory of national catastrophes, for deprecating national, sectional or only local scourges of any kind, and for imploring Divine aid against any perils.

In the centuries on the customs of which the old Rabbinical literature dilates, fasts for menaced or existing scourges were published and enjoined by the ecclesiastical authorities. To resist them by non-compliance was, indeed, no culpable act of religious recreancy. But it showed at any rate a decided repudiation of the aforesaid religious conception.

That in the time of Jesus all those occasional public fasts were already a set custom, is not to be questioned. The apostles can, from the above quotation, not be supposed as having observed them. Nor can they, in view of the same quotation, be reasonably assumed, as already remarked before, to have paid any regard to those mentioned in Zechariah.

It might be opposed that the above question of John's disciples allows of an allusion to self-imposed private fasts. These were doubtless also customary in those days. Not only for perturbing dreams, but for conscious sins, and even as supererogatory penances, we are, from respective statements and intimations in the Rabbinical literature, warranted to assume that private fasts had been in vogue in Jesus' time. John's disciples, of the Essenian or an Essenian-like ascetic sect, may by their Master have been taught to undertake frequent fasts in connection with other exercises of *repentance*, that the sins obstructing the arrival of the kingdom of Heaven, to hasten which was his arduous aim, would the more thoroughly be wiped away; comp. Matt. xi. 18. Jesus, on the other hand, having after following up for a time the theoretic teaching of John, arrived at the self-confident conclusion that he was himself the real Messiah and the practical inaugurator of the Kingdom,— incipient, but steadily growing under his hands,—could, as it is to be surmised from his answer to those disciples, not see the necessity of austere penances for the coming of the Kingdom in the full bloom of glory. It was already blossoming forth apace. To help on its maturity, his own recommended ethical-religious method, unencumbered by exterior rites, would suffice. Besides, as he is reported to have argued against John's disciples (ib. v. 15), he would hold it inconsistent that "the children of the bride chamber (the friends of the groom) mourn, as long as the bridegroom is with them," by which title he, without any shadow of doubt, meant to designate himself. This construction of the remonstrance of John's disciples with him would indeed be admissible, and perhaps commend itself in preference to any other, were it not for the unambiguous words "but thy disciples fast not," which allow of no other interpretation than that they slighted all Jewish fasts,—that of Atonement day perhaps excepted, as observed above.

That the disciples of Jesus had, while they were connected with him, not any regular devotional exercises, either, at least not until the time when they, according to Luke (xi. 1), asked him, "teach us to pray," and received in answer the advice recorded there also, would appear as conclusive from this quoted passage. From it is surely to be inferred that they had not been practicing the three fixed daily devotions of the orthodox Jews, the ritual of which had positively existed since centuries, nor those initiatory to and closing the Sabbaths and festivals, nor the many other doxologies established for various occasions and events.

Neither is it at all certain that they, from the time forth when he, according to Luke, proposed to them, in compliance with their request, a certain formula,—the so-called Lord's prayer,—adopted the latter instead of the traditional Jewish ones, as having to answer all their devotional purposes. That the later Christian church appropriated and introduced it as the set devotional formula, is by no means a convincing indication that his immediate disciples had already adopted it. The relative gospel contexts surely do not sufficiently warrant such assumption. For, as Keim says (l. c. iii. 342), the words "after this manner" (Matt. vi. 9) mean "thus briefly," and "in such a sense;" and Jesus' directions are not, "do pray," but conditional, "when thou prayest" (ib. 6). Keim urges, farther, that there is no trace in the New Testament that Jesus instituted that formula, which he holds to be genuine though as to its composition for the use of his believers: it was first named "the legitimate and regular prayer" by Tertullian and Cyprian.

If there was with the disciples of Jesus no ordinary Jewish praying, can it be imagined that they wore phylacteries or tassels, or affixed 'mezuzoth' at the entrances of their houses, not to say, of the several apartments of them? As to the first-named of these rites Keim remarks (l. c. p. 343), "the gospels know of prayers in the chambers, but nothing of the phylacteries." The same may confidently be asserted regarding the two other rites. For in the consciousness of the true Israelites all those three rites ranked about as equally important and sanctifying. They were the "threefold cord," the combination of which is in the Rabbinical literature designated a safeguard against sin (B. Menachoth f. 43).

Of less consequence was indeed the disciples' omission of hand-washing before meals, at which the Pharisees are said to have taken such deep offence, and which was, according to Luke (xi. 38). peculiar to Jesus, too. For however highly the Phariseic extremists, with whom taharoth, "rules of ceremonial purity," were a foremost religious concern, rated it, it was in truth, as to real religious merit, inferior to any of the aforenamed observances. Moreover, we have shown in Note 41, that at the time of Jesus the rite of hand-washing was, at most, in an incipient state among the lay class, and its omission by the disciples could therefore not have been made a subject of reproach by his opponents.

However, from all the other points of exposition given above, it should clearly result, that the apostles and other votaries gathered round Jesus, had very little practical Judaism about them. The year or two of Jesus' public activity was almost solely taken up by his Messianic aims and movements. Jewish religious observances came in, whilst he was engaged in this his life's work, for a very slim share of attention on his part. They were to him of secondary consideration. And so they were to be and, we insist, were, to the apostles, who are amply known to have proved themselves so very responsive to his claims and teachings of Messiahdom. An affinity of thought about the latter gradually formed itself between teacher and pupils, which must have prompted them to make all other things subserve to it, in the same manner he did.

As to the Sabbath, too, they had, as already observed above, undoubtedly familiarized themselves with the theory of his Messianic power of emancipation or temporary dispensation from its obligation, namely, that he was the "lord of the Sabbath," already before he enunciated its affirmation against the Pharisees. That they acted upon this affirmation on more than one occasion with that laxity of observance which its import and scope would convey to their Messianically excited minds, may safely be presumed.

In this connection we will be permitted to give to the reader another of our views, which he will hold at once important and pertinent enough to be subjoined in this place. We maintain that a distinction is to be made between Jesus' address to the people at large who were gradually to be gained over to and educated in his Messianic system, and the teaching to his narrower circle of adherents. The latter he would, on Messianic grounds bearing as well on the present as on the future, wholly dispense from serious care about Jewish observances. In the then imagined state of fast transition to the new order of things,—the kingdom of Heaven with the rule of the Messiah, resurrection, Judgment, and recreated world for the tsadikim "righteous,"—their engrossing care should be turned to, and such things be done for, the preparation towards it, as would be most expedient for making the balance of Judgment dip in their favor, that they would be allotted the privilege of entering that future world. The close followers of Jesus would indeed, from every evidence in the gospels, devote themselves with absorbing zeal to the problem of the Kingdom with all its appurtenances of doctrine and hope. For the uninitiated, however, that is, those standing yet at some distance from, though fairly susceptible to, the belief in his Messiahdom, a discreet indulgence of their customary adherence to ceremonial religion had to be devised and observed. In this way we can, e. g., account, on the one side, for the dispensation from fasting which he saw proper to give to his disciples (Matt. ix. 15), and, on the other, for his at least provisional allowance for it in the Sermon on the Mount (ib. vi. 16). The latter, we propose, was intended for outside hearers who were yet ceremonially scrupulous and diffident to join his band, for the notorious deviation from orthodox Judaism that subsisted within it. The same explanation may fairly be given regarding his stern and sharp repudiation of the material Temple worship, as contrasted with his provisional countenancing of sacrifice in the Sermon (ib. v. 23, 24), and the often quoted advice to the leper, ib. viii. 4.

And the same holds good to explain his fierce arraignment of the Phariseic-Rabbinical traditions (ib. xv. 3 sq.), and the opposite encouragement of the people to heed the injunctions of the Phariseic teachers and sages (ib. xxiii. 3).

To divide his teaching into esoteric and exoteric branches is by no means hazardous. It is not only perfectly warranted by Matt. xiii. 11. (comp. ib. x. 27), but analogies of this method are offered in the secular philosophies of paganism, as well as in the pursuit of old Rabbinical school-learning.

By this view we would not only have gained a mode of harmonizing the partly conservative utterances of Jesus about some ceremonial rites, with others showing his antagonism to them, but also be able to trace more justly the disciples' ceremonial indifference to that continuous strain of Messianic reasoning, which is naturally supposed to have been, within the confines of the narrower circle, carried to as high a pitch as would correspond to the overwrought thoughts of the Master and the feverish mood of the disciples. The latter being continuously trained in his all-absorbing Messianic teaching, and initiated in its mysteries, would for this reason all the more readily take to his mysterious dispensation of themselves from ceremonial observances which he offered to them, as long as they devoutly gave themselves up to the sole spiritual occupation with the questions of his Messianic kingdom. And to them, too, we surmise, the claim of his Messianic lordship over the Sabbath, uttered in the above-discussed controversy, was at the point of time when it occurred, not new any more. They had without doubt privately heard it before, and were completely conversant with it, so much so that they acted on its strength in the way stated in the record of that controversy, in Matt. xii. 1.

CHAPTER XV.

THE SABBATH WITH THE DISCIPLES OF JESUS AFTER HIS DEATH.

The Master had passed away. His execution had cast a deep consternation in the hearts of his faithful apostles and adherents. However, they were not left, or did not allow themselves to be left, to utter despair. Though parted from him in reality, they were united to him in sentiment. If his suffering and parting were a bitter blow to their sympathetic hearts, it was yet, on the other hand, as they firmly believed, the stepping stone to the structure of the Kingdom, which they expected soon to see fully realized by the Master's coming again in glory and at the head of angels.

The intelligence of his resurrection on the third day coming to them from two of his female devotees (Matt. xxviii. 8), made an end to their brooding over the hard stroke visited on them, and set them thinking over the gradual verification of his various Messianic predictions. Dejection thus gave way to hopeful reflections, and they began to compose themselves again. Jesus himself had, after being apprised of the Baptist's fatal end which produced in him the presentiment that his own could be neither much different nor very distant (see Matt. xvii. 9-13, and comp. Luke xxiv. 6, 7), prognosticated his coming resurrection to three of his apostles, and foretold it again to all of them as to happen on the third day (with reference, we suppose, to Hosea vi. 2), before his entry into Jerusalem (Matt. xx. 19). This prediction the Son of man had, as they believed, made good; see Matt. xxviii. 6. It was even tangibly proved to the eleven, as they fancied in their overwrought spirits, when they had followed the advice of going immediately to Galilee, where the resuscitated Messiah would appear to them again (ib. v. 16 sq.).

His other prediction about himself, that he would be sitting at the right hand of power (Matt. xxvi. 64, Mark xiv. 62),—" power," Geburah, was also by the Rabbis of old often used to denote the Deity,—was likewise beginning to be consummated. For he was, as they believed, after that appearance to them, "received up into Heaven and sat down at the right hand of God" (Mark xvi. 19; comp. as to the same dogma, at a later period, Acts v. 31, vii. 55, 56). All that yet remained to be fulfilled was, his second Advent, which he had predicted to be in the clouds of Heaven (Matt. xxvi. 64).

And it was to this future coming as the all-powerful Messiah, so repeatedly taught them in his lifetime, that they eagerly looked forward. The second Advent was as fixed a persuasion with him, as was that of his future sitting on the right hand of God, which he brought forward by the application to himself of Ps. cx. 1, which psalm, in passing, he was particularly infatuated with, since he deduced from it his own divine lordship, and, implicitly, his divine sonship, too (see Matt. xxii. 43-45); and as was, further, the self-conscious exaltation of himself to the dignity of the Messiah in his first or one of his first public sermons, by applying to himself the words of Isaiah xlii., picturing forth the destiny of the "servant;" see Luke iv. 16-21. Those three points of Messianic dogma were interconnected. The last-named was the starting-point, the other was the intermediate, and preparatory to the first-named.

The resurrection and the ascension having, as they fancied, come to pass, which preliminaries were in their minds unmistakable phases of the developing Kingdom, the height of which was to be the Master's coming again from Heaven, they could partly console themselves for the bitter loss they had endured in his personal withdrawal. Meanwhile they were not entirely left to themselves. They were not wholly abandoned by their Master. The belief was, that he promised to be with them "alway, even unto the end of the world" (Matt. xxviii. 20). Furthermore, his sorely missed presence was, as the notion had formed itself soon after his demise, supplied by the attendance of the Holy Spirit which, as the pretense was, Jesus "hath poured forth" from his celestial station (Acts ii. 33), and this not only on the apostles, but on all that had joined or would join (see ib. v. 38) the ranks of the believers. So much was this, indeed, the prevalent presumption after his death, that in Mark (xvi. 16-18), the promise is put in the mouth of Jesus after his alleged resurrection, that all baptized believers would subsequently become perfect thaumaturgists, competent not only to cure diseases and cast out devils, but to speak in all thinkable languages, and also proof both against the sting of serpents and the deadly grip of poison. In addition, the mere laying of hands by the apostles on baptized converts passed for having the virtue of imparting to them the Holy Ghost (Acts viii. 17).

As to the healing effects of their thaumaturgic efforts the supposition was, that they would be unfailing, provided the person on whom the supernatural act was to be performed, had faith in the *name* Jesus: for then, as is to be gathered from the theory put forth by Peter (Acts iii. 16), the name Jesus retroacted in making that person whole.

That the spell in magical cures centered, let us here observe, in the *name* Jesus, appears from various Jewish as well as extraneous sources, see Jer. Sabb. ch. xiv.; Tosifta Cholin ii., and comp. Acts iv. 30, also v. 41. Therapeutic marvels were the indispensable attendants of Messianic agitations. They inseparably accompanied the cry of the Kingdom, alike with John the Baptist and Jesus. The same combination was enjoined by the latter on his apostles (Matt. x. 7, 8), which they, indeed, faithfully discharged during, and most extensively after, his lifetime. Even the philosophical Paul could not dispense with miracles in the course of preaching his gospel, see 2 Cor. xii. 12, Rom. xv. 19. In fact miracles, in especial therapeutic ones, were the prominent characteristic of Christianity, throughout the whole apostolic and postapostolic ages.

The apostles could, after the death of Jesus, best beguile the dreary days of the personal separation from him, by taking to the practice of those "signs of an apostle" (so in 2 Cor. l. c.). They could pursue no more suitable occupation than this, to make the melancholy suspense concerning his return from Heaven fairly supportable. And, what was chiefest in the continuation of the Master's Messianic work, they could, with the aid of such miraculous performances, propagate, like unto him in his lifetime, the belief in his Messiahdom with the safest promise of success. Compare Origen, Against Celsus, I. 46, who surely says the true thing when he asserts: "The apostles could not without mighty acts and miracles have induced those to whom they gave new doctrines and precepts, to leave their paternal, and embrace the new ones, with great perils to their lives."

This combined Messianic profession of preaching the Kingdom and healing, they doubtless followed with ardent endeavor, as soon as they had returned from Jerusalem to their native district, Galilee. And, we hold, this event took place shortly after Jesus' execution. For Jerusalem will, after the dire experience they had passed through, not have appeared to them as a safe abiding place, if they were to continue in the teaching of Jesus' Messiahdom. This seems even to be intimated in Matt. xxviii. 7, 10.

The true substance of the statements in these passages seems to us to be, that the instinct of the women nearest to Jesus, as well as the shocked sentiment of his immediate family, suggested to the entire company that had espoused his Messianic cause, to make for home again and await there the progress of Messianic events.

This company will without doubt have soon begun to establish themselves into a regular community or Church. They consisted of Jesus' brothers and mother, and the apostles (Acts i. 14; on the latter's names see Matt. x. 2-4, with which compare John xxi. 2 and Acts i. 26), and the rest of Jesus-believers attached to them, who were all of them Galileans, too (see Acts i. 11, ii. 7). The number of this whole first Christian body may not exaggeratedly have been stated as being one hundred and twenty persons (ib. i 15), considering that a good number of women had also joined the Christian brotherhood (see Luke viii. 3, where the company of Jesus is stated to have included three women who are given by name, and "many others;" comp. ib. xxiv. 10, also 1 Cor. ix. 5). Possibly there were "above five hundred brethren," as Paul mentions (1 Cor. xv. 6).

This Christian body most likely settled themselves in the town of Capernaum, which had also been Jesus' fixed central station of activity. That Galilee had a settlement of Jewish Christians in the first third of the second century, appears from a passage in the Midrash, which we will adduce at a later point. Keim (l. c., v. 2) observes, too, with reference to 1 Cor. xv. 6, and Acts ix. 31, that a Galilean church consisting of Jesus' adherents from that province existed in the apostolic period. We may in view of these notices the more properly assume that the seat of the first Christian church was Capernaum, and that this town was selected, out of deference to the memory of the Master who had made it his home, by the returning Christian company soon after his departure, as the resort and plantation of apostolic Christianity. The settlement of the apostles and other leading personages of the Palestinian Jewish Christian church in Jerusalem occurred, we maintain, at a later date.

That the apostles and other early professors of Christianity were, after the death of Jesus, watched with intense concern both by the representative schoolmen and the ecclesiastic-judicial magistracy, suffers no doubt. Not only was any new irritation of the Roman authorities by Messianic stirring to be cautiously prevented, but the apostolic propaganda, having assumed a character antagonistic to the fundamental principle of Judaism by the more and more growing deification of Jesus, was to be met with vigorous resolution. His divinity came, in consequence of his own various relative claims uttered in his lifetime, and in especial through his august pretension of being the Messiah, the son of God (Matt. xxvi. 64, Mark xiv. 62, and comp. Matt. xvi. 16, 17; xxii. 42-45), to be an article of faith with his adherents after his death. Not only in Paul's writings and the fourth gospel is Jesus elevated to the quality of a superhuman individual,—in them he is even exalted to the eminence of divine pre-existence,—but the dogma of his being the son of God was held by all the Jewish Christians. Even the Ebionites, though they denied Jesus' sameness and consubstantiality with God, because he was "begotten," have adhered to the title son of God, as proper to him; see Epiphanius, Haer. xxx. 13, 16 and the Clementine Homilies.

That passage in Matt. xxviii. 18, "All authority hath been given unto me in Heaven and on earth," which is surely a later interpolation, does yet serve as a sufficient evidence of the construction put by the believers of Jesus on his supernal state after his death. They conceived it not alone as one of divine majesty, but of a most comprehensive divine sway. They attributed to him a divine domination which, in their exuberantly admiring souls, increased in magnitude with the increase of time. It grew brighter, the more the remoteness of time had dimmed the memory of his terrestrial life. That this was to the orthodox Jews the most obnoxious and alarming part of the profession of Jesus' early apostles and adherents, is unquestionable. It was not the avowing by all the earlier Jewish Christians of the dogma of his sitting on the right hand of

God in itself that excited the profound and bitter antipathy of the orthodox Jews against them. Whenever that dogma was—if it ever was—abstracted from the additional notion of his exercising a divine power in his sainted state, it could not well have had a moment of Jewish religious offence. In this case it could have been held no more heterodox than was the saying of the Rabbis in the Talmud, B. Sabb. f. 152, that "the souls of the righteous after their death are kept hidden by God beneath his throne of glory." Compare also Josephus, Wars iii. 8, 5. What made that dogma so odious to the orthodox Jews was, that usually a divine potency was along with its enunciation assigned to Jesus. See especially Acts v. 31, where Peter designated him Prince, Savior, and Remitter of sins; comp. also ib. x. 43, and the previous verse, where he re-asserts him as the Judge at the coming resurrection.

Connected with and based on the quality of remitting sins was, we suppose, the apostolic usage of the invocation of his name at magical cures, which has already been noticed before. Since these cures were the professional acts of the apostles, such invocations must have occurred most frequently of all their efforts at propagating their Christianity, and consequently have most often given serious scandal to the orthodox Jews and their authorities. Under the same category came the speaking or teaching "in his name;" see ib. iv. 18, and in other places. All this shows sufficiently that a high degree of divinity was ascribed to Jesus already at the earlier epoch of the apostolic church. This must have had an appalling effect on the orthodox Jewish people everywhere. They were to nothing more sensitive and vulnerable than to the infringement of their monotheistic principle. They were by nothing more deeply galled than by the defection of any of their community from this vital condition of their faith,—a faith which they were at any time ready to seal with their own blood.

On the reprimands, menaces and chastisements (on the latter see Matt. x. 17, xxiii. 34; Acts v. 40 and comp. 2 Cor. xi. 24), which such deifying attitude of Jewish believers in Jesus have called forth, we can here not expatiate. The conspiring causes of criminal inquisition made against some, and of mortal doom executed on a few other primitive Jewish Christians, we have surveyed elsewhere. We will here only state in general that serious collisions of the disciples of Jesus with orthodox Jews had inevitably to ensue from their heretical doctrines. Even if their conduct was not of a defiant or insolent anti-Jewish nature, such, for instance, as were the assaults of the impetuous Hellenistic Christian, Stephen, they must have felt in their hearts a vehement sting at the mere profession of those doctrines.

That collisions about Jewish religious observances too will, even after the Master had departed, have occurred, we may take for granted. ,For we hold that, in the main, the apostles trod, as to them, in the steps of the Master. Consequently we have to maintain that ceremonial rites were to them, as to him, of a subordinate import, as compared with the paramount cause of the Messianic kingdom of Heaven and the preparation towards it. He had taught them their relative unimportance, and they would doubtless bring the lessons to bear on their whole line of conduct. We have already in previous chapters adduced and discussed instances partly of their disregard and partly of their levity as to the Jewish ritual and customs. That now, after the removal of the Master, a change should have set in in their sense and estimate of ceremonial religious duties, is not probable. All that might be proposed in this respect is,—and we will treat of this hereafter,—that they, after the death of Jesus, became more observant of them out of policy and prudent yielding to unpropitious circumstances.

Let us assert here that, in truth, they were and remained Jews to the core as to the belief in the obligation of the sacred sign of the covenant and seal of the national-religious communion, circumcision. They held it so indisputable that they would even not receive any Gentile converts as on an equal footing with themselves, who did not submit to that rite and with it to that part of the Mosaic-Jewish ceremonial, which had yet authority with them; see

Acts xv. 1, 5. In the latter verse that insistance is, indeed, ascribed only to certain of the Phariseic Christians. But since its author attests himself the demand of circumcision for Gentiles on the part of "certain men" who had come from Judea to Antioch, which certain men were assuredly no other than those sent by the head of the Christian church, James (Gal. ii. 12), it is apparent that it was a sentiment and principle of the entire body of the Jewish Christians, and that consequently his statement in v. 5, limiting it to "certain of the sect of the Pharisees who believed," is inaccurate.

The apostles were, too, as Baur urges ('Paul' i. 203), equally as antagonistic to Paul for his antinomian teachings among Jews and Gentiles in Grecian communities, as the orthodox Jews themselves were. He deduces this not only from Acts xxi. 21, but also from Gal. ii. 12, and supports it, further, by reference to the hostile feeling of the Ebionites against him. He remarks there also (p. 204), that the author of Acts himself presented against his will the historical truth, that "the Jewish Christians in Jerusalem saw in the apostle Paul an apostate from the Law, and a preacher of this apostasy among both Jews and Gentiles."

The Sabbath, also a sign of the Divine covenant and with circumcision forming, in the consciousness of faithful Israel, the two greatest fundamental rites of Judaism, the apostles held in reverence, too. That is to say, they estimated it as of that authority which, while they did not, as little as their Master, hold it Divine, the reverend antiquity of its origin, as well as the traditional conception of its being a corner-stone of Israel's religious constitution, and its continuously manifest sacred import, almost absolutely brought with them. With this consisted, on the other hand, primarily because they did not hold it as having come from God, that arbitrary deviation from its observance which is directly recorded about them (see above).

The Mosaic festivals they no doubt kept also, though certainly regardless of the sacrificial ritual ordained for them. And, we may mention here, as little as they can be supposed to have attended to the offering of victims prescribed for individuals on the three pilgrimage feasts, so little will they have cared about the non-sacrificial oblations required to be brought to Jerusalem, such as the so-called second tithe, the fruit of trees and vines in the fourth year of their plantation, and the first-fruits, which latter were portions due to the priests and were solemnly borne into the city and Temple, their regular appointed season being from Pentecost till autumn. (According to Philo a sort of festival was made of the occasion at the end of every fifth year.) That they will already in the first few years subsequent to the death of Jesus have substituted for the sacrificial Passover ceremonial on the eve of the fourteenth Nisan, the sacrament of the Eucharist, is most likely. The (real) apostle John who, by the way, has no doubt contemporarily with Paul set himself industriously to Jewish Christian mission-work among the Gentiles of Asia Minor, as likewise Peter has, on his part, done at the same period in Antioch and other cities of Syria, and even in Corinth (see on this 1 Cor. i. 12), as, possibly, also in Rome, seems, from various reliable notices (as to which the writer refers to Hilgenfeld, 'The History of Heretics, etc.,' p. 601 sq., and to Baur, 'Ecclesiastical History, etc.,' p. 156 sq.), to have introduced this rite, with the Mosaic date of the Pascha, among those Asiatic churches. To it they, indeed, clung immovably for many centuries afterwards. Now if the Christian Pascha with the Mosaic date was habitual with Gentile converts, much more justly may we assume this date as unalterable within the apostolic Jewish Christian church. Again, in this church there was doubtless observed the eating of unleavened bread at that religious love-repast (see on the same observance by the Ebionites, Epiphanius, Haer. xxv. 16, in Hilgenfeld, l. c. p. 432), and, we presume, also during the rest of the seven days of the feast, which there is every reason to believe that they did not leave off celebrating in all after time, and that fairly in accordance with the Mosaic appointment.

On the whole, then, there can be little doubt that in the apostolic sphere the feast of Passover was kept, as to date and partly as to ceremonial rites, conformably to the Mosaic import.

The feast of Pentecost, too, may at a very early date have by the apostles been infused with Christian elements. That they celebrated it, on the whole, for its being an ancient Mosaic institution, appears from Acts ii. 1. While we can not lay much score by any of this author's reports, it is yet quite possible that the alleged effluence from the sublimated Jesus of the Holy Spirit over the devout assembly (ib. v. 33), put by him on the day of the first Pentecost after Jesus' death, has at any rate the historical basis of the *ecstatic belief* existing with those gathered together for devotional exercises, that such imparting of the spirit did really then take place. That they will thenceforth have annually celebrated this pretended event on the feast of Pentecost, we can readily believe. But we have at the same time to hold firmly to the view that, strongly tinctured with Christian bearing as that old Jewish feast had no doubt become to them, they never attempted to remove it from its Mosaic foundation. Both the Mosaic and the new, Christian, purport may have been blended in their conception and usage; though, we farther incline to think, rather with a preponderance of the Christian, because the Mosaic could, for their opposition to the Temple ceremonial, offer to them no clear motive for sacred observance. It is therefore possible that the Mosaic character of the feast consisted with them merely in the perpetuation of its prescribed date.

As to the feast of Booths, we have no reason for questioning its observance by the apostolic church, either. Whether some Christian elements were mixed with it, we are not able to affirm, because every relative information or indication is wanting. With regard to the feast of the first day of Tishri, we may justly surmise that it shared attention with the rest of the traditional Jewish solemn days. Whether they fasted on the Day of Atonement, on this we reflected already before. The doubt of their having done so in Jesus' lifetime may, as will hereafter appear, not attach to them for the period after his death.

To these considerations we may add some indirect evidence from the following places of Paul's Epistles. In Gal. iv. 10, he arraigns those converts having relapsed into Judaizing by the observance of solemn days and seasons. In Coloss. ii. 16, he takes issue with him who would cavil with his fellow-believer about his non-observance of "holyday, new moon or Sabbath;" compare also Rom. xiv. 6. Now the cogent consequence from those two places (the Ep. Rom. is by some notable authors of our day held as written to the Jewish Christians of Rome, and could accordingly not be turned to account in the argument we here propound) is, that if Gentile converts were observant of the Jewish sacred days, much more must their teachers from the Judaic church, the apostles or their agents, have been observers of them. That Paul's reference should in those passages have been exclusively to the Ebionites as a class of sectarians, cannot be upheld, as we will by and by demonstrate. Even if it had been, it would not invalidate our argument. For the Ebionite missionaries, whom Paul may have held polemically in view, can have been no other than those authorized and delegated by the leaders of the apostolic church, who were themselves largely imbued with Essenian doctrines, to preach the Jewish Christian gospel to the Gentiles.

As to rules of religious purity the apostles can, for their unquestionable opposition to the sacrificial ritual, not be supposed as having been straightly guided by the relative ordinances of the Mosaic code. In all instances of personal impurity requiring sacrifice (see Lev. xii., xiv. xv.), or in those for which the "water of separation" is prescribed (Numb. xiv.), they will consistently have omitted these rites. Still a reverent regard to many Mosaic propositions of defilement they can fairly be expected to have had. We advisedly say, many, and not, all, for we cannot imagine that they will in their zeal of Messianic propaganda have, for instance, shunned the touch of a leper or an impure woman, any more than their Master did. Nor could we reconcile it in our mind that they should in their missionary intercourse with pagans have avoided, even if they felt such anxiety, every one of those pollutions termed as such in the Pentateuch. Yet for all that there is reasonable ground to believe that they will have looked to the Pentateuch as the general guide in matters of religious purity; see also our Note 34. While we concede this, we have nevertheless to state it as probable, that alike in their doctrinal and practical course the Essenic rules of purity predominated. Not that they would or could regularly, in their public activity, carry into practice the extreme conceptions of purity of that sect, which, as is well known, left even the Mosaic ones behind. But there are certain indications showing, that they had Essenic prepossessions and will, therefore, whenever, as we remarked, their Messianic missionary work did not interfere, have followed out the Essenic rules of purity rather than the Mosaic-Jewish. We will not, in evidence of this, quote Paul's "Handle not....nor touch" (Col. ii. 21, 22). For these phrases admit as much of a direct Mosaic as of an Essenic or Ebionite bearing. Indeed, Paul may there have alluded to some respective prohibitions explicitly set forth in the Pentateuch. But there are other pertinent indications for it. We have in the before-cited Note endeavored to make it probable, that three out of the four apostolic decrees had pre-eminently an Essenic basis. And if we be permitted to retrace the many injunctions of bodily purity in the Ebionitic Clementine literature to the apostolic church which, as may be set down for certain, prominently leant on Essenism, we are all the more entitled to assert the postulate, that within it the Essenic rules of purity enjoyed a superior estimation. Was not, it may yet be observed, the rite of baptism itself, so greatly exalted by the apostles, originally a prominently Essenic or, at any rate, Essenic-related symbol of regeneration?

Connected with the rules of purity, alike in the spirit of Mosaism and evidently also, to judge from the Clementine Homilies (vii. 4, 8), in the thoughts of the Ebionites, were the Jewish food restrictions. It is safe to presuppose the same connection in the minds of the apostles. As to the observance of those restrictions, the consequence is easily drawn from those four decisions for proselytes to Christianity recorded in Acts xv. (see on this, Part First, p. 118, and Note 34 of the present treatise), that they surely abstained for themselves with horror from those kinds of flesh named there as part of the resolutions of warning to converts. For if the apostles ordered those points for converts from paganism, much more must themselves have heeded them. To those kinds may at once be superadded the flesh of dead animals, which the Peter of the Clementines, too, joins to the rest of restraints appointed for Gentile converts (see Homilies).

True, our view is, that three out of those four apostolic decisions were principally suggested by Essenic theories. But there are apart from them other inferences and accounts, showing forth the apostles' religious regard, in general, to the Mosaic dietary prohibitions. We will produce such from some of Paul's Epistles, and from Acts.

In Col. ii. 16, Paul reprobates the temper of those converts censuring their fellow-believers for not observing the laws about "meat and drink." In Rom xiv. 2 sq., he likewise warns those "weak" enough in not indiscriminately eating, out of religious scruple, every sort of food, against criticising others already strong enough in their faith in Jesus not to have to pay any regard to such distinction. Now that Paul polemically alluded in those passages to the Ebionites, as is the opinion of many modern writers, we may readily allow. We may agree with them that in his reflection on the question of lawful food in Romans, he alluded to the Ebionite rejection of flesh-meat. Even in his using, in., v. 14, the epithet "unclean," he may have thought of such Ebionite notion. Likewise may the before-noted passage of Colossians have the same Ebionite bearing. For the repudiation by the Ebionites of animal food is variously and strongly attested; that of wine, too, would appear from the testimony of Epiphanius (Haer. xxv. 16) who reports, that they celebrated the annual sacrament of the Eucharist by using water only (instead of wine). The ascetic custom of combinedly avoiding flesh-meat and fermented liquors they had in common, if not with their Jewish Essenic stock,—for whether such rules subsisted with the Essenes is matter of dispute among various learned authors of the present day,—at least with the Buddhists (according to Koeppen, 'The Life of Buddha,' in Bunsen, 'The Angel Messiah'). Yet apart from the consideration that there is no conclusive intrinsic evidence that Ebionite allusion is to be traced in those passages, for we hold it quite as possible that Paul thought, in those Epistles, of meats and drinks offered to idols, and meant to pass on the non-sectarian, generally Jewish notion, that they pollute the eater (meats and drinks offered to idols were Rabbinically reckoned equal to "sacrifices of the dead," and not only interdicted for eating, but for any use whatever; see B. Abodah Zarah f. 30; they were also considered polluting the human body, some Rabbis declaring their impurity of the same degree with that of a corpse; see ib. f. 32 and Cholin, f. 129), and this in view of his standpoint of indifference concerning idol-meat vented in 1 Cor. viii.,—we have, even if that sectarian Ebionite allusion be allowed, at all events to insist that it cannot have been exclusive in those entire passages. This becomes plain from the circumstance that Paul reflects in one same strain in the Colossian Epistle on the observance of "feast, new moon and Sabbath," and likewise in Romans on the regard for "days." Surely no one will be stolid enough to give out those sacred and solemn days as peculiar to the Ebionite sect. Nor can it for one moment be supposed that it was solely Ebionite propagandists who taught Christian neophites to observe them. No, indeed. Any Jewish Christian teacher, with the exception of the Paulinists, will have made it his aim to propagate their observance among new converts. The bearing in these passages of Paul's Epistles as to sacred days can accordingly be no other than a generally Judaic one. From this it clearly results that, even if Paul's remarks on religious eating restraints were personally aimed at certain Christian zealots who chanced to be Ebionite sectarians, he nevertheless had, in putting them down together with those on the sacred days, before his mind at large the national Jewish scruple about all those ordinances of the Mosaic-Jewish religious ritual. It vexed him, as we must judge from his relative objections, that they were persistently being transplanted into Gentile Christianity by Jewish Christian emissaries, who came from the seat of the apostolic church. His opposition was, we conclude, by far not so much to Ebionite sectarians as, on the whole, to the Judaizing propaganda carried on by the determination of that church. In the latter, then, we infer for our purpose from Paul's polemics, the Mosaic eating laws must have been treated with religious regard, or its emissaries could not have urged their observance on Gentile converts, or on converts at all.

We will yet adduce some other indications of such religious regard having subsisted in the apostolic church. Let us first notice Peter's alleged dispensation from Mosaic food injunctions by a voice from Heaven (Acts x. 13). We may without hesitation reduce it to the significance of self-dispensation, accompanied perhaps,—if there is at all any historical ground to that entire story, even when stripped of the vision related there,—by the delusion of himself, before he set out on the missionary journey to the preponderantly pagan city, Caesarea, that the divine spirit privileged him to indiscriminately partake of the meats prepared by pagans. For our immediate purpose we assert, that that account shows incontrovertibly, that Peter was at least until then observant of the relative Mosaic prohibitions. Farther, it is to be deduced from that very author, that at the same conjuncture all of the apostles and their church held to them religiously: for they are said to have taken Peter to task for his trespass (ib. xi. 1, 3).

All this holds good on the supposition that Peter had indeed violated Mosaic eating prohibitions on the occasion of his visit to Cornelius, or on any other. But there are, in fact, serious doubts about the respective reports that he did so. Acts is not in the least authentic. Its tendency is to make of Peter a Pauline universalist and partial repudiator of Mosaism (see especially ib. xv. 9), and of Paul a true or at least a fair respecter and observer of it. Its author has possibly taken the motive for that fantastic account rendered in ch. x., from the noted passage of Paul's Epistle Gal. ii., improving it for his object in the way he did. As to Paul's own statement in the Epistle, while we are far from calling in question the substantial occurrence as brought out by him, we would yet propose that there is no necessity whatever for construing it into bearing any other sense than merely that he saw Peter eat in the company of Gentiles. What he ate must for this reason not have been Mosaically prohibited food. That Paul charged him with it, does not signify that his reproach rested on fact. He may have simply judged on the impression which the superficial notice of his eating in the society of Gentiles made on him. But by so eating and yet at the same time abstaining from impure meats, his trespass was merely against the Essenic-Ebionite canon (see Clem. Hom. xiii. 4), or the Phariseic-Rabbinical rule, but not against a Mosaic inhibition. Putting the case even that Peter did at Antioch actually take some illicit freedom with regard to certain Mosaic eating prohibitions, we have at all events Paul's own testimony that at that point of time the observance of them was the indispensable norm within the body of the Christian church. For he presents Peter and others as having "drawn back" from the Gentiles, that is, from their tables, after the arrival of the Jerusalemite deputation sent by the head of the church, James, through fear of being detected by them eating unlawfully.

It is readily seen from all the foregoing that in general, a religious regard to the Mosaic food laws, amalgamated with the respective Essenic precepts, was a fixed norm with the primitive apostles. They adhered to them to such a degree, that they would not only hold themselves

liable to them, but, as we believe, impressed the same
liability on all those converts to Christianity aspiring to a
full communion with them. Nevertheless, we can perceive
the possibility that the missionary intercourse of some
apostles and sundry agents of theirs, had gradually brought
about a certain relaxation as to some of those laws, to which
they, ascribing no Divine authority to any of them at all,
would attach only an inferior importance. They may in
mixing with pagans for objects of conversion have soon
ascertained that it was impossible to be any longer so
observant as they could be and were among themselves, in
their secluded, uncolliding Palestinian homes. In the first
place may hunger have often urged them to relax this or
that ritualistic food restriction (comp. Acts x. 10). Again,
it must have seriously thwarted the end they pursued;
which was, to win converts from among the pagans, had
they persistently refused to join in any of their meals, or
been critically particular as to every dish served on the
tables at which they attended. Such a demeanor would
have had a decidedly repulsive effect on would-be converts.
It is therefore plausible that they will have indulged some
latitude about the observance of the food laws, when conversing with Gentiles on Christian missions. Moreover, it
is quite probable and at the same time agreeable with our
general view of the Jewish Christians, from Jesus onward,
to presume, that the apostles or any Jewish-descended professors of the new faith were at no time, even previous to
their Gentile mission work, very scrupulous about the
Mosaic-Jewish food laws, at least those which did not rank
with them as of unquestionable religious value. Was it at
all to be expected that they were so scrupulous, when we
have to judge of them as depreciating the authority of the
entire Mosaic ritual from the common Jewish orthodox
acceptation of directly Divine, to angelic or merely human?
And, let us amplify the question, was, in view of this fact,
a scrupulosity about any ceremonial rites, even those which
they, on the whole, yet prized religiously, to be at all

expected from them? That they did so depreciate the authority of the Law, we not only assert on the general supposition of disciples ordinarily following their master, but there is valid Rabbinical and other testimony for it.

From the passage in the Talmud quoted above p 149, and which is indisputably historic, it appears that the Mineans recognized only the Ten Commandments as Divine or angelic. We affix the latter clause, because that Talmudical relation is not explicit enough, allowing the interpretation that the Mineans regarded them, and them only, as directly promulgated by God, as well as the other, that even the Decalogue was enunciated by angels, and not by the Deity himself; see our Excursus B. The latter apprehension would be more adequate as concerns the Jewish Christians who, as was also illustrated above, limited the Decalogue, while nominally reverencing it as such, practically to a Hexalogue. It is not reasonable to suppose that this reduction to the range of Six Commandments would have been attempted by any, who attributed an immediate Divine authority to the entire Decalogue.

Now as to those Mineans there is in our view, indeed, no direct evidence that Jewish Christians were solely meant by this title in that context. Essenes and other like heretics, particularly Gnostics of Jewish descent, might, too, have been included. Even men of the type of Philo—the spiritual father of Gnosticism—who, while they were outwardly observant Jews and also sincere in their religious practice, had yet fallen away from the orthodox conception of all the Mosaic laws being immediately commanded by God, as well as from the pure and stern monotheistic doctrine of God alone, without any intermediate spiritual powers, having providentially acted and enacted laws, as represented in the plain words of the Pentateuch, would by the ancient Rabbis have promptly been denounced as Mineans; see Excursus B. Yet for all that we are justified in prominently, if not primarily, detecting in that term and its connection in the aforementioned Talmudical passage,

Jewish Christians. For of them, and the Gentile Christians following them, we know also from other sources that they held, and dogmatically and unhesitatingly pronounced, the nominal Decalogue as the Law proper.

To continue our above argument we have further to urge, that scrupulosity as to that or any other part of the Mosaic ritual Law was not to be expected from Jesus' disciples for this other reason, that their enthusiasm for the Kingdom endured unabated after his death, occupying their minds, as we presume, to such a degree that only a moderate attention, and one insignificant in proportion to that principal Christian cause, could be spared for ritualistic duties. Besides, all the other Messianic-prophetical notions which we produced above as presumably prevailing on Jesus to treat ceremonial observances with indifference, are likewise fairly supposed as having passed to his disciples. All these elements may have concurrently met in the minds of the disciples, and brought forth a certain ceremonial laxity, the same we discerned in their habits in the lifetime of their Master. With this consisted well their avowed adherence to, and even ordinary practice of, those portions of the Mosaic ritual named above, and, perhaps, to some more ceremonies to which their minds were religiously partial. But, we are to maintain, they valued, for the most part at least, only their essence, and were not much concerned with the way of their observance, established of old and by aid of tradition. Farther, they practiced them, or most of them, not with the common Jewish-religious sentiment at heart, but with an intent of their own; not because they felt themselves bound in their conscience to thereby discharge religious duties owed to God who had himself enjoined them, but from a capricious motive of choice and preference, how pure and reverent soever it might generally have been. Religious arbitrariness, however, never fails of creating sooner or later an inconstancy, prone to turn into careless relaxation, when the problem of expediency intervenes, of whatever nature this may be. In the case of the disciples the expediency, we are ready to admit, bore, for a large part, a kind of spiritual or ideal mark. But it doubtless interfered all the same with the regular and prompt exercise of their Jewish religious duties. At all events it is clear that all those combined moments of dogmatic dissent which we brought forward before as having operated on their minds, must, if they continued to exist with them after Jesus' death, have considerably, nay essentially, detracted from their practical, serious attention even to the limited Jewish ritual which they had yet upheld.

Those, therefore, who with the Author of 'Supernatural Religion' pronounce the apostles after the departure of Jesus as observant Jews with the distinction only of their being Jesus-believers, are widely astray. That Author advances : "At the death of Jesus the Twelve remained closely united to Judaism....They were simply Jews believing that Jesus was the Messiah... , and if the influence of Paul enlarged their views upon some minor points, we have no reason to believe that they ever abandoned their belief in the continued obligation of the Law. Paul never succeeded in bringing his elder colleagues over to his views." Now, let us say, he is surely correct in the latter assertion, also partially in the other, that they "remained closely united to Judaism." For, in very deed, they never renounced allegiance to Judaism. They never, for all we can gather from the extant sources, openly spoke with disdain, or pretended to the abrogation, future or present, of the Mosaic economy, as Stephen and Paul respectively did. But that their union to Judaism was a close one, we have decidedly to negative. Their ceremonial religious conduct was at no time since their attachment to Jesus conformable to the established Judaism, nor was their faith the untarnished monotheistic one of the body of the Jewish people. Surely, they were not considered by the true Jews as merely harmlessly dissenting from them on the problem of Messiah. They were, on the contrary, classified by the Rabbis as Mineans—an opprobrious designation generic for heretics, and this almost uniformly in view of their known or strongly suspected ditheistic or polytheistic beliefs. With that title the professors of Christian doctrines were already branded, as we propose in our work on the Mineans, at a rather early date.

The Rabbinical doctors legislated against the intercourse with them under that title, as well as they had them doubtless included—whether prominently or only equally with other heretics, cannot be determined—in the formula of imprecation issued about the earlier part of the second century, C. E. The cause of this was, we hold, mainly the various proclamations by the Jewish Christian sectaries of the divine qualities of Jesus.

Were the Twelve, then, "simply Jews," with the only divergent mark of the belief in Jesus as the Messiah? By no means. They were schismatics, with aims and tendencies subversive of the pure Jewish Monotheism, and at the same time with a religious practice, resistant to a large portion of the Mosaic ritual, inasmuch as they unquestionably opposed sacrifice and all the appertaining or connected observances, and lax in many other ceremonial rites, but the initiatory one and probably, besides, the precepts of religious purity with the inclusion of food restrictions which, mixed up with Essenic or Ebionite theories as they presumably were, they were most apt to heed, in the ordinary course of their communal life, with the minuteness peculiar to those sects.

Baur, 'Paul,' i. p. 204, maintains, too, that the Jewish Christian community—his observations are on the period as late as the trials of Paul under the procurators Felix and Festus—were not greatly differing from the rest of the Jews, and merely distinguished from them by their own Messiah-belief. Now if after all that has been set forth in this and previous chapters, a claim of Jewish orthodoxy is yet to be put up for the disciples of Jesus, we have to insist that the religious test by which they must be tried to be found thus qualified, can assuredly be no other than that of an extra-Jewish critic, trained in the Pauline faith-system. But as far as we are able to judge of the true Jews who were their contemporaries, we are most safe in asserting that from their pious standpoint those Christians were not ranked along with themselves as orthodox, but stigmatized with the title of heretics.

On what grounds should the apostles have been held orthodox Jews? Had, perhaps, their appearance in the Temple, that is, on Solomon's porch (Acts v. 12; comp. ib. ii. 46), which porch was situated on the east of the outermost court (see Keim, l. c., and Ewald, Hist. of Israel, vi. 360), indicated such orthodoxy? Zeller, in his 'The Contents and the Origin of Acts,' observes concerning the various assertions in Acts of the apostles' attendance in the precincts of the Temple, that "we have the more reason for giving credence to them, as the Acts declares the primitive apostles and their church as rigidly adhering to the Mosaic Law; xv. and xxi. 20 sq." But, we have mainly to object, the testimony of a writer whose whole composition is, as is practically done by Zeller, pronounced a sheer tendency-work, can be of very little historical merit. If he invented from his own mind in so many instances, he must consequently be expected to have done so yet in a few more. Again, we have to ask, what of it, if they really appeared habitually on that porch, at times even at the hour of prayer? First, we affirm, their meeting was, judging from the context of the relative reports of Acts, primarily or solely for performing their miracles and for "teaching and preaching Jesus Christ" (see ib. v. 42), and not for devotions. Secondly, the apostolic hours of prayer, or stations, as they were afterwards called, were, from relative indications (see ib. x. 9, iii. 1; also Tertullian, 'On Fasting'), entirely different from the Jewish hours of devotion. That their prayers were, thirdly, not those of the established Jewish ritual, has already been said above. Fourthly, let us ask, could the apostles' appearance on that porch, even if it had been purposely for devotional exercises, have impressed the orthodox Jewish observers as an evidence that they were Law-abiding, when they otherwise knew them as so averse to the national Temple service?

Let it again be stated in this place,—we have set it forth at length in another published essay of ours.—that a fair measure of reverence for the Temple as the fixed *national* Jewish centre of Divine service, consisted in the minds of the Essenes and the Ebionites (see on the latter, Clem. Hom. ii. 17, 22), as well as of Jesus and all the Jewish Christians, with an utter disdain for the *sacrificial* service actually conducted in it. We maintain in that disquisition, that the antinomian and antinational tendencies must be held apart from each other in our judgment as well on Jesus as on all the Jewish Christians. From this point of view, we urge, the anti-Temple utterances of Jesus have to be considered. The same distinction of the sentiment on Israel's national sanctuary as such, from that concerning the established ritual carried on therein, is to be upheld for his disciples, to whom, doubtless, the Master's view on the Jewish Divine service passed as an unalterable dogma. Only Stephen and Paul and such like philosophizing Hellenists who were opposed to every hand-made temple, could not well have cherished any reverence for Israel's Temple in Jerusalem, even only in the abstract, that is, disjoined in thought from its sacrificial worship.

We have, then, to reject the argument from the apostles' appearance in the Temple, put forth in favor of their Jewish orthodoxy, as unavailing. We aver that such appearance could, in any case, not have the virtue of redeeming them, in the sight of true Jews, from the odium of heterodox innovation and pernicious doctrinal heresy, which they had otherwise drawn on themselves.

More in harmony with our view which we have evolved with authentic statements and indications, as well as by way of inference, is the following sentiment of Keim (l. c. iii. p. 328): "The first apostles were not absolutely faithful to the Law; compare only Peter, in Gal. ii. 12, and also the transgressors of the Law, even James, in Josephus, Ant. xx. 9, 1." He allows this in the face of his previous remark, that the apostles "did not see that Jesus had in his innermost genius overstepped the limits of Judaism." On this latter assertion we have already passed above.

We insisted there, that their comprehension in respect of the emancipation from the burden of ceremonial observances was by no means less capable than that of Paul and John, whom he credits with "fully developing the spirit of the teaching of Jesus." As to the same author's before-cited references to Epistle Gal. and the Antiquities of Josephus, to prove that the apostles were wanting in absolute faithfulness to the Law, we have, too, to direct the reader's attention to the opinion we advanced on them in the respective places of the present treatise. He could certainly have added many more direct or inferential indications that the apostles were, on the whole, lax in the practice of even those Mosaic-Jewish ceremonial rites which they, in substance, professed as valid for themselves as born Jews, and kept embodied in their new, Christian, usage.

Let us here, as we are to produce the sum-total of the estimation and practice of Jewish ceremonial rites by Jesus' disciples after his death, pause awhile and meditate on the possibility, that our conclusions brought out by critical methods have been drawn too sternly. We are conscientiously aware that we owe justice to persons of antiquity no less than to our own coevals. Nay we hold that they, being removed from the scene on which they might vindicate themselves from our perhaps one-sided and strained criticism, deserve even a larger measure of considerate judgment than those who, because living, have ample opportunity of righting themselves before our critical tribunal.

That the aphorism, "like master like pupil," is on general grounds applicable also to Jesus' disciples, is not to be questioned. Nay it would seem that it holds of them all the more appropriately, as we know that the later Ebionites made use of Jesus' own respective saying,—though in a different sense from the one in which he had propounded it,—"It is enough for the disciple that he be as his master" (Matt. x. 25 ; see Epiphanius, Haer. xxx. 26, and our Part First, p. 123). This was the mode of reasoning with the Ebionites to defend their strict adherence to the rite of circumcision against those Christians who opposed it. Let us say that it is but fair to infer that they resorted no less to the same apologetical argument with regard to their fulfilling other Mosaic religious precepts according to the Master's custom. While we are only informed of that sort of argumentation being employed by the Ebionite sect, it may be assumed confidently that not only they, but all the Palestinian Jewish Christians, strove to follow, in their outward religious practice, in the wake of Jesus. Accordingly we would have to maintain that they followed him not only affirmatively, but also negatively, that is, as to the discriminations he made between what he held obligatory and what seemed to him indifferent or objectionable; and also, that they fully embraced and put into practice all Jesus' theories on the ceremonial law, those independent of Messianic notions as well as those relating to them.

Yet all this is only an anticipation, however strongly and solidly it rests on relative indications or inferences, as also on the directly provable analogous fact, that Jesus' supernatural claims too were amply adopted by the disciples. For if it is indisputable that they made his teaching about himself their own, is it not most likely, too, that they espoused also his various position on Jewish religious rites, as we have illustrated it in previous chapters? And is it not in especial likely that, as regards his Messianic dispensatory pretension, its effect continued with them fresh and vigorous, in proportion to the undiminished glowing Messianic enthusiasm that filled their souls even after his death?—a circumstance that was also brought forth above.

All this granted, it is none the less well and fair to view, in this our inquiry into the outward ceremonial religious attitude of the disciples after Jesus' death, the availability, in their favor, of another aphorism: "Circumstances alter cases." Let us see whether, in the totally changed condition in which they were placed after his departure, there may not have been created motives for a more observant course—the ineradicable, constitutional Christian opposition to sacrifice and its connected rites always excepted.

Before we essay to investigate this problem, let us again remember that the teaching time of Jesus was but one or at the most two years, viz., between 33-35 C. E. (so Keim). It might accordingly be going too far to expect from that short space of time of the disciples' connection with him, a real elaborate and extensive system of practical religion that could suffice them in all later conditions and complexities of life. Not even for a thorough tuition in all the details of the Messianic religion, such as we ascribed to him above, might that limited period have been adequate. And this in particular, when we farther consider, that he had from the start of his public career met with or involved himself in frequent polemical struggles that grew more vehement as time went on : so that a successful leisure, even only for the private instructions to be imparted to his disciples, cannot be maintained for any time of his public labor. Moreover, a feeling of perturbance about his own fate, too, must, since the imprisonment of his cognate southern preacher of the Kingdom, John the Baptist, have been pungently preying on his mind. With this perturbance, while it did not prevent him from continuing resolutely and even at all hazards, his Messianic activity, could yet not consist that intellectual composure in which alone a teacher may advantageously mould his manifold ideas into a compact, well rounded system. The excited days he passed through were, then, little favorable for explicit elucidations on problems of religious practice. To be sure, it could, on the other hand, not take the disciples long to learn from him the general lesson of the relative unimportance of outward Jewish religious rites, in the transitional state in which he represented the world to be in his time. This lesson they could quickly and readily succeed in comprehending. Yet we believe at the same time, that not only were his particular utterances on this or that law or custom, put forth on sundry occasions, for the most part only fragmentary and desultory, but they could naturally not be sufficient for every future state and phase of life that lay in his time in obscurity, and could not possibly be forecast. When they were therefore, after his departure, left to themselves and without the teacher to whom they might turn for instruction in all questions of conscience, they must many a time have been perplexed as to the proper decision to be made on points of religious practice. On these the Master's reflections were only occasional. Their memory could therefore have retained only a number of stray utterances that lacked systematic arrangement and completeness. It results that, when in their altered condition new questions of such a character turned up on which the Master had not expressly given his opinion, they were compelled to strain their memory for an analogy that would approximately cover the new case, whatever it might be, and assist them in being as conformable as possible to his view and wish. At times, however, even the utmost taxing of their memory will not have availed them to recall an analogy that would aid them in finding an authentic thread, by seizing and following which they would be able to realize an identity with his spirit. In such instances, then, in which either no direct reference to the Master's own precepts could be made, or no analogy from his lifetime be discovered for their guidance, they were urged to take up with the verdict of their own mind. This will, it is fair to presume, have on the whole been a strenuously aimed accommodation to the liberal, ceremonially unincumbered Messianic religion of Jesus; but it may, on the other side, have also been considerably tempered by the pressure of unfavorable circumstances, by which we know them to have been unremittingly confronted.

Such circumstances existed all along since Jesus' death. His tragic fate itself must have struck a deep terror in their breasts. They saw, from his precipitous end as well as from the previous fatal doom visited on the Baptist, how perilous Messianic movements were in the Jewish land, from south to north. The execution of Stephen for his resistant and defiant denunciations of the existing Jewish worship and institutions, as well as the persecution of other Hellenistic Jewish Christians with and after him, must, too, have had an overawing effect on their minds. They themselves were from the Master's departure forth continually subjected to close surveillance and inquisition, if not persecution. They became more and more singled out as heinous suspects for assigning divinity to Jesus, which conflicted so irreconcilably with pure Jewish Monotheism. This cloud of suspicion overhung them thickly and was, indeed, never dispelled. Furthermore, severe visitations befell some of them in Agrippa I.'s reign. It may therefore be fairly supposed that from the latter epoch forward, they made up their minds to a more cautious and wary way, alike in their Messianic profession and mission, and in their outward religious conduct. Their Messianic avowal and propaganda may from thence not have been so clamorous, nor their Jewish religious practice so lax any more, as before.

This supposition holds, if not of the bold apostles Peter and John (comp. Acts iv. 13) and of James the Just, who succeeded the ill-fated apostle James in the presidency of the mother-church and fell himself a victim to hierarchal violence, at least of the majority of the apostles and the generality of the Palestinian Jewish Christians in the apostolic age (see also Strauss, Life of Jesus, i. 295, who suggests that the terrible fate of Jesus and Stephen produced the "effect of Jesus' followers abandoning the dangerous position which he had occupied, and retreating several steps, etc." He advances this as a certain conclusion. We on our part give it, however, only as a possibility. Nor do we date this possible retrogression from the epoch named by him. We rather propose for it the time of Agrippa I.'s persecution). This view will surely appear yet more acceptable, when we bear in mind that those votaries of Jesus must have realized more and more that there was no trifling with the overwhelming power standing over against their little band. They must by degrees have become aware that, if they wished to retain the seat of the church in Jerusalem, they must cautiously abstain from any scandalizing of the Jewish public, either by defiant breaches of Jewish ordinances, or by an ostentatious deification of the Master. The formidable arm of the supreme magistracy of the Jewish nation could, as they must have felt more and more, crush and annihilate them at any moment, if they newly attempted any headlong provocations of the innermost religious sentiments of all its orthodox people. True, the right over life and death was in those days taken from the Synhedrin and reserved to the Roman procurators (see Ant. xx. 9, 1; John xviii. 31). Yet there is no doubt whatever that that supreme court could at any time and in any case, except in one like Paul's, obtain easily the procuratorial sanction for a sentence of death against a Christian delinquent, if it was minded to pass it and have it inflicted. To presume that the then still powerful Jewish Senate, the prominent doctors of the Law, and their many influential disciples, together with the bulk of the Jewish lay people, were afraid of the few hundred Christians, is, to say the least, most absurd. Different it is with the danger the representatives of the Jewish nation really apprehended from the spread of the new doctrines of the renegade church. It was too obvious and imminent not to notice and be alarmed at it. But they were, we contend, alarmed only insomuch, as their purpose was to do no bodily harm to the adherents of Jesus. Else the danger could have been removed by a few decisive strokes.

As far as the Roman rulers and people at large were concerned, they would surely have been most ready to lend their strong help to violent persecutions of the Christians, if the Jewish people had been inclined to such severe measures in the period after Agrippa's death. For it is well known and variously verified that the Romans hated the Christians intensely, and that, mainly, for their Messianic doctrine and belief. Their name alone constantly suggested to them a mutinous spirit and disposition. For Christian meant "kingly," and this implied to them the tendency to rebel from the all-powerful empire; see our First Part. Note 20, and Tacitus, Annals, xv. 44, who, in speaking of the Christians as "hated for their vices" and as animated by the "hatred of mankind," seems to allude chiefly to their characteristic name and their doctrines about a Messiah-king, whom they not only believed to have come, but fervently expected to come again ; compare also Ep. Pet. ii. 12, iii. 16.

It is questionless that the Jewish people and their Senate had autonomy and power enough left to them to the last days of their State, to plague and punish the Christian schismatics, if these continued to excite their intolerance by any demonstrative negation of and assault on the Jewish creed and ritual. This it is to be surmised the Christian believers of the Palestinian church realized more and more. It is therefore not amiss to suppose that they, after the time of Agrippa's persecution, gradually left off their former temerity as to Jewish religious conduct and became more observant than they were since their connection with Jesus.

Possibly this at first insincere policy of greater caution, developed by degrees into a fairly conscientious mode of Jewish observance. While the change was not spontaneous, it can yet be conceived that the persecutions they underwent, and the animosity that prevailed against them, struck their conscience to the quick, and made them gradually bethink themselves better. By degrees they may have subsided into more sober judgments on their Jewish religious obligations. Their veneration for the Master, it is true, did not diminish aught after his departure. It assumed, on the contrary, more and more deifying dimensions. Their Messianic enthusiasm lost, neither, any of its fever height after his personal withdrawal, but continued to be very strong and all-absorbing. Yet there is no reason why the many serious obstacles which they continually encountered during the early growth of the church, should not eventually have turned their former inconsiderateness as to all things lying outside the Messianic scheme, which had outrun their prudence as well as their sense of obligation as born Jews, into a more thoughtful regard for their native religion and its ceremonial precepts.

Those more sober judgments may, moreover, have gained greater substantiality in view of the circumstance, that the Master's living word and actual example were no more with them, by leaning on which they could formerly, in his lifetime, feel themselves compensated in their conscience for various ceremonial shortcomings. The "bridegroom" whose presence had to them such convincing and reassuring dispensatory authority, had personally gone from among them, so that direct dispensations could no more be got from him. This may have worked a thorough change in their attitude toward the Jewish ceremonial and, together with the before-noted other adverse causes that operated on them, urged them to return and settle down to a more strict observance of it, the same in which they had been bred up in their parental homes. What they had valued slightly or treated with levity in the short interval of their personal alliance with Jesus and yet some time thereafter, may from that later period on which we suggested before, have again been regarded by them with a fair sense of obligation. What they had abandoned in their early immediate Messianic excitement, they may later have re-adopted as really compatible with their Messiah-belief, and as obligatory on themselves.

All this we advance, however, as a mere hypothesis, with the purpose, as stated above, to be as fair as possible in our judgment on the early Jewish Christian sect. The fact remains nevertheless, that the indications to the contrary are heavily on the other side of the balance.

As regards the Sabbath, while there can be no question that the apostles and other Jewish Christians of their age kept it, in the main, holy, we are yet not inclined to admit promptly the premise, that they may after Jesus' death have retrograded to the Jewish orthodox way of observing it. Not only in view of the various moments put forth above to illustrate Jesus' impugning of the genuine Jewish conception of the authority and obligation of the Sabbath, and the apostles' partial levity concerning it which they evinced while connected with him, are we reluctant to concede that premise. But, aside from these points of consideration, we think ourselves entitled to conjecture, on the ground of a Rabbinical passage to be reproduced immediately, that the customary Jewish reverence for the Sabbath was, as time advanced, even more and more lessened within the Jewish Christian church. We will let the reader judge for himself of its admissibility for argument and proof in this question.

CHAPTER XVI.

THE JEWISH CHRISTIANS RIDE ON ANIMALS ON THE SABBATH (?).

In the Midrash Rabboth on Ecclesiastes, ch. i., we read : "Hanina, the nephew of Rabbi Joshua, went to Kephar Nahum (Capernaum, the old Jesus-town). There the Mineans (Christians) preformed a magic cure on him.[51] They brought him riding (or made him ride) on a donkey on the Sabbath. Coming to his uncle, Rabbi Joshua (whose residence and school was in Pekiin; see B. Synh. f. 32), the latter applied an ointment to him, and he got well. He then told the nephew : 'Since the wine of that wicked one has been stirred in you, you dare not stay any longer in the holy land.'"

The whole of this narration sounds genuine. The occurrence set forth in it belongs to the period of either Trajan's or Hadrian's reign. Now we are well aware that there is no direct warrant for concluding back from this later period to the earlier of the nascent Jewish Christian church. Nevertheless, since we had all along in this treatise to maintain, on the whole, the principle of continuity as to religious theory and practice from the public life of Jesus throughout the earlier ages of Christianity subsequent to him; and, farther, since we know Jesus to have been so antagonistic to Phariseic-Rabbinical injunctions,—the so-called traditions,—we may not propose amiss that the levity of riding on animals on the Sabbath dates back to the earliest professors of Christianity.

Its prohibition was one of the Sabbath restraints, Rabbinically denominated Shebuth or Sheboth, meaning "rest." The ancient Jewish sages imposed many such restrictions on the people to serve as hedges, preserving them the more securely from the temptation to such infractions of the Sabbath as are real labor, that is, either the kind expressly forbidden in the Pentateuch, or coming by traditional rules of Scripture interpretation under the head of the general command, "thou shalt do no manner of work." It seems that riding on animals was, since the earliest times of the second Commonwealth, regarded as the gravest of all the Shebuth-restraints. The Talmud (B. Betsa f. 36), in discussing the cause of this prohibition, propounds first, that it was instituted by the sages to prevent the severer trespass of exceeding the Sabbath-limit of two thousand cubits (see our Part First, p. 17), but rejects again this proposition, deciding that it was a measure intended to ward off the trespass of cutting a twig off a tree and using it as a whip. From whatever cause it may have been forbidden by the sages, thus much we know for certain, that it passed with olden Rabbinism universally for a most grievous violation of the Sabbath. It was provably treated as such already in the Maccabean period, and very probably since the days of the ancient Sopherim "Scribes." As to the Maccabean period, we may adduce the following Talmudical relation to substantiate our statement: "Rabbi Elazar, the son of Jacob, states (as by authority), that a Jewish Senate may inflict judicial penalties for transgressions of Jewish observances, though not prescribed in the Mosaic code, and that for the purpose of erecting by it a fence to its direct commands. As an instance in point may serve, that once, in the time of the Syro-Greeks, a Jewish man rode on horseback on a Sabbath and was brought to the Senate for trial, who passed and executed on him the sentence of death by stoning. This was done, not because the offender was really liable to such punishment, but for the urgency of the then circumstances" (B. Yebamoth f. 90). Rabbi Elazar's report of such rigid proceeding in the troubled days of the Maccabean uprisings, when Hellenizing apostasy had made such pernicious inroads upon Judaism, and filled the pious with deep alarm about the future of Israel's pure Monotheism, is in itself very acceptable. It gains yet the more probability when we compare with it a passage of the Midrash (Rabb. Gen. ch. lxvi.) which bears, in the main, the stamp of unquestionable authenticity. It is said there: "Jakum of Tseroroth (the notorious Alkimos), the nephew of Jose ben Joezer,[52] was riding on horseback on a Sabbath, when they carried before him the beam on which his nephew was to suffer crucifixion. Jakum said to the latter (mockingly): 'Look at the horse which my lord (King Demetrius who had conferred on him the high-priesthood) has given me to ride on, and look at thine which thy Lord (God) has prepared for thee, etc!'"

While there is, perhaps, in this relation the anachronism of putting crucifixion as the mode of execution carried out at that conjuncture, which really belonged to a later, Roman, period, there is otherwise every reason to believe that the occurrence narrated there is historical in substance. It shows forth the habit of the frivolous Hellenists in the dismal days in which Alkimos was high-priest, to deeply offend the sentiments of the pious Jews by publicly riding on the Sabbath day. Like that degenerate ecclesiastic, there were no doubt many other triflers with Judaism who paraded the thoroughfares on a Sabbath high on horse, boldly demonstrating their irreligious license. Such state of things, intolerable to the pious, may have induced them, after they had gained the ascendency over the renegades, to decree capital punishment on all those who would not cease disregarding the Sabbath in that offensive manner, though they committed thereby no breach of the Mosaic enactment, for which alone mortal punishment was legally provided. The precedent stated by Rabbi Elazar in the above-cited Talmudical passage, is accordingly easily referrible to a tradition, one of the historical backgrounds of which was the narration of the Midrash in point.

However this may be, we are at all events warranted in assuming that riding on animals in public on the Sabbath, was already in the times of the Syro-Greek dominion held as a most reprehensible obliquity and dishonor of that sacred day. The same applied to every one of the high festivals. They shared all restraints with the Sabbath, except those of labor in preparing the meals of the day. The threads of such vigorous condemnation of that exercise on the holy days reach, we suppose, back to the days of the earlier Scribes.

An analogous instance of austere perception of the religious regard due to the holy days, may confirm this supposition. There was a serious dispute on the permissibility of the rite of the laying on of hands on the victims offered by individual Israelites on the festivals, kept up for a period of about one and a half centuries, between either of the several presidential pairs of the national school of Jewish learning in Jerusalem, who lived and succeeded one another during that period. It lasted from the time of the above-noted Jose ben Joezer till that of Shammai and Hillel and the divided schools of these two sages. It was only through the interference of Baba ben Buta—himself a Shammaite, but later convinced of the error of his school—that Hillel's opinion was authoritatively adopted as the correct one, to be followed in all the future ritual practice (Jerus. Chagigah, ii.). This opinion was, that the rite might and should be performed on the festivals: for, he reasoned, any sacrifice Mosaically ordained for a certain day must necessarily have the virtue of vacating it as to all rites pertaining to it (B. Betsa, f. 20). This view of Hillel was consonant with his other, and one, by the way, that made his name so famous and his station so prominent in

Judea,—that a sacrifice prescribed for a "fixed season" cannot but make the Sabbath restraint recede before it (B. Pesachim, f. 66). Thus he argued to dispel the scruples of his contemporaries about killing the Passover victim, if the fourteenth Nisan happened to fall on a Sabbath day.

We have to keep in mind that the laying on of hands on living animals was only prohibited by the sages and classed under the name of "Shebuth," coming, according to the commentator Rashi in B. Betsa, f. 19, under the category of "making use of animals," the same as riding on them does. And yet, so profound was the awe of the Mosaical holy days, and the apprehension lest they might be profaned by that rite, that it took so long a space of time—from Jose to Hillel—to overcome the objection of its possible unlawfulness, though it were performed on such victims as had to be offered up entire, being thus an act pertaining exclusively to Divine worship. This proves conclusively what a severe sense was in the remoter ages of the second Commonwealth put on the use of animals on holy days, even when they would not do any labor themselves, which alone involved an infraction of the Sabbath law (in accordance with Exodus xx. 10).

The riding on animals correlated, according to that commentator, with the laying on of hands as regards the ceremonial offence involved in the act, was doubtless as early as this rite considered a serious violation of the holy days, though neither could be classified as labor in a Mosaical import.

If the riding was in public, it was unquestionably considered a still greater offence. For not only was it a leading view with the olden Jewish teachers, that any irreligious act done openly, in the sight of piously observant coreligionists, was intensified by the scandal thus committed against their individual religious susceptibilities, as well as the affront thus offered to the paternal, Divinely instituted religion itself. But the appearance of a Jewish person bestriding the back of an animal on a sacred day, and traversing the streets and quarters where a general solemn quietude prevailed, will, besides, have the more forcibly roused the indignation of the pious brethren who beheld him, because they must have been impressed by it, that the perpetrator was of a defiant mind, and prompted by the base motive of showing ostentatiously, that he had cast behind his back all reverent recognition of the day.

These several notions on the use of animals on Sabbaths and holy days were without question transmitted through successive ages, as we find them embodied in the Rabbinical literature. Consequently, we judge, has such a transgressor, all through those ages, drawn on himself the utmost detestation of every orthodox coreligionist.

If, therefore, our proposition above advanced, that Jewish Christians made no scruple of publicly riding on the Sabbath day, can be accepted as probable, there can be no doubt that the true Jews, holding such an act a real and serious violation of its obligatory rest, will have spurned at them the more for their setting at naught, additionally to their other notorious levity, an observance that had such great moment with them.

Let us yet mention that to about the same period with the before-discussed narrative of the Midrash on Ecclesiastes, belongs the apostasy of Elisha ben Abuyah, the Gnostic heretic, by the Rabbis nicknamed Acher, that is, one fallen away to alien and false religious belief and worship; see on him also our Excursus B. We will in this place produce a notice of his disregard of the Sabbath, exhibited by the same frivolity as we premised to have marked the Jewish Christians. Our conjecture that one motive may have been common to both, we will bring forward by and by.

To dilate on that Rabbinical doctor's heresy would carry us beyond the bounds of our present purpose. We do it in our larger, unpublished work, in the division: 'The Gnostics as Mineans.' Here we must confine ourselves to the brief assertion, that he leant strongly on Gnostic ditheism or diarchy, or had actually turned Gnostic. His Gnostic bias was probably created by reading Mineic works, that is, those of the Platonic philosophers, and, in particular, of the many Christianizing Gnostics flourishing in his day.

It is said in Jerus. Chagigah, f. 77, that he once on a Sabbath passed on horseback the school of Rabbi Meir, in Tiberias. This Rabbi was his intimate friend and former pupil. On being told that Elisha had passed the place, he suddenly broke off his discourse and went out to meet him. He overtook and followed him some distance out of town. Before parting he entreated him to retrace his steps of apostasy and return to true Judaism. Elisha replied that he could not possibly do it, for he had heard once, when riding on horseback on a Sabbath which happened at the same time to be Atonement day, an oracle announcing to him the verdict, that he was irreclaimable and abandoned by God.

This account cannot here be scrutinized and tested on its historical merits. True, without doubt, we remark, appears to be the mention in it, that he was habitually slighting the Sabbath by holding cheap the customary restraint of riding on this sacred day. For the Talmud relates, besides, previously, that it was he who, during the Hadrianic persecution, when the Jews were by the Romans compelled to break the Sabbath by labors done for them, schemed to see his wretched compatriots coerced into positive violations of the Sabbath law, whenever they attempted to evade them by some mechanical shifts which they had contrived in their pious anxiety and awe of the Sabbath. It may, in view of such Rabbinical representations of Elisha's character, be safely affirmed as historical, that he was sharply at odds with the traditional observance of the Sabbath. We at least hold it inconceivable that olden Rabbinism should have coupled his name so directly and repeatedly with circumstances of dishonor to the Sabbath, had there been no foundation for it in authentic tradition.

Now it is quite possible, we hold, that Elisha came to value the Sabbath slightly by his Gnostic speculations that landed him on the verge of the heretical notion, that the supreme, good God was distinct from the Creator and Giver of the Mosaic Law. If the latter proceeded from an inferior Deity, then the Sabbath could claim no superior sanctity or, at any rate, no inviolable obligation. This conclusion would readily be made on such a supposition. By it, moreover, he would little by little be led to a levity in the observance of the Sabbath, such as is noted about him in the Talmud.

Possibly there was some affinity in this regard between him and the Jewish Christians. These may, consistently with the implicit denial by their Master of the Divine authority of the Sabbath law, have held it of little consequence to treat it in some respects with that license, born of the thought that they were any way not liable to God for its violation. As one mark of such license may be accounted their regardless riding on animals on the Sabbath, which, while it was no labor Mosaically prohibited, passed yet in the minds of the orthodox Jews for a most frivolous slight of the high honor due it from "the children of the covenant."

NOTES.

³⁴ Even Keim, by-the-by the most learned, profound and comprehensive modern historian of the life of Jesus, who in various passages of his voluminous work tries hard, yet most inconsistently and therefore unsuccessfully, to sustain the pro-nomian position of Jesus (comp. iii. p. 113 ; 315 ; 323, 24 ; 427 ; 362, 63, and chiefly his summary in vi. p. 401), cannot help detecting in that re-asserted opposition of Jesus to the law of divorce, a repudiation of Moses. We have here a concession by the foremost critical writer on Jesus, that the latter had in the instance in point really and decidedly seceded from Mosaism. Space does not permit us to argue with him on his assertion that Jesus "arrived," in that instance, "for the first time at the point of repudiating Moses" (v. p. 30). What we will have to dwell on as to our present purpose is, his proposition, on p. 31: "Here was a point discovered on which he could in fact be indicted before the Sanhedrim."

Keim does indeed not mean, that the repudiation of Moses as such made him liable to be capitally tried by the Jewish high court. Nor would there be the slightest shadow of a warrant for an assumption like that, could we even think him capable of entertaining it. For neither the Pharisees nor the Sadducees would ever presume to elevate Moses to the dignity of a divine-like, prophetical being, such as the Essenes professed him to be. It was only this philosophico-ascetic sect that made a blasphemer of Moses punishable with death (see Josephus, Wars, ii. 8, 9). That this was, on the one hand, due to their overwrought Neo-Pythagorean reverence for the *teacher* Moses, which reverence, in passing, we discover likewise in Philo, who calls him now all-great, now all-wise, and, again, most sacred, and, on the other, to their anxious caution lest the primacy of that greatest and "true prophet" (so he is designated in the Clementine Homilies) might be questioned and infringed on by the rival claim of any one of their own order, which had itself bred so many would-be prophets, and the sacred and secret books of which contained without doubt so many precepts and predictions of their own illustrious, prophetically inspired lights, we incline to hold, rather than seek for the motive for such severity of legislation in their religious reverence for the Law itself. For we know from some of their otherwise Jewish heterodox doctrines, that this could not have been the case.

No, Keim was not so extreme as to connect the indictment of Jesus with his repudiation of Moses, from the view of the disparagement of his person. He had, on the contrary, in mind his own peculiar construction which he later, in vol. vi. p. 46, puts on the accusation brought against Jesus, of "seducing the people," adopted by him from Luke xxiii. 2, 5. This accusation of being a Mesith, "seducer," he lets there arbitrarily precede the actual deposition of the testimony of the witnesses, mentioned in Matt. xxvi. 60, 61. The charge implied in that criminal term is to him, that he was "an inciter to disobedience to the Mosaic ordinances."

Now that the Synhedrin could not have tried him on the charge, nor surely convicted him of the crime, of being a 'Mesith,' for mere incitation to ceremonial transgressions, might the accusations even have been drawn, as he gives it on p. 47 of the quoted volume, from the "rich mine of the strong earlier-uttered invectives against the hierarchy as a whole," should be known to a learned writer like him. The relative penal provision on the strength of which Jesus could have been criminally tried on the charge of being a Mesith, sets forth directly a seduction to false worship (see Deut. xiii. 7, sq., and Mishnah Synhedrin f. 67), and not to "disobedience to the Mosaic ordinances." (As to our own account of the provisionally supposed criminal charge of seduction laid against Jesus, by a legal inference drawn from his contempt for the established Temple worship, we have to refer the reader to our above-cited dissertation on the Essenes, in which this subject is discussed*).

And yet, while we have to confute Keim's sarcastic reflections as impertinent in the question of the charge of religious seduction brought against Jesus, we cannot refrain from suggesting that his anti-Mosaic utterances and, partly, practical course, may not only have hastened his arraignment before the Synhedrin, but even been judicially charged against him, though no mention of it is made in the gospels.

And here we will express a view, which will at least throw some light on the obscure New Testament narrations of the capital incrimination not only of Jesus,

---

* See Excursus C.

but also of other Christian men after him, in the same century, a view which is, moreover, associable with our assertion, with which we started our present treatise, that Jesus denied the Divine authority of the Law.

It is possible, we hold, that his anti-Mosaic utterances have drawn on him a charge of blasphemy which, though Rabbinical tradition has not handed it down in the relative penal rubric in the Mishnah, Synhedrin f. 55, 56, may yet have passed as a capital felony with both the Pharisees and the Sadducees, alike within and without the Synhedrin. We mean that blasphemy, on which the statute appears in Numbers xv. 30, 31: "But the soul that doeth (aught) presumptuously, . . . the same reproacheth the Lord ; and that soul shall be cut off from among his people. Because he hath despised the word of the Lord, and hath broken his commandment, etc." Now while the later Rabbinical interpretation of this somewhat indefinite statute was, that it was either directed against the polytheist and idolater, or against the same blasphemer of God of whom Lev. xxiv. 15, 16, treats, (see B. Kerithoth, f. 6), there is, on the other hand, a sufficient warrant from another place in the Talmud (B. Synhedrin, f. 99), showing definitely that it was as well, and we believe rather commonly, employed to cover cases of antinomian heresy, general or particular. The sentence of the Mishnah (ib. f. 90), "He who declares that the Torah is not from Heaven (God), has no share in the world to come," is there substantiated in the name of previous teachers by reference to that Mosaic statute. In another relation, also credited there to antecedent teachers, even he is denounced as a "despiser of the word of God," who denies the Divine authority of only one verse of the Pentateuch, nay even of Rabbinical injunctions derived, by the established rules of interpretation, from its text. On this last exaggerated clause we need indeed not reflect here. For not only have the Sadducees never consented to and accepted as obligatory such derivative Rabbinical ordinances, even the Pharisees themselves have not pushed their exaltation of the "institutions of the Sages," or of the periodical ceremonial restraints of Rabbinical councils, to such an extreme, as to hold transgressors of them, or deniers of their obligation, liable to mortal punishment, by virtue of the statute in question. They will never have raised their own injunctions to the dignity of the "word of God," so that a despiser of them could become guilty of real blasphemy, and incur the penalty prescribed for it in that statute. That the Talmud mentions once a single case from the Maccabean period of infliction of capital punishment on the violator of a Rabbinical Sabbath restraint (B. Yebamoth f. 90, and Synhedrin f. 46), a case which we discuss at another point of this treatise, does by no means contradict our assertion. It confirms, on the contrary, as all exceptions witness to existing rules, the order prevailing among the Pharisees, that only those offenses were to be capitally punished, which come within the province of Mosaic provisions. To deviate from it would have been an anti-Mosaic innovation, of which those pious and devoted Jews could certainly not make themselves guilty. The less so, since they would by it have opened the door to the Sadducean method of inflicting penalties from personal discretion, which method the Pharisees so positively marked as heretical (see Megillath Taanith). That single case must accordingly have been unwarranted in the minds of the Phariseic doctors at large. It was doubtless only a measure of a momentary impulse and excessive zeal at a certain juncture, at which froward irreligiousness prevailed among a certain class of the community. This view is evidently held by the olden Rabbis, too; see the cited passages of the Talmud. The above-quoted Talmudical saying which comprises heretical opponents of Rabbinically derived decisions under the title of "despisers of the word of God," must, then, be pronounced as an extravagant theory, and can at best only mean, that such men are deserving non-judicial reprin and, or, at the most, a light punishment, but not the penalty provided in that statute.

Different it is, however, with the other part of that saying, relating to the enactments and general contents of the Mosaic code. The proposition that deniers of their Divine origin came under the head of such "despisers," and were to be accounted blasphemers, must by no means be regarded as a mere theory of Rabbinical doctors. There is the strongest probability that it rested on a settled norm transmitted from former ages, in which grave religious offenders were actually incriminated by the authority of a powerful Senate. *We maintain that such a norm, based on the statute in question, actually existed in the times of the Synhedrin, and that antinomian heretics were called to account and criminally tried on the strength of it, by this judicial body of the Jewish land.*

At what period of Jewish history the Synhedrin may have first made a practical application of that statute against open assailants or derogators of the Law, can no more be ascertained. That the Christian schismatics should have called it forth for the first time, we cannot think. For the apostatizing Hellenism, in the Maccabean times, was certainly serious and grievous enough to have demanded a rigid interference on the part of the religious authorities of the land, and also the practical enforcement of that statute, provided it was employed in a really penal sense. Nor must the special legislation against Mineans,— presumably Jewish Christians, though Essenes and kindred sectaries could as justly have been included in that designation, as we set forth in our work on the 'Mineans,'— which is reported in B. Abodah Zarah f. 27, and confirmed as historical by external literature, viz., the prohibition of intercourse with them, etc., induce us to suppose that that statute, too, was, by way of special enactment, first called into requisition with the rise of Christianity, to be used as a judicial weapon for dealing with this new heresy. For that legislation belongs to a more advanced age of Christianity, about the latter part of the first century, when the destructive antinomianism of Paul and his consummate deification of Jesus (see Epistles Eph. and Col.; Phil. ii. 10; Rom. x. 12, 13), as also the intrusion of overbold Gentile Christians into the Church, had cast a bitter dismay into the hearts of the faithful Jews, and when, further, the pretension of miraculous cures in the name of Jesus by every Christian who claimed to have the Holy Ghost with him, had more and more increased, and threatened to make dangerous inroads upon the illiterate part of the Jewish people.

With much less justice could the teaching of Abbahu, the learned Palestinian Rabbi of the third century C. E. (see B. Abodah Zarah f. 26), that "the Mineans, dilators, and apostates need not be tried before the high court" (this is, we contend, the real meaning of the words "we-lo maalin;" there is to be supplemented, 'le-beth din' or 'lirushalaim'), be brought to bear on our point, as being an analogy of a special legislation concerning Christians. For it was merely a decision of an apparently private character, and belongs, moreover, to the later time when Gentile Christianity had been habitually manifesting a furious hostility not only to the Jewish religious ceremonial, but to the Jewish nation as such. Nor is it so very certain at all, that Christians alone are to be understood there by the term Mineans.

We have to remark, further, that Maimoni's dogmatic systematizing in his commentary on Mishnah Synhedrin xi. 3, can be of no direct avail in the question before us.

He has there only worked out Talmudical statements and sentiments, coming as they do from different epochs of later history, which do not warrant an historical conclusion being made from them for the times of early Christianity.

We will, nevertheless, reproduce the substance of his casuistic reasoning, for we have in view the object of making it appear the more probable, that the respective theories he advances there in a combined form, re-echo fundamentally and rather accurately the disposition of the ancient orthodox Jews towards those who denied the Divine authority of the Mosaic Law, or assailed or exposed any of its appointments.

Respecting the sentence of the Mishnah quoted above, that "a denier of the Divine authority of the Law has no share in the future world," Maimoni propounds, that "this class of unbelievers are kopherim "renegades," and deserve death the same as the atheists or those disputing the existence of Moses (as the deliverer of the Divine commands). Such men have broken away from Judaism, and stand without its pale." They are to him ' Mineans,' who have by their apostasy forfeited their lives.

May we not justly, according to all that we know of the orthodox Jews of antiquity, assume that this representation of Maimoni, though drawn and condensed from the later theorizing Talmud, was approximately the standard by which the legal religious authorities in the time and century of Jesus guided themselves, and that they may have adopted as their judicial norm for dealing with antinomians that statute of Numbers xv. 30, 31, by which such delinquents might be treated and tried as blasphemers?

We may, further, find some support to this supposition in the comment which a prominent Rabbi of the Hadrianic and Bar Cochba period, Eliezer of Modin, made upon the sentence of this statute: "Because he hath despised the word of the Lord, and hath broken his commandment." He observes on it: "He who profanes the holy things (sacrifices), reviles the festivals (that is, the Sabbaths and holy days; for the former are included in the term moadoth "festivals," as is clear from Lev. xxiii. 2, 3), and breaks the covenant of Abraham, our ancestor, though he have many counterbalancing deserts, is worthy of being cast out of the world." (This reading seems to be the original; see Sifre, Numb. sect. 112. The enlarged version in the Mishnah of Aboth, iii. 15, appears to us inauthentic).

Now while we are not so dogmatic as to regard this post-Synhedrial exegesis of a Rabbi of the second century as the exact norm translated into judicial practice by the former high courts,—although it is, on the other hand, possible that that doctor's youth reached back to the time when the Synhedrin yet existed in Jerusalem, and he accordingly spoke from the remembrance of his own anterior notice of its real practice,—we are nevertheless perfectly warranted in asserting, that he has by his commentation sounded the keynote of the pious Israelitish sentiment. What to him was a mere theoretical estimation of the relative offenders' liability to capital punishment,—since the capital jurisdiction of the Jewish Senate was assuredly out of the question at the time when he uttered that exposition,—was, we suppose, in the period of the Synhedrin's actual and, later, pretended power of life and death, that is, till the last days of the Jewish State, a real cause for a legislative infliction of it.

Sabbath and circumcision were since the cessation of sacrifice undoubtedly held as the most important and sacred rites of Judaism. This can be proved as well from multifarious Rabbinical, as from external sources. In the Temple times sacrifice was pre-eminently ranked with those two rites. As the sacred provision for constantly procuring expiation and atonement, its rite was commonly esteemed of paramount import. As to sacrifice, we have indeed to note, that in that Rabbi's lifetime the exegetical observations made on it were no more of any practical consequence. For it had ceased since the ruin of the Temple, the only remnant of it having been the ordinance concerning the bechor "first-born animal," which was respected as of perpetual validity, the ex-priests receiving the animal, indeed, as their obligatory portion. He can therefore scarcely be understood as having alluded, for practical objects, to this mere remnant of the former extensive sacrificial ritual. Yet we must not for one moment assume that the discontinuance of sacrificial offerings had interfered aught with or diminished his reverence for them. It was with him as with all other pious and devoted Israelites as intense and fervent after the destruction of the Temple, as it ever was before this national catastrophe, and this at once from their reverent valuation of the respective Divine ordinances and their strong, unbounded hope of the speedy restoration of the Temple. Are we consequently not entitled to deduce from Rabbi Eliezer's exposition, especially since his lifetime was surely not very remote from the period of the flourishing Temple service, that he interpreted by it the ground-sentiment of all pious Israel of the past, and no less of their judicial religious representatives, the national council? Is it not perfectly plausible that the supreme tribunal of the nation will in the days of its power, have rigidly avenged any direct and open "profanation of holy things," which that Rabbi designated as a delinquency worthy of death?

What he meant by such profanation is, we aver, not the infraction of the appointed time and place of sacrifice, both of which were Rabbinically included in the ordinance of Lev. xix. 8 (see B. Zebachim f. 28), or its defilement, which three trespasses, judging by the representations in the Rabbinical literature, have likely passed as the principal ones among the many which rendered sacrifice "abominable," nor any delinquency incurred by any other of the various conditions of ceremonial abomination, so much as the express opposition to and obvious antagonistic neglect of sacrifice. For not only do the parallel propositions in the Rabbi's declaration point to the latter-named meaning, but the analogy, for example, of the phrase "profaning the Sabbath," which everywhere in the old religious literature denotes an actual breach of its law by forbidden labor, compels us to assume that he had before his mind an apostasy from sacrifice, at once by avowed opinion and exhibited disuse. Such a profaner of holy things or of sacrifice, together with the reviler of festivals and the violator of the rite of the Abrahamic covenant, Rabbi Eliezer, then, esteemed worthy of being cast out of the world. May we not infer from this, that the judges composing the Synhedrin of the past held the same view, and practically made such antinomianism a capital offence, too?

If we should hesitate to presume this of its Phariseic members, since the later Rabbinical codes offer no evidence of such penal construction of the statute, and, further, since that sect was withal distinguished by a mild legal disposition, is it not at any rate easily supposable that the Sadducean members interpreted it in such sense and purport, denouncing religious delinquents of those descriptions, as well as others whose anti-Mosaic demonstrations were held grievous enough to call for a deterrent visitation, as *blasphemers*, equally punishable with the blasphemers of the name of Jehovah? And may we not, therefore, fitly suppose, too, that the Synhedrin instituted an indictment for blasphemy against Jesus for his antinomian utterances and acts, proceeding in this penal course upon the authority of that statute, although there is no mention in the gospels that this was a direct issue at his trial?

A further support to our view, and one which is of no little moment to us, we find in the Synhedrial punishments inflicted on some Jewish Christians after Jesus, some of which at least must be recognized as historical. Let us start with Stephen, whose incrimination fell one or two years after the death of Jesus. The penalty of death visited on him was stoning, as is recorded in Acts, vii. 58. The charge preferred against him was, speaking against the Temple and the Mosaic laws (ib. vi. 13, 14). That this double offence was treated as blasphemy, as Hausrath (l. c.) asserts, we could by no means allow, if that kind of blasphemy were to be understood which is set forth in Lev. xxiv. 16, and which the codified Rabbinical treatise of Synhedrin (vii. 5) has, as we are compelled to presume, preserved as the only crime of this denomination for which capital punishment is prescribed. Unless Stephen's judges can be supposed as having indicted him capitally on the same indefinite grounds on which the enraged priests, prophets, and common people declared the prophet Jeremiah worthy of death (Jer. xxvi. 8, 9), we cannot see how the charge of blasphemy for the attack upon the Temple and the Law could have been sustained against him, provided, at the same time, that we adhere to the view collected from that Rabbinical treatise, that no other dereliction fell under the head of capitally punishable blasphemy than that stated in the quoted place of Leviticus.

Now that the supreme tribunal of the Jewish nation can not be thought, at that advanced period of systematic jurisprudence, to have resorted for their guidance to that old mob precedent, will readily be admitted by all. Baur ('Paul,' i. p. 52 sq.), too, has vindicated that Jewish court of justice from the imputation of mob irregularity and defiance of legal form. He even rejects on this account, among some other reasons advanced there, the statements of Acts vii. 57, 58, as ungenuine. His conclusion is, that the whole affair was merely a tumultuous popular insurrection againt Stephen, to which he fell a victim by stoning. Now while we will not dispute the possibility that a multitude of Jews exasperated at the "trenchant public utterances" of that pugnacious Hellenist, should have taken justice in their own hands and attempted to avenge on him pre-eminently either his attack on the Jewish national worship, as Baur maintains, or his threat of the entire abolition of the Mosaic Law by the returning Jesus,— though lynch justice was at no time during the judicially regulated second Commonwealth popular with the Jews, and they were ordinarily most jealous for any capital cause being tried according to the fixed forms of law (see Ant. xiv. 9, 3),* — we yet could not understand why the penalty chosen by them was stoning, unless we attribute it to his final exclamation by which he apotheosized Jesus (ib. 56). This may indeed have been held as blasphemy by his executioners, for the implied imputation to the Deity of having a progeny or a second in the being of the risen Jesus. Yet it is a fact, that the charge of such blasphemy was not included in the testimony of the witnesses. Their evidence turned only on the two above-named points (ib. vi. 13, 14). We, then, have to ask, for what purpose were these two offences charged against him, if not with the view of visiting them with capital punishment, if they were really committed? And when we further inquire, under what Mosaical category did they come, what will we decide.?

That it should have been seduction, is out of the question. For this applied only to him who attempted to lead away others to the worship of alien gods, which attempt is, however, not provable from the respective sources as having been made by Stephen. Even if we should assume that the accusing party worked out such a charge by the aid of the same association which we have provisionally laid down for the cause of Jesus (see our essay on the Essenes), namely, that Stephen had taught others to follow Jesus, as being the son of God, which suasion might, indeed, have been construed as seduction to false worship, it is yet to be objected, that there is no indication whatever in the records that he ever did publicly teach such doctrine. Since, therefore, the charge cannot have been that of seduction, we have to look for another statutory provision which could easily have been employed in Stephen's case. This we find readily, in accordance with our view held forth above, in the statute of Numbers xv. 30, 31. By it Stephen's transgression was amply covered. Having been an assaulter of the Temple, he was surely to be treated as a " despiser of the word of God." In this word of God— the Mosaic Law — was not only frequently enunciated the dwelling of God in the national sanctuary, but was also contained a large portion of the ritual of sacrifices and other sacred offerings constituting its worship, all of which precepts were implicitly reviled by Stephen in his open assault upon the Temple. Again, as a most decided "despiser of God's word" he assuredly proved himself by his insinuation, that Jesus would, at his Parousia, change the entire

---

* See also Excursus D.

Mosaic dispensation. This defiant disparagement of the whole system of the Mosaic religion, in which he really was the "precursor and prototype of Paul" (so Edward Zeller), was certainly a flagrant *blasphemy* in the eyes of the orthodox Jewish hearers. That they actually held it as such a felony, is reported by the author of Acts himself (ib. vi. 11, 13).

Such an impious attack must have wounded the inmost affections of the faithful Jews. It was the rankest heresy that could be uttered. It sacrilegiously negatived one of the most essential principles of the Jewish belief, viz., that the Mosaic economy was in all its parts of Divine authority. As it was impossible to conceive that, what God had once commanded, could at any time be repealed, the cogent conclusion from Stephen's heretical discourses was, that he denied the Divine origin of the Law.

If the objection should be made, that the author of Acts made out the witnesses as false, we reply, that Stephen's speech itself, as reproduced by him, incontestably shows that the charge as to the Mosaic Law was genuine and true. For let us inquire, how does he therein represent the Law? As revealed by God? By no means. He designates it as "lively oracles" (not as "dibhre elohim chayim," to accord entirely with Jeremiah xxiii. 36, but merely as "debharim chayim"), and those communicated by an angel (ib. vii. 38) or by angels (v. 53)—a heterodox notion, which likewise occurs in Paul's Ep. Gal. iii. 19. This notion was in itself to the orthodox Israelites a downright blasphemy. It was yet increased and intensified by the threat of the imminent abolition of the Mosaic Law, which Stephen had uttered, according to the testimony of the witnesses. It may, then, readily be assumed that the executioners, if they were laymen out of the multitude,—which hypothesis of Baur we can however not accept,—had recourse to the discipline which the Synhedrin presumably used to apply against public assailants of the Mosaic Law, namely, the statute of Numbers forming the subject of the present dissertation. Let us yet state here that, notwithstanding the above-noted objection of Baur against the representation, in Acts, of Stephen's trial by the Synhedrin, and several other more or less weighty objections made by him and other critics against the whole relative account, we yet fully believe in his execution by the sentence of that high court. As the execution itself is left unquestioned even by such critics as Baur and Zeller, we are inclined to regard some details of the narrative that render a judicial trial very doubtful, as an addition by the late Pauline author of that work (there is according to Zeller no trace of its existence before the year 170 C. E.), rather than surrender the prosecution of Stephen by the Synhedrin as unhistorical. Since it is possible that the affair happened after Pilate had been recalled (whether the latter event occurred in 36 or 37, is disputed), and the new procurator had not yet appeared on the scene of his official activity, we can well conceive that the preponderantly Sadducean Synhedrin improved the interval to proceed exemplarily against that religious offender.

As to Baur's further objection that the Synhedrin had then no autonomy for executing a capital sentence, and that "this supreme spiritual tribunal must certainly have had sufficient fear of the Romans to pay some attention to legal form," we reply, that the analogy of the execution of James the Just, by the younger Hanan, the son of the ancient high-priest, Hanan, in the year 63, sufficiently justifies the assumption of a like speedy judicial interference, in the absence of the governor appointed, in the cause of Stephen.

The affair may, as Hitzig (Geschichte des Volkes Israel, quoted by Keim l. c. vi. 227, 28) proposes, have occurred under Caiphas' successor, Jonathan, whose hasty and harsh Sadducean legal justice impelled him to use the opportune interval between Pilate's departure and the arrival of his successor, Marcellus. And it may, too, in passing, as the same author suggests, have been by reason of that act of judicial usurpation of the high-priest, that he was afterwards deposed by Vitellius (Ant. xviii. 5, 3), as likewise the before-named later high-priest, Hanan, the younger, was removed for the same abuse of power.

Having, by the foregoing argument, as we hope, sufficiently educed from the capital indictment of Stephen for his impious assault upon the Temple and the Law, a support to our view, that the Synhedrin of old made any public derogating attack upon the entire or only a part of the Mosaic Law a capital offence, we will continue our observations on the other judicial persecutions of some early Jewish Christians after Stephen, to strengthen it yet more. But instead of directly turning to the problem of the execution of the apostle James the Less, which was nearest in time to that of Stephen, we will at once attach the accusations against Paul, as being more akin to those brought against his congenial precursor, Stephen.

That Paul was in his polemics against the Mosaic Law much advanced on Stephen, should be observed before we go on in the consideration of his offences. Stephen had, in his speech, deferred the change of the Law to the time of the returning Jesus. Paul, however, declared it already abrogated. His leading doctrine of justification by faith in Jesus, which he boldly derived from Gen. xv. 6, moved him more and more onward in his opposition to the Mosaic religion. Not only did he, like Stephen, proclaim the heterodox opinion, that the Law was given by angels, and not directly by God, he even reduced the Law below the level of equality with the "promise,"— the associate doctrinal term of his main theory,— in the notorious contrast set forth in his Epistle to the Galatians, iii. 16-20 (see on this Baur, 'Paul,' ii. 196 sq.). He, further, positively and repeatedly declared the whole Mosaic dispensation as unavailing towards acceptance with God (Gal. ii. 16; Rom. iii. 20); as having multiplied transgressions (Rom. v. 20); and, in fine, as being abrogated by Jesus and through his death (Gal. iii. 13; Col. ii. 14; Eph. ii. 15).

As to special commands of the Law, he certainly opposed violently the chief one, the initiatory rite, which signalized in the consciousness of Israel, and no less in that of all the rest of the Jewish Christians, himself and a few Hellenistic followers only excepted, the participation in the covenant of God made with Israel's ancestor, and stamped each Israelite a ben berith "child and member of the covenant." This opposition he put forth not only in the question of the admission of Gentile converts to the Christian community, but for Jewish converts as well (Gal. v., and see Baur l. c.). Nay, he preached against circumcision even among Jews; Acts. xxi. 22 (Edward Zeller finds in Gal. iii. 10 and v. 2 sq., the Pauline doctrine, that none who adhered to Law and circumcision had any share in the kingdom of the Messiah). In the place of the ancient covenant Paul had devised a new, universal one (Gal. iii. 17), that should embrace all nations having faith in Jesus. This covenant was to him the *promise* made to Abraham: "in thee shall all nations be blessed" (Gen. xii. 3, being so rendered in Gal. ib. 8), which promise— enlarged by him by-the-by with the aid of a disconnected phrase in Gen. xiii. 15, so as to represent it as not alone being made to Abraham, but also to his seed, which seed was to him none other than Jesus himself (Gal. iii. 16)—he lets be centred in Jesus, and in his believers made one with him. In this covenant-promise, he teaches, every one from all the nations is to share, if he has faith in Jesus.

His judgment on Sabbaths, festivals, and eating laws, in Cor. ii. 16, 17. compared with Gal. iv. 9-11, certainly shows his utter disregard for those Mosaic-religious institutions, as far at least as their obligation on his converts was concerned. Even the eating of idol-meat—that gravest abomination in the sight of Jews, as well as Jewish, and, later, Gentile Christians—he declared to be an indifferent thing for firm Christ-believers (1 Cor. x. 27).

His sentiment on the Temple worship was doubtless about equal to Stephen's, see Acts xvii. 24, and comp. 2 Cor. vi. 16, also Acts xxi. 28, and our Note 34. [The statement in Acts xxi. 23 sq., also that of his taking a vow, ib. xviii. 18, and the double mention in this work of Paul's festival journeys, which would appear as standing out to the contrary, inasmuch as he is in those accounts more or less directly made to reverently value and adhere to the Temple ritual, are either ungenuine and mere productions of its late author, whose Pauline apologetic tendency is maintained by the best critics of our day; or, if they should have to pass for historical, they must be pronounced as imputing to Paul a "contemptible hypocrisy," by which he stood incomparably more condemned than Peter (if Peter's action—see Gal. ii. 12—implied at all a transgression): for he would then, aside from the undeniable violent attempt at undermining and destroying practical Judaism in the whole course of his teaching, be condemnable also for the grossest inconsistency in professing at one time things as true and obligatory, which he would at another disparage or negative. Such inconsistency, it may yet be noted here, is not unlikely in him, though, judging by his own assertion in 1 Cor. ix. 20, and, again, by his solemn declaration at his alleged trial before the governor, "believing all things which are according to the Law, etc." (Acts xxiv. 14),—provided, of course, that he understood by the Law which he pretended to have all along been observing, the Mosaic-religious ritual, and not the few moral precepts which Christianity had adopted from Mosaism,—which declaration is so strikingly at variance with the remorseless polemics he carried on against the Mosaic Law during his missionary travels, whereby he so sorely scandalized alike the Jews and those Jewish Christians outside his own small following]

The cast of his theological doctrine about Jesus, too, largely exceeded, as to the intense deification of the latter, the notion which the primitive apostles and the Jewish Christians in general entertained about his divinity. Is it then to be wondered at, that the Asiatic Jews accused him as a teacher of apostasy (Acts xxi. 28)? His assaults upon circumcision and the Law made in Grecian communities, had doubtless become known to the Hellenistic Jews residing at Jerusalem. These had, besides, frequent occasions of personally noticing his antagonism to the Mosaic Law (see Acts ix. 29; this passage is by Baur, 'Paul,' i. 111 sq, declared inauthentic, however).

His antinomian assaults are further attested by the statement in Acts xxi. 21, that the body of the Jewish Christians themselves were scandalized over the report, that he was "teaching all the Jews which are among the Gentiles to forsake Moses, saying that they ought not to circumcise their children, neither to walk after the customs." The implication of this statement in vv. 20, 21 is, as Baur suggests, that he would have to fear the worst even from the Jewish Christians. How much the more must not the Asiatic Jews, and, through their information, the rest of the orthodox Jews of Jerusalem, have been exasperated at that greatest foe of their ancestral faith and forms of religion?

That the Asiatic Jews have really brought the charge mentioned ib. xxi. 28 against Paul before the Synhedrin,—presided over though not by Ananias (ib. xxiii. 2), if the son of Nebedeus be meant (see Jos. Ant. xx. 5, 2), but most likely by Ishmael, the son of Fabi; see Ant. xx. 8, 8,—may safely be accepted as substantially historical, to be gleaned out of the vast mass of accessory and additional matter reaching from that passage of Acts to the end of ch. xxvi. That he could not have stood "before the high council on a charge of violating a temple by-law," as Hausrath (l. c.) somewhat contemptuously and superficially remarks, should, after all that we have premised, be readily allowed by every thinking reader. No, he stood before the Synhedrin charged with being a teacher of religious apostasy, to be "judged after the law" (ib. xxiii. 3; comp. xxiv. 6), and that, as it would further appear from xxiii. 27-29, capitally.

The accusation laid against him is, in a more generalizing and, as we hold, less reliable form, repeated ib. xxiv. 5, 6. The main charge seems to have centred in his teaching and offending against the Law and the Temple; see ib. xxi. 28, and comp. xxv. 8.

(As to the additional charge of speaking against the people, ib. xxi. 28, this could surely not have been accounted a capital offence. But that it was well founded, appears from the following. He positively rejected, in Ep. Gal., the merit of circumcision as the condition of Israel's prerogative over other nations. In his argument he aimed to establish the bare level between Jews and Gentiles. The highest point of this his position is reached in Ep. Rom., which was in the main addressed to the Jewish Christian church of Rome. In it he aimed radically to disabuse its members of their sentiment of primacy over the Gentiles; so Baur, l. c. In a sense, his speaking against the people may even be found implied in his polemics against the Law. For in Eph. ii. 14, 15, he propounds the theory of the breaking down of the partition wall between the Jews and Gentiles, which he explains as identical with the abolition of the Law).

Now as regards those chief points of accusation, we have to ask, on what penal grounds were they based? As a Mesith "seducer" in the Scriptural sense, he might indeed have been arraigned, and was perhaps so arraigned in Greece, before the tribunal of the proconsul Gallio; see Acts xviii. 13. For he not only proclaimed the ordinary Jewish Christian dogma of the divine Sonship of Jesus, he even raised him to the proportion of "Lord," Kurios (Jesus had already virtually applied this title to himself, in Matt. xxii. 44, or rather its Hebrew equivalent, "adon;" it was yet left to Paul to identify his Christ even with the Jehovah of the Hebrew original, in Rom. x. 11-13), who should be "called upon" by his believers (1 Cor. i. 2; Rom. l. c.), and worshipped (Phil. ii. 10, 11). Nay he exalted him to the dignity of "Creator of all things" (Col. i. 16; 1 Cor. viii. 6) and "Ruler over all" (1 Cor. xv. 24 sq.), acknowledging still, it is true, the supremacy of God. (Compare our relative remarks in Excursus B.) Yet we find no evidence in the respective accounts that such charge was really brought against him in Jerusalem. There is, then, no other alternative left than to assume that his cause was antinomianism, his indictment resting on the statute in point, of Numbers xv. 30, 31, by which his guilt could be defined as blasphemy. His derogating (and profaning) of the Temple was already in itself, in accordance with what we observed above, a "despising of the word of God," apart from his having committed this latter offence, in its general sense and in the most aggravating degree, by his radical teaching of the abolition of the whole Law through Jesus.

This consummate antinomianism was a most decisive, crushing blow, aimed at the jealously cherished belief of Israel in the Divine authority of the Law. By it he exposed himself to the penalty of death, the infliction of which the preponderantly Sadducean Synhedrin, in its high function of punishing offences against God, claimed, as we suppose, to be its judicial prerogative, because Holy Writ had adjudged kareth "extermination" for such despising, which penal sanction there is no evidence whatever that the

Sadducees had not intrepreted in the sense of execution by the hands of the legally constituted high tribunal of the Jewish nation (compare on this the sequel), especially since Leviticus xxiv. 16 had, in ordaining such execution for the direct blasphemy of God, offered to them an available analogy.

That he escaped that penalty, because the procurators of those days and their subordinate officials cared nothing for the religious heresy charged upon a Jewish offender (see Acts xxiii. 29), as long as no political misdemeanor could be urged and proved against him (comp. ib. xxi. 38), is well known. ——

A little later, in 62 or 63 C. E., James, surnamed the Just, and brother to Jesus, was put to death by sentence of the Synhedrin convened by Hanan, son of the elder Hanan or Elchanan, as he is named in the Tosifta. [Whether this James was Jesus' brother or only relative, on this the modern writers are not agreed. Doellinger, ' First Age of Christianity,' identifies him with the apostle who was the son of Alphaeus or Clopas, and calls him the cousin of Jesus. See also Renan, 'Les Apotres,' p. 42 Strauss, l. c. i, p. 260, maintains that he was Jesus' real brother. This writer is, moreover, let it be said in passing, the only one of all the theological scholars known to us, who does not separate the two James. He was without doubt decided in this identification by Ep. Gal. i. 19, where the personage commonly taken for the apostle James, who was martyred under Agrippa I., is designated "the Lord's brother." This stands out, indeed, against the ordinary acceptation as authorized by Eusebius' Church History. This ecclesiastical writer treats of them as of distinct persons, speaking in ii. 9, of "the apostle James, the brother of John" (both the sons of Zebedee), and in ii. 23, of "James, the brother of the Lord." The former is known as one of the three leading apostles—the three pillars, as Paul styles them (Gal. ii. 9). He was most likely the leader of the earliest Church; see ib 12, Acts xv. 13, xxi. 18. The latter passes in Church history as a later saint, and is supposed to have become the head of the Church after the death of his namesake, the apostle.]

In those troubled days in which the fanatical Sicarii, in their fiery hatred of the Roman supremacy, had caused so much disorder (see Ant. xx. 8, 10), and Messianic pretenders had all along kept the Roman authorities in suspicion of rebellious attempts (see our Note 20, and especially Acts xxi. 38), it is not strange that a pontifex of the family of the Sadducean tyrant, Hanan the elder, should have summarily proceeded against the head of the young Christian church, who may have been more profuse than the rest in unguarded language concerning the second coming of Jesus as the Messiah. Hegesippus, in Eusebius, Eccles. Hist. ii. 23, does indeed make James proclaim, while placed upon a wing of the Temple, that Jesus "was about to come on the clouds of heaven,"—a testimony to Jesus which he had doubtless frequently spoken forth, and which had, as that writer reports in the same place, practically aroused a *tumult* at the time of which he speaks, so that the rulers became fearful of the "danger, that the people would now expect Jesus as the Messiah." Or it may be, that that pontifex singled him out as a terrifying example, for being the representative of that body of Jews whose chief dogma was, the past and future Messiahdom of Jesus. Says the Author of "Supernatural Religion," iii. 120, seq.: "There can be no doubt of the reality and universality of the belief, in the Apostolic Church, in the immediate return of the glorified Messiah and 'speedy end of all things.'" That the primitive Apostles, also Paul, fervently cherished such expectation, is evident from 1 Ep. John ii. 28, iii. 2; Apocal. xxii; Ep. James v. 7, 8; 1 Ep. Peter iv. 7, 13, and comp. Acts ii.; 1 Thess. iv. 15, seq, v. 23; see also 2 Ep. Peter iii. Nor can we doubt that the Jewish Christians made no secret of this doctrine. There is all likelihood that they openly and loudly avowed it. Now as to this intense Messianic expectation it is very probable, that the Sadducean ruler had strongly and bitterly resented it from political motives alone. It bore too decidedly on the delicate relations of the Jewish people to the Roman authorities, affecting directly his own interests, as also the existent national establishments generally. Nor is it at all unlikely that he with his other Sadducean colleagues had taken grave offence at the Christian resurrection-belief, which was so closely connected and so expressly urged with that doctrine. Yet all this may not have appeared to Hanan a sufficient cause for instituting a judicial prosecution against James, the chief of the Jerusalemite Church. He therefore, we suggest, brought that general charge against him, which Josephus reports, that of Law-breaking (Ant. xx. 9, 1). [To the Greek term employed by Josephus, "antinomianism" corresponds. The older Rabbis stigmatized a Law-breaker either as Epicurean, (see Sifre., Numb. 112) or, more frequently, as Mumar "turned away from the Law." The latter title was denounced as well for a partial as for the entire apostasy from the Law. If it was of the gravest nature, a falling

away to polytheism or idolatry, then the stigma was usually
'Min'—the etymology of which term we discuss in our
work on the Mineans. For Min the Rabbis used at
times the scornful name 'Sadducee,' because the Sadducean
sect too were by them held as real heretics]. If this
accusation was no mere pretence, but had some foundation
in the fact of a real offence or offences, we may look for it
in his Essenic antagonism to the sacrificial Temple
worship. James was unquestionably a sectarian Ebionite,
or Christian Essene. Whether or not the partial Essenism
of Jesus and the Ebionism of James, his brother, may be
tracked to their parental family (Essenes lived in every
city; see Wars, ii. 8, 4), of whom Hausrath, 'N. T. Times,'
ii. 130, asserts that "their tendency towards strictness can
be recognized in the Essenic-coloured ascetic life of Jesus'
brother, James" (which view, put into our own words—for
we apprehend the Essenes as an heterodox sect—would be
equal to this, that the family professed heretical Essenism),
thus much is at any rate sufficiently well attested, that
James was an adherent of the Ebionite sect. Hegesippus
states about him, that "he drank neither wine nor fermented liquors, and abstained from animal food."

This was surely a pronounced trait of Ebionism. Aside
from this individual peculiarity, we have to declare it as
indisputable, that the leading spirit of the entire primitive
Jewish Christian church, presided over first, as it is supposed, by the apostle James, and then by James the Just,
was prominently Essenic. The Essenic disregard for the
goods of this world and the communistic system, were not
only *constitutional* in it, but would even without this
organic peculiarity have naturally been produced by the
belief of those Jewish Christians in the speedy end of the
then world (see Renan, 'Les Apotres,' p. 64).

We discover, further, a remarkable trait of affinity of
that Church with the Essenic sect in the well-known
decrees of its earlier council, headed by the apostle James;
see Acts xv. This council is there reported to have laid
down four points of precept for the admission of Gentile
converts into the Christian community. Their genuineness
has indeed been called in question by several modern
critics of note. We cannot here estimate their various
opinions and arguments. The conclusion we, on our part,
have reached concerning them is, that they are authentic
so far,— but only so far,— that the council of the Jerusalemite Church issued them as a norm for the conversion to
the new creed of those Gentiles, who would not submit to
the initiatory rite and with it to the observance of that

range of Mosaic laws held incumbent on every Christian. They were devised in about the same manner, as the so-called seven Noachian precepts were introduced by the orthodox Jews for the reception of those Rabbinically designated 'Gere Toshab,' or, as they were also, though less frequently, named, the 'God-fearing,' from the Gentiles. As little as these attained, by the acceptance of the seven precepts, to the perfect title of 'sons of the covenant,' and in especial to the privilege of unimpeded intermarriage with born Jews, so little, we hold, were those converts to Christianity, for whom the four decisions of the apostolic council were framed, ever intended to be regarded as fully and equally incorporated members of the Jewish Christian community. It is this comparative authenticity alone that we can accord to those decisions. Yet, on the other hand, we strongly incline to maintain for them this degree of authenticity, rather than totally reject them as unhistorical, as to the period to which they are credited, as Renan, Baur and others have done. For they not only occur three times in the same work (Acts xv. 20, 29, xxi. 25), and recur, in the main, in the later Ebionite production, the Clementine Homilies, vii. 4, 8 (which work, even if we may not regard it with Clement of Alexandria as the authentic record of Peter's preaching, is at any rate a true exposition of Ebionite views and regulations), as directions given by Peter for the conduct of the Gentile Christian converts of Tyre and Sidon ; but their entire tenor and internal interconnection seem to us to point unmistakably to Ebionite principles, prevailing with the three "pillar apostles," one of whom, James, was the chief of the primitive Church.

Now to consider those four decrees as the "ensemble of Noachian precepts" (so Renan; they are enumerated in B. Synhedrin f. 56), would in our opinion be going too far. We own the resemblance of the former to some of the latter. Their intent may even, on the whole, be construed as identical in both. But since four out of the seven precepts do not at all occur in the apostolic decrees, viz., robbery (theft), murder, blasphemy, and Mosaic judicial laws, we cannot take them as a direct imitation and embodiment of these requirements for Gentile converts handed down by Rabbinical tradition.

We prefer to assume that the apostolic council in devising those four decrees, acted entirely independently of those seven precepts. This would appear to us clearly already from Peter's before-noted direction for Gentile converts, in the Clementine Homilies. He adds there the warning against eating dead flesh and that of strangled beasts—a prohibition not enumerated among those seven precepts, but which is yet prescribed for proselytes in Lev. xvii. 15. He, further, in the direction for Tyre, enjoins on the converts the abstention from "all unclean things," the same "which the God-fearing Israelites have heard," that means, all or at least most of the ordinances of religious purity prescribed in the Mosiac code, of which he names in particular, in the admonition for Sidon, washing after coition, and menstrual female purifications; compare Lev. xv. 18, 19. From this it is evident that the Peter of the Homilies was not guided by the Rabbinically transmitted regulations for proselytes, but framed his own, partly on the model of the Pentateuch, and partly on the ruling principles of the Ebionite system. Like him, we hold, was the real apostle Peter, as also John and James, determined in the fixation of the four rules, not by the Rabbinical tradition, but on the one side by a direct reference to the respective Mosaic ordinances, and on the other by the prevailing doctrines of the Essenic sect.

These four rules appear to us as bearing pre-eminently an Essenic stamp, that is, a demonological relation. We cannot here attempt to illustrate how much of the dualism of the Essenes and the Apocryphal literature had already got hold of the thought of Jesus. But we have to assert as immediately to our purpose, that at all events the minds of the chief apostles were, judging by three out of the four decrees for proselytes, preoccupied with those dualistic notions.

We take on ourselves to affirm, that *the interdiction of idol-meat, flesh of strangled animals, and blood, points chiefly to Essenism.* As to idol-meat, it is to be remarked that alike the Gentile and Jewish Christians of the first centuries condemned and abhorred it as the "table" or "repast of the demons" (a stigma that took its rise, perhaps, from the Septuagint in Isa. lxv. 11); see Origen, Against Celsus, viii. 30; Clem. Hom. l. c; 1 Cor. v. 21. That the two other injunctions have also a demoniacal bearing, may be gathered from the declaration of Origen in that place: "What is offered to idols is offered to demons, and man devoted to God must not become a companion at the table of the demons. We should, further, abstain from strangled meat, because the blood which it is said is the food of demons, is not separated; that we may not partake of the food of the demons."

That the apostolic framers of the four decisions entertained about the same sentiment on the three aforenamed of them, we have no doubt. It was pre-eminently, we hold, Essenic demonological impressions that prevailed on them to enact those three injunctions for Gentile converts Their theosophic abhorrence of every sign and vestige of spiritual association or contact with the devils, was mainly active in their legislating in that manner.

We are at the same time far from denying that the fundamental tone of the sentiment of those apostolic legislators was the common Jewish one of those days. The ordinary intense Jewish antagonism to every form of pagan worship rested as well on the conception that the gods of the heathens were no-gods, as that they were evil spirits; see Deut. xxxii. 17; Ps. cvi. 37, and in especial the Septuagint in several places. The enactment of the three ordinances in question was accordingly properly Jewish and unsectarian in the outlines, inasmuch as it laid down as indispensable the total renunciation of every trace of heathenism. Even in the fourth, the negation of heathen ways may readily be found stipulated. For the moral profligacy and corruption among the heathens of those centuries was wide-spread and deeply settled, and had become most intolerable and shocking to the pure minds of godly Jews; compare the very frequent connection of idolatry with fornication as peculiar to heathendom in the vast Rabbinical literature. The term "porneia" of that fourth ordinance certainly corresponds to the last-named vice, which, in the original generic Jewish designation, "zenuth," includes doubtless incest and unlawful marriages (the "gilui arayoth" of the Rabbinical literature.).

Yet for all that we cannot fail to discover an Essenic predisposition in the apostolic enactment of the three ordinances in question. Their combination obviously involves both a polemical reflection on the demons of the heathens and an extravagant apprehension of their existence and power, which the bulk of the Jewish nation, for all the demonological notions infused into their minds in the centuries of the second Commonwealth, did positively not share. We have not the slightest evidence that the ordinary Israelite of those days rejected the eating of blood from a religious horror in a demoniacal sense, such as we have to impute to the framers of the four apostolic decisions with regard to two of them. The generality of the Jews surely abhorred blood only for the Mosaic reason, that "blood is the soul."

In support of our proposition that those three decisions had principally a demoniacal bearing, may yet be urged the repudiation by the Ebionites of animal flesh. They account for it themselves by reference to evil spirits, and the voracity of these after the blood of animals. In the Clementine Homilies we meet with three different accounts for their rejection of flesh-meat; see ib. viii. 16; xii. 6 and 12 (still another is given by Epiphanius, Haer. xxx. 18, but it is scarcely historical.). We advert principally for our present purpose to the last-noted passage of the Homilies. In it Peter sets forth the eating of animal flesh as first introduced by the giants—the bastards born of fallen angels and women of the earth; see Gen. vi. 2. "They," it is said there, "not being pleased with purity of food, longed after the taste of *blood*. Wherefore they first tasted flesh." About the same sentiment is expressed in the book of Enoch, vi. 4-6. It is mainly from the occurrence of this sentiment in both works that Hausrath, 'N. T. Times,' i, p. 166, concludes an affinity of thought between the Essenes and other mystics, whose tendencies were similar to those of the apocryphal author of Enoch. We, on our part, would base on this circumstance the supposition, that among the various theosophic classes of ancient Judaism, whether the Essenes or their Christian cousins, the Ebionites, or the mystics of the Apocrypha generally, the notion prevailed, that the use of animal flesh is to be abominated chiefly for the blood it contains and for the necessity of shedding it to obtain the flesh, blood being considered as the food of the demoniac beings of the legend of Genesis.

By this mystical apprehension the apostolic prohibitions of strangled meat for converts on account of blood, and of blood itself, are easily explained. These two prohibitions have, then, the same relation as that of idol-meat.

It will now, we expect, appear very plausible to the reader that Ebionism or Essenism inspired the enactment of those three conjoined apostolic decrees. Should he even have any hesitation to regard the leaders of the primitive Church, prominently the apostles James and Peter, as real Christianized Essenes, he will at least recognize with us in that enactment the adopted spirit and tendencies of Essenism. From this we may be permitted to draw the farther conclusion that, as the rejection of animal flesh and of sacrifice was, as Zeller, 'The Philosophy of the Greeks,' iii. 2, points out, always combined in the theory of the ancient ascetics, and, further, as such combination is positively and variously attested of the later Ebionites who, as well as the earlier, sprung from the Essenes, or, at any rate, adopted the doctrines of this sect, the opposition to the sacrificial Temple worship was peculiar to all those early Jewish Christians who manifested an Essenic or Ebionite affiliation or leaning. If then, as we suggested, dualistic Essenism underlies the three out of the four apostolic decrees, we may safely account the three apostles Peter, John and James, the last-named in particular, who was the chief of the council in which they were enacted, as direct antagonists of the Temple ritual from that sectarian predisposition alone, aside from the other consideration, which should always be kept in mind, that they must have strenuously aimed to imitate the example of their Master, who was a very decided opponent of it.

And in like manner, but with yet stronger probability, we may infer that James the Just, Jesus' brother, was a pronounced antagonist of sacrifice. For of him does Hegesippus directly assert, that he rejected animal flesh. With such rejection that of sacrifice was doubtless allied in his mind and teaching.

A clue would, then, be offered to the real cause for which he was tried and condemned to death by stoning by the Synhedrin of the high-priest Hanan. We may fairly suppose that, as a stanch Ebionite, he repeatedly, openly, and vehemently inveighed against the prevailing worship of the Temple. That rigorous Sadducean president of the high court, we further surmise, availed himself of the temporary freedom from Roman surveillance, to visit on the assaulter that capital punishment which the Synhedrin had already in former times, as we take it, been inflicting on violent antagonists of the established Temple ritual and the Mosaic institutions generally, and that in pursuance of the statute of Numbers xv. 30, 31. By it James could be indicted for *blasphemy*, and condemned to that mode of execution which the law, Lev. xxiv. 16, had provided for direct blasphemy of the name of Jehovah, the difference of the species of crime not interfering, as we believe, with that Sadducean pontiff, so long as the same denomination could be seized upon to meet his case. To the offence of assaulting the Temple service, Josephus alluded, it may be, in the account he gives of James' persecution. That offence can be understood by the charge of "Law-breaking," brought by the high-priest himself against him and other offenders; see also our Excursus C.

We must indeed, in our effort at strengthening our argument of antinomian assaulters having by the Synhedrin been prosecuted as real blasphemers, not pass over the account of Hegesippus who mentions nothing of the charge of Law-breaking, but lets him be martyred for his Jesulogical Messianic testimony. The penalty of stoning which he reports as having been inflicted on James, would at the first glance, judging by his entire description of the case, point only to the deification of Jesus as the cause of his incrimination. This deification could, in fact, have brought on him the charge of blasphemy that came under the statute of Lev. xxiv. 16. To meet this objection from the account of Hegesippus, we suggest it as probable, in view of Josephus' statement and our own previous argumentation, that the felony of "despising the word of God" formed at least part of the accusation, and that, if Hegesippus' report can claim to be genuine, he was arraigned for both species of blasphemy, that of which the aforementioned ordinance of Leviticus treats, and the other described in Numbers xv. 30, 31. Not only is this probable, but we would, by this explanation, yet gain the advantage of harmonizing both the accounts of Josephus and Hegesippus.

The deification of Jesus for which, in conjunction with his antinomian blasphemy, as we now proposed, the Synhedrial judges may have awarded the penalty of death against James, is attested by the latter writer who attributes to him the declamation of the Christian dogmatic phrase, current then as before, that Jesus was " now sitting in the heavens, on the right hand of great Power " (God); comp. Acts vii. 55, 56. This exaltation of Jesus was no doubt severely resented by the orthodox Jews and penally avenged by the authorities, since it was ordinarily attended by express epithets of deification. It was yet aggravated by the Ebionite antagonism to the Mosaic institution of sacrifice, which we imputed to him before. ——

A trial for antinomian blasphemy by the statute of Numbers xv. 30, 31, likewise in conjunction with the accusation for blasphemy of Jehovah by the Christian assertion of the dogma of the divine sonship of Jesus, might be suggested also in the cause of the apostle James, the son of Zebedee, who suffered death under Agrippa I., the grandson of Herod, about the year 44 C. E., were we not informed in Acts xii. 2, and in Eusebius, l. c. ii. 9,—the latter reporting from Clement's seventh book of the 'Institutions,'—that he was beheaded.

We demonstrated above the apostle's Essenic sectarianism or leaning. It is therefore not too much to suggest that he as well as James the Just, exhibited an open and aggressive opposition to the sacrificial Temple service. As a valuable support to this supposition we mention the Ebionite tradition based on a book bearing the apostle James' name, that he "spoke against the Temple and sacrifice, also against the fire on the altar "— quoted by Hilgenfeld, History of Heretics, etc., p. 431. It was thus he could have drawn on himself the accusation of being a "despiser of the word of God," and consequently a "blasphemer." With it there might have been associated the charge of blasphemy, and perhaps also of "ditheism" (abodah zarah), for publicly professing Jesus, in speeches as well as at performances of miraculous healings which were always attempted "in the name of Jesus," as the son of God. While this must in theory appear as probable, it is yet to be objected, that the punishment with which the apostle's offence was visited, would not tally with our supposition. He was decapitated. This penalty he could not have incurred for antinomian blasphemy, or for blasphemy at all. It is, moreover, to be remarked that, considering the apostle's cause by itself, it would appear that the proceeding against him was not at all by the ordinary tribunal, the Synhedrin, but that he fell a victim to the arbitrary act of the king Agrippa. See Renan, 'Les Apotres,' p. 201, who says: "The affair was not presented as a religious one. There was not an inquisitorial trial held before the Sanhedrin. The sentence was pronounced by virtue of the arbitrary power of the sovereign, as it had been the case with John the Baptist."

When we contrast both proceedings, the one against the Baptist by Herod Antipas, and the other against the apostle James by his nephew, Agrippa, and hold in view that in both instances decapitation was decreed, it will indeed seem quite possible that both autocrats acted on their own discretion and independently of the Synhedrin. Likewise seem both to have been mainly actuated in their fierce resentment and decision, by political motives. Possibly the cry of the impending return of Jesus as the Messiah — the continuous anxious watchword of every Christian since his death — had jarred too dismally on the sensibilities of king Agrippa, in particular in view of the exciting effect it must have produced on his illustrious patron, the emperor Claudius. This emperor's vehement intolerance to Messianic movements is set forth above, pp. 58 and 98 sq.

Decapitation was withal, judging by Rabbinical tradition, a very rare mode of execution with the Jewish legislative authorities; see Mishnah Synhed. ix. 1 sq. Its repeated infliction by Roman officials in Palestine, on the other hand, suggests the idea, that those Herodian rulers had copied that method from their Roman masters. (See on Theudas' decapitation, perhaps yet in the same year, 44 C. E., by the procurator Fadus, Ant. xx. 5, 1, and on the same punishment of a Roman soldier by Cumanus, a few years later, ib. 4).

Accounting thus for the proceedings against the apostle James by the individual determination of king Agrippa, we would have to eliminate his case from those instances adduced for our leading argument, viz., that the statute of Numbers xv. was the Mosaic legal enactment, upon which the Synhedrin based their title of criminally prosecuting antinomian Jewish Christians. While this would in no way invalidate it, we would yet prefer, if possible, to range James, the apostle's, cause with the others discussed before. We venture indeed to attempt it, the foregoing contrary points notwithstanding. Agrippa, we propose, may not have proceeded against him exclusively from political considerations. Nor is it unlikely that he had at least some Synhedrial coadjutors in bringing him to justice. The action against him may, then, have partly at least borne an authoritatively judicial character. And the provocation to it, too, may partly have lain in what was construed as blasphemy, alike anti-monotheistic and antinomian, in the manner explained above.

That Agrippa's action may not have been entirely political, but caused by religious motives as well, might be assumed from the extent of his persecution of Christians. For not only the apostle James suffered it at his hands, but also Peter was designed by him as a victim. In view, then, of his severe attempts on more than one leading personage of the new Christian sect, the supposition will not appear too remote, that the charge of religious delinquency was strongly co-active in the cause of James, the apostle, too. (Baur's remark, that Peter's unexpected release was perhaps due to Agrippa's notice, that his execution of the apostle James was after all not so popular as he imagined, is as noteworthy as it is acceptable. Here we hold it pertinent to produce yet the important opinion of the critics Schneckenburger, Zeller, and Baur, that Agrippa's persecution of the Jewish Christians towards the end of his reign was the first of its kind since the death of Jesus, the previous one, started with Stephen, not having affected any other than Hellenistic Christian schismatics).

To resume the main thread of our argument, we contend that the statute of Numbers in question was well fitted to be used as authority for penal proceedings against antinomian offenders. As such were surely considered the Essenes with their opposition to sacrifice, and also the

Jewish Christians sharing this opposition. That the Synhedrin will, in order to deal rigidly with such "despisers of the word of God"—and as well with other defiant assaulters of the Law or parts of it—have resorted to that statute, is, while not directly provable, most probable at least. We hold that it was brought to bear and put in practice in the several prosecutions of Jewish Christians, from Jesus to James the Just.

The objection that no record of the judicial execution of that statute against criminally arraigned antinomian Christians is extant, cannot count for anything. How many reliable accounts of the real judicial practice of the Synhedrin since the time of Jesus have been preserved at all? What do we know for sure about the actual method of trials and course of proceedings in those days of Saducean supremacy and majority? As to the relative expositions and traditions delivered to us through the later Rabbinical literature, we may lay it down as indisputable that they are, in the main, nothing but self-made and scholastically evolved theories on points of judicial law. The Saducean Temple nobility with the president of the council from their own rank and party, may, for all we know, have followed, in the prosecution of Christian schismatics, either their old, at one time abolished, but possibly, on the restitution of their power, again revived "code of decisions," or devised new rigid measures by way of more or less direct derivations from Mosaic provisions of judicial law. They may, moreover, have acted very arbitrarily in cases of antinomian inquisition—a supposition to which one is easily led by comparing the mode of execution of the apostle James (provided the Synhedrin was connected with the infliction of his doom), decapitation, with that of Stephen and James the Just, which was stoning. That the later Rabbinical rubrical enumerations of points of criminal law were for the most, or, at least, a large part, mere theories, which cannot have been the actual standard by which the Synhedrin judged when in power in the first century, may be proved from the following.

Jesus' trial and condemnation practically took place on the first day of Passover. So the Synoptics report, especially Matthew, concerning which Evangelist we quote Strauss' view (A New Life of Jesus, ii. 314), that if he "did not hesitate to assert that Jesus was condemned and crucified on the first day of Easter, we may fairly be satisfied with his statement." Now it was well known that there was a Rabbinical canon, that no trial should be held on the Sabbath or any holy day (Mishnah, Betsa, f. 36). That

Rabbi Akiba should by that proposition in Tosifta Synhedrin xi. 7, "and they bring them to death on the feast," have intended to contradict and upset that canon, is a most erroneous opinion of some writers. It is maintained by the before-quoted Strauss (l. c. p. 312). Even the erudite Jewish author, Dr. Joel, fathers and elaborates it in 'Blicke, etc.' ii. 62 sq. He would account for Akiba's disregard of the established rule, by what he alleges as his acquaintance with the precedent set in the case of Jesus. The knowledge of it, he affirms, came to him through the report of the Synoptics, since "the evangelical books were known in this (Rabbinical) circle." He lets Akiba generalize from this single precedent, and extend the permissibility, nay the obligation, of execution on the holy day proper, to a number of delinquents.

But all this is nothing but airy sophistry, wanting every solid support. We on our part presume to vouch, that Rabbi Akiba never thought of countenancing a breach of a holy day proper by the execution of a criminal, such as is imputed to him by reference to that passage in the Tosifta. Nor, we insist, will he have antagonized the established prohibition of holding court on Sabbaths and holy days (see the aforecited Mishnah), so that he could, as Joel pretends, be supposed to have found and declared the trial and condemnation of Jesus on the first day of Passover as perfectly in order, and at the same time as forming a precedent, justifiable to be copied in subsequent legislation. That Akiba should have had such a divergent, liberal view is utterly impossible, especially in regard to capital cases, in which it was besides prescribed, to have two recording clerks for writing down the whole proceedings of the court (B. Synh. f. 34). That no ancient Rabbi can be conceived to have approved writing on a sacred festival, admits of no question whatever. To harmonize therefore that scholastic utterance of Akiba in the Tosifta, with his otherwise unquestionable orthodox position on all points of Jewish law and custom, we have to explain it to refer not to the real holy day, but to the half-holy days of Passover and Tabernacles, which intervening days were Rabbinically designated "regel," too. As to the Feast of Weeks, it is easy to suggest that Akiba, if he included this festival at all, thought of the six days following it, on which the executions enumerated in that passage might take place. For these six days which together with the Shabuoth day itself made up a week, were for ritual objects accounted as appendages to this festival (comp. Moed Katan, iii. 6). In the case of the execution of a delinquent set for the Shabuoth season, Akiba may accordingly have intended to propose, that it has to take place during the six supplementary days belonging to the festival.

Reverting now to the before-mentioned point that Jesus' trial occurred on the first day of Passover, it will not seem necessary to assert, that in it no regard was had to the Rabbinical rules that were, in the manner explained before, to be affected by it. Nor is it likely that in his case the other Rabbinical canon, "no condemnation without previous warning," was complied with. At any rate, there is no mention that such warning was given him. But this was positively a disregard of the precept, that no one should be executed or even corporally punished, without such previous warning. It was a most weighty one with the Rabbis of old. The clemency of the Pharisees—on it, see Mishnah Synhedrin, f. 40, and B. Maccoth f. 7—had devised all sorts of humane pretexts to evade the carrying out of the stern letter of the Mosaic penal law. To it was also due the institution that no judicial punishment should be inflicted, without that a proper dehortation was before given to the delinquent. We are yet to observe that possibly, in the cause of Jesus, even the Phariseic doctors did not deem a dehortation necessary, since he was no doubt regarded as a Chaber, "an instructed person" (distinguished from the vulgar), always supposed to know what is unlawful, without any expostulation with him concerning the matter in question (see on this B. Maccoth f. 9); or that, if the criminal charge laid against him was seduction, the question of previous warning was waived even by these doctors, because, according to the Talmud, the rule had prevailed that to a 'Mesith' no such consideration is, for the eminent gravity of his trespass, to be accorded (see B. Synhedrin, f. 80). On the other hand, it is to be noted that we possess no authentic proof, that such distinctions had already been made or gained legal recognition at the early period in which Jesus lived, even among the Phariseic party.

There are some other divergences from Rabbinism that could be mentioned as striking us in the accounts of the proceedings against Jesus. We will here only yet point out the rule, stated in the Mishnah Synh. f. 32, that no decision must be rendered in any capital case on the same day of the trial. This was surely not kept in Jesus' trial.

All these foregoing remarks tend to show conclusively, that to judge from the literary discussions and decisions on points of criminal law preserved in the Talmud, back to the real practice followed by the Synhedrin when it had a Sadducean majority, as was the case in the first Christian century to the end of the Jewish State, is in the highest degree unwarranted. The Sadducean rulers in the council were either not aware of, or paid no heed to, the various theoretical devices for evading rigid judgment, which the Phariseic schools had brought forward. This holds good as well with regard to the incrimination of Jesus as of the other accused Jewish Christians.

To object dogmatically, therefore, that, because the extant codifications of judicial law, coming as they do from Rabbinical doctors of a later age, furnish no analogy for certain Synhedrial proceedings, that may yet, on the other side, be set down with perfect propriety as prevailing with those Senates composed mostly of Sadducees, is unreasonable, indeed. Our proposition, then, that Jesus, Stephen, Paul, and the two James were incriminated for the blasphemy of "despising the word of God," and sentence of death was passed on them by a Sadducean majority of the Synhedrin in accordance with the statute in question which treats of such offence, will not in the least be invalidated by the fact, that the Rabbinical rubrication in the Mishnah does not contain any provision of judicial punishment for antinomian blasphemy, the Rabbis having uniformly interpreted 'kareth'—the penalty denounced in that statute—as to be inflicted by God and not by any temporal power. Who, we have to ask, can bring forth any evidence that the Sadducean judges, in their lofty and stern conception of the Synhedrin being the substitutes of the Deity for carrying out his Law, did not presume to act as its competent avengers themselves, and decree and execute with their own hands the "extermination," which was the Mosaic, and, consequently, Divine, judicial verdict enunciated for antinomian heresy? And this in especial, since, as already observed before, they might refer for a warrant to the enactment of Leviticus xxiv. 16, appointing death by stoning as the penalty for the crime of the same denomination?

It may here be added that not only can we not reliably conclude from judicial ordinances laid down in the Mishnah, back to the actual norm of procedure maintained by a previous, largely Sadducean Synhedrin, we must even not be too positive in our inferences from them to the course followed by former Phariseic Synhedrists themselves, in those days, namely, when they happened to be in the majority, or only in a strong, determining minority. We will adduce only one out of several instances to demonstrate the incongruity of later Rabbinical theory with earlier Phariseic practice. In the Mishnah, Synh. vi. 4, it is directly asserted that Simeon ben Shetach, who as president of the Synhedrin had eighty witches hanged on one day in Askalon, acted against the established custom of trying only one criminal case a day. He differed, too, from the view held by the " wise doctors " mentioned in that Mishnah, who maintained that women should not be hanged at all. We may state in addition, that he dissented from the later Rabbis also in this respect, that he put those witches to death by hanging, while the Mishnah at least had recognized stoning as the mode of execution of witches (Synh. vii. 4). When we find such practical divergences of older Phariseic courts of justice from later Phariseic-Rabbinical judicial institutions as embodied in the code of the Mishnah, how can we use the latter as authority for ascertaining the criminal practice of the Sadducees in the days when they were in power? It is an indisputable fact that we know very little about the criminal justice of this sect. It is well-nigh enveloped in obscurity. To resort, then, to later Rabbinical theories as proofs for settled judicial norms prevailing in the Jerusalemite Synhedrin of anterior times, must seem impertinent to the inquirer after true historical facts.

To convince the reader that we are not alone in holding such view, we will mention Weiss' relative discussion in his " Dor Dor, etc.," i. p. 151. He declares it evident from diverse instances, that the legal concepts and canons of Rabbis of the post-Synhedrial times can by no means be set down as representing those of the anterior Synhedrin, when the senate was invested with real jurisdiction and punitive authority. He refers there to the trial of Herod for the slaying of Hezekiah (see Jos. Ant. xiv. 9, 4). Surely, he argues, there were not observed in this case the Rabbinically delivered judicial rules, that a delinquent must be forewarned by the two accusing witnesses, and he himself must verbally admit to them his knowledge of the liability to death for the particular crime against which he was warned, else the penalty of death cannot be carried out against him. For, he asks, how can it be supposed that there were then two men found in the whole of Galilee, who had courage enough to stand up and give evidence against the powerful tetrarch of this province?

As another instance of the incongruity of later Rabbinical judicial theories with the practice of the former Synhedrin, Weiss quotes a case of execution by burning to death of an adulteress from a priestly family (by the enactment of Lev. xxi. 9), attested as an actual occurrence by a Rabbi of the earlier period,—the latter part of the first century C. E. The way in which this doctor reports the execution to have been managed, conflicts with that theoretically adopted by the other Rabbis, and which is indeed laid down as the norm in the Mishnah (see B. Synh. f. 52 and 53).

With this author's congenial view we will close this dissertation, hoping that its leading idea of the practical application by the Synhedrin of the statute of Numbers xv. 30, 31, in cases of antinomian heresy, will meet if not with the unqualified assent, at least with the appreciation of the thinking, critical reader.

[35] Even Keim, who strains himself to the utmost to represent Jesus' position in reference to the Law half-conservatively, concedes that "the moral precepts dominate in the Sermon on the Mount, even in Matt. v. 33, 37, just as they do in the controversy ib. xv. 3 sq., and in the speech to the young man, ib. xix. 17; comp. also ib. xxii. 34 sq." We agree with him on the domination of the moral precepts, but have to assert it as being exclusive of all ceremonial laws. This he himself almost directly admits towards the end of his work, in vol. vi. p. 401, where he says: "The Law . . . had long lain on the ground as breaches made by his prowess. This he has accomplished by laying stress merely on the moral truths of the Law and disposing of the Old Testament like one who has authority."

[36] A considerable number of celebrated critics, quoted by Keim, l. c. iii. 322, regard these two verses as a later Jewish Christian, anti-Pauline interpolation.

[37] This estimation occurs also in Ecclesiasticus, xxix, 11, 12, only that no reference is there made to the future world.

[38] It is true, Jesus gave the cry of repentance, at times at least, the turn, not of actual sorrow for real religious and moral delinquencies, but of a change of mind from being insusceptible to the belief in his Messiahdom, to espousing his cause with that reliance which he gave out to be so fully justified by his miraculous works. In the same sense he even uttered his reproach against the disbelievers in John the Baptist; see Matt. xxi. 32. Yet for all this we see that he invariably made use at least of the term repentance as the nominal subject of his utterances. By so doing he but entered upon the commonly prevailing notion, that the realization of the Messianic hopes depended on it.

[39] That Jesus should not have held an absolute end of heaven and earth in the times of Messiah, as Keim l. c. iii. p. 301 contends, we can not approve. Matthew xxiv. 3, 35,

are too decided evidences to the contrary. Furthermore, Jewish tradition had too confidently derived this view and belief from Isa. lxv. 17 and lxvi. 22, and also the Christianity after Jesus had too firmly grasped it (see Rev. xxi. 1; 2 Peter iii. 13), to suppose that he remained strange to or discountenanced it. The less so when we bear in mind, that the second Isaiah was apparently his favorite for his own Messianic inquiries. Alone the adoption and employment of the phrase in question in the noted passage of Matthew, which recurs again ib. xxiv. 35, is sufficient evidence that he was well conversant and even impregnated with the popular Jewish notion of the destruction and recreation of the world in the Messianic period.

[40] We would conjecture that even in Matt. xi. 13 the word heos "until," is a false Greek translation of the original. This particle of time gives an intolerable sense. It is much rather supposable that the original had the Hebrew or Chaldaic preposition "le" attached to the name of John, or to yemoth "times," in connection with this name. As an example corresponding to the original reading we here suggested, may serve the Talmudical sentence, kol hannebhiim lo nisnabbeu ela limoth hammashiach, "all the prophets prophesied only for the times of Messiah" (B. Synh. f. 99). The particle "le" in such a construction denotes "for" or "toward." The Greek translator, we surmise, misunderstood this particle, and rendered it with 'heos.' That by substituting le, "for," the context gains a much better sense, is clear. Jesus wished, then, to convey that the olden prophets pointed to the period of John, whom he introduces in the following verse 14, as Elijah revived. He may accordingly have referred in mind, in vv. 13, 14, to Malachi iii. 23.

[41] The gospel accounts of controversies held by Jesus with Scribes and Pharisees are on the whole very suspicious. While occasional collisions and altercations with some pious sages of the Jewish people have doubtless occurred, we cannot accept as authentic the representation of a systematic conflict with them, such as the gospels put forth.

As worse than suspicious, even as ludicrous, we must declare the report of a commission of Scribes and Pharisees being purposely deputed by the Jerusalemite authorities to the Galilean abode of Jesus, to inquire into the cause, why "his disciples neglected the tradition of the elders" in not washing their hands before meals (Matt. xv.).

Not wishing to argue here on the production by the later and less reliable Luke and Mark of Jerusalemite doctors on the scene of Jesus' Galilean ministry, in instances in which

Matthew mentions merely Pharisees and Scribes (comp. Mark iii. 22 with Matt. xii. 24; and especially Luke's "Pharisees and doctors of the Law from all Galilee, Judaea and Jerusalem," v. 17. [see on the latter also Keim, l. c. iii. 215] with "certain of the Scribes" in the corresponding account of Matthew ix. 3), we will confine ourselves to a reflection on the above relation of Matthew.

. Is it conceivable, we ask, that an authoritative embassy of Scribes and Pharisees came all the way from Jerusalem—it was at least a three days' journey; see Josephus, Life, sect. 52—to investigate Jesus' attitude regarding one Phariseic-Rabbinical custom, the washing of hands before meals?

Had the commission been for a general investigation of his public activity and teachings, we might credit it. Especially if, as Keim proposes, it took place towards the close of the Galilean activity, and previously to his journey to Jerusalem, late in the autumn of 34 C. E. At this juncture many grave objects calling for a serious inquisition had accumulated against him. But that the authorities of Jerusalem should have held it important enough to dispatch an embassy of inquisitors to Galilee for the apostles' omission of hand-washing, which was merely a late Phariseic-Rabbinical observance, is for us impossible to believe. We have, despite Keim's unquestioned acceptance of it as "certainly and manifoldly attested" (l. c. iv. p. 17), to reject it as most inauthentic.

The more so when we hold in view, that in Jesus' time the rite of hand-washing before eating can hardly have been commonly adopted by the Jewish people, so that its neglect by Jesus' disciples might be reproved by the Rabbinical authorities as a religious dereliction. There is a well warranted relation preserved in the Talmuds (B. Sabb. f. 14; Jer. Sabb. f. 3), that Hillel and Shammai, the scholarchs of Jerusalem in Herod's time, established the rule that priests should have to wash their hands before eating their consecrated food, the Terumah, even if they were not conscious of being defiled by any contact with unclean things. It was one of the many preventive restrictions, peculiar to the punctilious Phariseic Rabbinism, that laid such superior stress on Levitical purity. That it must needs have taken some time before this rule of the scholarchs could gain a fairly wide acceptance, even among the priests of the Phariseic sect, may safely be anticipated. And that the Sadducean priests who were doubtless in the majority, will not have allowed themselves to be dictated to on that point by Rabbinical authorities whose statutes they otherwise, on the whole, discountenanced, admits of no question, either. There is every reason to assume that, after it had once been firmly established, some austere casuists in the schools of Jerusalem—the names of the authors are not transmitted—proposed that the same restriction which those scholarchs had enacted for priests, should prevail with lay people as well. They too should observe it before eating their meats, though profane and not really requiring such scrupulous care.

Whether the motive for this later ordinance was a reverent regard for holy things, namely, as it is set forth in B. Cholin f. 106, to inure the priests, seeing that ablutions were required even of laymen before eating their profane meats, to be the more exact in regard to the rite of hand-washing for their consecrated portion; or whether it was urged by a mere pious rivalry with the priests and the intent of observing the same rule of purity as was ordained for them, this much must at all events be allowed by all, that it cannot have been passed long before Jesus' activity, if at all before his time. For the view we advanced above on the original restriction, that from the theoretical legislation to the general practical introduction of a rite, a considerable time must elapse, surely holds no less as to the second. Accordingly it will not be amiss to aver, that very few of the Jewish lay people knew of this second restriction, which, by the way, passes in the Talmud as a "statute of the Wise" (B. Cholin f. 106). The custom became, it is true, general at a later time. But at the period of Jesus it had positively not become so yet. It may not even have been enacted anterior to or even during Jesus' lifetime, so that we could expect it to have then been observed by the Jewish people at large.

How, then, could Jesus' disciples and he himself have been made subjects of recrimination for its neglect? Furthermore, if the hand-washing before common meats was, as the Talmud suggests (see above), instituted for habituating the priests to greater exactness of purity with their own consecrated meats, it is even possible that in Galilee, where there were no priests (see Rashi in Nedarim f. 18), the necessity of such legislation did not appear at all, and that consequently the rule that had its origin in Jerusalem, gained no acceptance in that province, in Jesus' or at any other time. And if the Rabbis and other pious people of Galilee emulating them, did not know anything of it, or, at any rate, saw no necessity of observing it, were, we ask, the fishermen and other unlearned folks who formed Jesus' narrower and wider circles, expected to know and heed it?

Again, let us say, if at a discussion in a later Babylonian academy the authority of the rite of hand-washing for common meats was freely questioned, because it was thought contradictory to the original Shammaic and Hillelic ordinance which was expressly passed for priests only (see B. Chagigah f. 18; comp. also Tosifta Berachoth vi. 3: "en netilath yadayim lecholin"), is it reasonable to suppose that any one in Jesus' time, when the additional Phariseic restriction could at best have but recently been introduced, was authoritatively called to account for omitting it?

It is true, that a case of violent inquisition for the rejection of this rite, is reported in the Mishnah as having occurred within the province of Judaism itself. A Rabbi, Elazar ben Chanoch, is said to have been excommunicated, probably by Gamaliel II., the scholarch of Jamnia, who held this office from about 80 to 120 C. E., for disputing the obligation of hand-washing before profane meats (Aduyoth v. 6). But it has to be borne in mind that not only may such excess, due to the vehement temper of Gamaliel and other peculiar circumstances which cannot here be set forth, have been the only one perpetrated within the old Rabbinical jurisdiction as regards that rite, but, mainly, that stern measures of legal interference of this later time cannot be held out as an indication, that the same severe procedure or even only verbal reprobations on the part of the religious authorities, were entailed by the opposition to that rite at the much earlier period in which Jesus lived and taught. For in the latter's time the rite can at best, as we have shown above, have been in a state of incipient acknowledgment by the Jewish people. Persecution for its neglect can therefore not possibly be set down as having occurred so early.

We admit that a rigorous enforcement of the rite was attempted by Phariseic-Rabbinical authorities at the more advanced time when the first gospel was written. The author of Matthew—he wrote according to Hausrath, 'N. T. Times,' ii. p. 106, during the Jewish war; according to Strauss, 'New Life of Jesus,' some time after the destruction of the Temple—may have noticed in Jewish society cases of inquisition for the omission of that rite. Wishing to add another point of collision between the Master and the much berated Pharisees, this Evangelist would copy, as may be supposed, from those instances which he witnessed in his own time, and transfer one of them back to Jesus.

To antedate one of those occurrences with such combination, so as to set the Pharisees of Jesus' time in the worst possible light, was no matter of conscience with that gospel writer.

⁴² It must at the first sight certainly appear strange that the Pharisees are in the gospels represented as being such rigorous Sabbatarians, while we know that the Sadducees and Essenes were yet stricter in the Sabbath observance. As to the latter it is attested at least by Josephus, that they were more punctilious in it than any other class of the Jewish people (Wars, ii. 8, 9). In illustrating their Sabbath rigor he says : " They not only get their food ready the day before, that they may not have (or, be tempted) to kindle a fire on that day, etc." If this account means anything as peculiar to the Essenic sect,—for surely all the other Jews would consider kindling fire on the Sabbath as grave a violation as the Essenes,—it can mean only that with them all vessels had to be removed from the heating apparatus before the Sabbath, and were not permitted to be left there for keeping the food warm during the day.

In this respect they exceeded indeed the Sabbath scrupulosity of the Pharisees. For these were indulgent enough to allow for the comfort of having warm food on the Sabbath day. The third and fourth chapters of the Mishnah of the Sabbath treatise—if we may conclude back from this later Rabbinical compilation to the custom of the Pharisees in Josephus' time—show their mild position in that regard. Both the sterner school of Shammai and the moderate one of Hillel appear to have been agreed, that it was permissible to put pots with eatables on cooking apparatus before the beginning of the Sabbath, and leave them there for use during the day, as long as there was no fear that one might be tempted to rake up the unconsumed fuel, with which the fire was made and kept up on Friday. Likewise were evidently all the Rabbinical doctors of one mind on the permissibility of keeping food warm by wrapping such material around the vessels as would best preserve the heat : only that no material should be used that would increase the heat by the process of condensation.

It is thus plainly seen that the Rabbis—and they were on the whole identical in religious views and practices with the learned Pharisees of Josephus— were by no means so extreme in the Sabbath observance as the Essenes. Their view was, that the day should be distinguished by substantial comfort. The day should not be one of mortification of the body, but of serene delight. They therefore sought out different devices by which comfort and delight might be attained without any infringement of the law.

The mystical Essenes, on the other hand, dissented from such view. They held it perhaps an impairment of their most significant 'Hebdomad' (compare also Philo's frequent descanting on the number Seven in connection with the Sabbath) to disturb the mind on the Sabbath by the sensuous occupation of looking after the nourishment of the body, and providing for a meal that would become more palatable by a certain suitable temperature and attendance. Nor were the Pharisees so extreme as these ascetics, with regard to handling vessels on the Sabbath. Josephus attributes to them that "they dare not remove any utensil from its place" (ib.). That the historian knew from his own experience and observation that the Pharisees were not so strict as all this, is already clear from the contrast by which he sets forth this Essenic restriction. We certainly do not know exactly how the Phariseic authorities of his time had legislated concerning the handling and removal of utensils on the Sabbath. The decided relaxation regarding this point which is reported in B. Sabbath f. 123, as having been suggested by the Rabbis of the second century C. E. can, for the continuous variation of legislation upon it which is mentioned there, not be taken as a standard by which to judge of the respective view and practice that prevailed among the Phariseic doctors of Josephus' time. Yet thus much is certain that, however strict they may then have been as to the matter in question, their severity did not equal the Essenic which Josephus delivers. We may take it for granted that the Pharisees would never countenance such restrictions as could accomplish no religious ends, at the same time when they would deprive the Israelite of the feeling of serene delight and comfort, which was to be, in the Phariseic-Rabbinical mind, the concomitant of Sabbatic rest.

After the foregoing citations and arguments, the query may pertinently be put: Why are the Pharisees so prominently marked out in the gospels as austere and minute observers of the Sabbath, whereas the Essenes had notably a much stricter view of its law, and it should consequently be expected that Jesus collided with them at least as well on questions of its observance? In answer to it we would say, that the Essenes, being a retired, contemplative folk, aimed at evading every polemical encounter as much as might be, even in cases in which their own sense of the sanctity of life was provoked by any contrary conduct of coreligionists from the other sects.

As to Jesus himself who was without any doubt partially imbued with Essenism, he too will, we can readily understand, have purposely avoided every dogmatical conflict with them. Whether or not his points of doctrinal contact with them exceeded those of contrast, this may in any case be asserted with confidence, that there are many close doctrinal relations with them discernible in the essence of his teachings. This spiritual accord, though only partial, would surely prevail on him to eschew every dispute with members of their sect on any subject of religious practice. This accord, too, explains easily the absence of reports of polemics between him and this sect on questions of Sabbath observance, concerning which he differed with them so essentially, as is apparent to every one setting off his interpretation of it against the most rigorous one entertained by them.

The congeniality between Essenism and primitive Christianity so manifoldly attested, may withal be regarded as the cause why no disputations have come down to us as having occurred between one another, even in instances, such as slights of the Sabbath, which called for sharp rebuke by such strict observers as the Essenes were. It is this congeniality, too, that goes far to account for the circumstance, that Essenic sectaries are never brought into the arena by the Evangelists. This circumstance must inevitably attract the notice of every thinking person. It is surely as curious as it is significant. To us it signifies, by reason of abundant indications to support our notion, the congeniality of the body of the pristine Christians with that sect. There is indeed nothing that might explain the absence of collisions in the N. T. writings between both classes or any allusions to the Essenic sect, so well as this our point of view.

Here it seems to us opportune to cite the respective interesting remarks of Bunsen, "The Hidden Wisdom," etc.: "The mysterious fact that the Essenes are not mentioned at all in Scripture is best explained by the assumption, that in the first century of our era they were more or less identified with the Christians."——

As to the Sadducees, they too will, from the following, appear as more rigorous in regard to the Sabbath law than the Pharisees. Though they doubtless disregarded many, if not all, Rabbinical rules of Sabbatism (Shebuth), as well as, perhaps, the Rabbinical division of Sabbath labor into thirty-nine chief occupations (aboth) with their correlative derivates (toledoth), and no doubt rejected also the Rabbinical institution of the imaginary combinations called Erubh, by which artificial devices the punctilious Pharisees claimed to renew the Sabbath limit of 2,000 cubits from their local terminus, as also to create a dispensation for carrying things from one precinct to another (see on this Geiger, 'Sadducees and Pharisees,' p. 21), we are yet warranted in declaring them stricter in guarding the Mosaic Sabbath law from violation than the Pharisees were. Their standpoint was the direct Mosaic one, as it resulted from the literal sense of the respective commands. They rejected as not obligatory all the traditional accretions of Phariseism, existing in the form of new observances or preventive regulations. They were e. g. opposed to the Temple rites, on the feast of Tabernacles, of "libation of water" (nissuch hammayim), and the circuits made round the altar of burnt-offerings with willow branches, which were shaken in the hands of the bearers (wherefor the rite was called "chibbut arabhah;" see Graetz, Monatsschrift, Nov. 1887), and put up at the sides of the altar after the circuits were over.

In their stiff literalism they would accept no Phariseic addition to the written ritual. This alone had obligatory authority with them. Consequently they repudiated also those two rites, neither of which was prescribed in the Torah. They would though, as a rule, not omit them when they were officiating themselves as Temple functionaries. For they had to fear the indignation of the masses of the people who were Phariseic in religious belief and usage, if they designedly left them off. Yet their theoretical opposition to them they never concealed. And occasionally it may have happened, as we have an account at least of one ostensible slight committed with the water-libation (see B. Sukkah f. 48), that they gave it even a practical expression.

Their protest against the use of willow branches in the Temple on the feast of Tabernacles they exhibited specially by contending, that the rite must by no means take place on a Sabbath on which any one day of the feast might fall. Not even on the seventh, on which the solemnity reached its height by the discharge of seven circuits, should it be allowed (see B. Sukkah f. 43). The grounds on which they based their view were supposably no other than that the handling of willow branches was unlawful on the Sabbath, because they were an article set apart for use on working days only ("muktse," according to the Rabbinical terminology, which restriction they apparently held in common with the Rabbis). This shows certainly a much keener apprehension of the Sabbath restraint than the Pharisees had. To these the "chibbut arabah" ranked as high as any other of the Temple rites, before which the Sabbath law had to give way. They regarded it, we suppose, as an act "needful for the service of God" (tsorech Gaboah), and to be therefore performed on the Sabbath, like the entire sacrificial ritual of the holocausts ordained in the Pentateuch for this day (Numb. xxviii. 9, 10).

The Sadducees, on the other hand, distinguished between those Temple rites prescribed in the Law for the Sabbath, and others that were only traditional. To the former were counted the perpetual holocausts of the morning and evening, together with two additional ones for the morning (Numb. l. c.); the incense offering, directly ordered for every day, and certainly inclusive of the Sabbath (Ex. xxx. 7, 8); and the attendance on the lights of the candlestick, also distinctly understood from Exodus l. c. as obligatory on every day. It was to the Sadducees self-evident that all the labors required for those parts of the ritual—and there was, indeed, a considerable number of manual operations otherwise prohibited on the Sabbath connected with the victims of the morning and evening—should be done on the Sabbath, because they were integrant parts of the Divinely instituted worship. The traditional rites, however, could with this sect not avail to make the Sabbath law recede before them. The same principle upon which they opposed those rites in general, namely, that God has not ordained them in his written Law so as to be obligatory on the Israelites, was, we suppose, applied in their refusal to permit their execution on the Sabbath, if this implied a breach of its law.

We hold it even uncertain whether they allowed circumcision, or the Passover ritual, on the Sabbath. For though these were most prominent Mosaic institutions, there was yet no provision in the Law that they should take place also on the Sabbath. This becomes the more probable when we compare the Karaite inhibition of the same rites on the Sabbath (see Fuerst, 'History of Karaism,' i. p. 132). The Karaites were the doctrinal kin of the Sadducees. And though we may not be perfectly warranted to conclude from those later Mosaic literalists to the earlier literal legalists, the Sadducees, with regard to every custom and doctrine, there is yet all likelihood that the Karaites had a tradition from their doctrinal parents on the two before-mentioned points of religious usage.

Let us adduce another instance illustrative of the Sabbatic rigor of the Sadducees. They were evidently emphatically opposed to the Phariseic custom of cutting the firstling-sheaf on the eve of the Sabbath, as it was invariably customary with the Pharisees, if the second day of Passover—the Omer-day—fell on the Sabbath. According to the Sadducean interpretation of the relative Mosaic text the sheaf-ceremony had always to take place on the day after the weekly Sabbath, as likewise the feast of Weeks had always to be on a Sunday. Accordingly, their time of cutting the ceremonial sheaf never clashed with the Sabbath observance. It was always at the close of the weekly Sabbath. The Pharisees, however, holding fast to their interpretation of the Scripture text by which the day for offering the sheaf was the second day of Passover, on whatever week-day this might fall, absolutely allowed its cutting even on the Sabbath eve, if that day of the feast began with it. The man appointed for reaping the ceremonial sheaf had to call out demonstratively three times, "on this Sabbath?", if the second day of the feast happened to fall that way. This was done in a spirit of polemics and refutation aimed at the Sadducees, who insisted on Sunday being the invariable, lawful sheaf-day (Mishnah, in B. Menachoth f. 65).

From the challenging phrase "on this Sabbath?" we infer that there were constant carpings between the two sects as to the permissibility of cutting the sheaf on the Sabbath. The Sadducees, we suppose, decidedly declared it a sinful labor and a needless profanation of the day, since the Torah does not order it done immediately on the night previous to the oblation, were it even that the Scripture text admitted of the Phariseic perception.

We readily concede that in this case there was a great deal of sectarian animosity mixed up with the stern reverence for the Sabbath. Yet the opposition which the Sadducees made, bore at least the outward aspect of such reverence. Moreover, it certainly appears from all the other foregoing propositions that they had a very austere perception of the Mosaic prohibition of labor, surpassing, as to the letter of the Law at least, that of their antagonists, the Pharisees.

Why then are they not even once mentioned and held up as Sabbatic extremists in the N. T. writings, the same as the Pharisees, with whom Jesus or his apostles collided? We can account for it only by the circumstance, that the Sadducees were the Temple party whose intercourse with the populace was very rare. Jesus and his followers supposably met very seldom with any of that aristocratic class. Whereas the learned Pharisees were scattered all over the land. Their precepts were followed by the unlearned bulk of the Jewish people, though in some instances not completely in accordance with the standard of exactness to which they had raised them for themselves. The generality of the Jewish people were especially strict in the observance of the Sabbath. As it is once remarked in the Talmud : " While Israel—the am ha-arets " common people"—are to be suspected in matters pertaining to the observance of the Sabbatic year, they are irreproachable as to the proper heeding of the Sabbath restraints." The laymen did, then, not lag behind the learned in Sabbatic strictness. Phariseic or Phariseically trained and habituated Sabbath observers, Jesus will consequently have encountered in every town or village of his own native district, too. And it was such who would unremittingly resent any open breach of the Sabbath law, whether the written or the traditional. Of the Saducean party, however, he may never have met one during his Galilean activity. The passage in Matt. xvi. 1, 12, naming Saducees together with Pharisees, we have to declare as inauthentic. This does indeed not imply that Jesus must, whilst he lived in Galilee, have been unacquainted with the doctrines professed and the position occupied by the Saducees. No, indeed. We have on the contrary every reason to suppose that he learned about them at his previous stay at the Jordan, with John the Baptist ; see them mentioned in connection with the latter, Matt. iii. 7. Yet personal disputes with representatives of that sect he cannot be thought to have had till the latter part of his public career, when he entered the province of Judea and the city of Jerusalem. Even here he seems to have had but one doctrinal controversy with them. It was that about the resurrection, which the Saducees denied (Matt. xxii. 23 sq.). This controversy was probably started by them, as Geiger has rather ingeniously suggested (Judaism and its History, I. p. 118), because " he had emphasized the resurrection so decidedly by asserting the imminence of the future world, the kingdom of Heaven." Let us observe here in passing, that this is not at all an unlikely motive for the Saducean opposition to him, though it was by no means the only one. It may even be that the persecution of other early Jesus-believers was partly owing to the latent rancor which the Saducean sect cherished against them, for openly and continuously putting forth not only the resurrection of their Master, but the earnest and eager expectation of his second coming, at which period the general Messianic resurrection would occur.

On this occasion of discussing the Sabbatic standpoint of the Sadducees, it will be pertinent to annex some information on the Sabbath observance of the Dositheans, a Samaritan sect. It is known that the Sadducees and Samaritans had some sectarian doctrines in common. Both denied resurrection. With regard to the Pentateuch it is to be noted, that the former repudiated all traditional observances and statutes, attributing obligation but to those of the written Law. [See Josephus, Ant. xiii. 10, 6; 16, 2, and compare Geiger's partially adverse standpoint in "Urschrift, etc." p. 133 sq. Their maxim was, for all we can gather from the envious Rabbinical sources, that a doctrine, rite, or statute must be Mosaical ("min hattorah," or contained "battorah"), if recognition and obligation are to be claimed for it. Their agreement with the Pharisees on some points of Mosaic textual expositions does not affect the accuracy of Josephus' assertion]. The Samaritans had a similar position in reference to the Pentateuch. They recognized it only as sacred Scripture, rejecting all the other books of the Jewish canon as not having this character. In view of this doctrinal kinship between the Sadducees and the Samaritans, it will certainly seem appropriate to mark in this place the perception of the Sabbath law by a sect belonging to the latter nationality. Dositheus, a Samaritan reformer,—represented by Origen, 'Against Celsus,' as a Messiah-pretender of the apostolic age, previous to Simon the Magician, but in the Clementine Homilies and the Apostolic Constitutions, as a false apostle, contemporary with Simon,—is by the first-named writer, in his other treatise, 'On the Principles' (cited by Hilgenfeld, l. c. p 157), reported to have interpreted the injunction of Exodus xvi. 29, "abide ye every man in his place, etc.", that it exacts a perfectly still, motionless condition. "Every one," he expounds, "must remain in the same place and position in which he is found on the Sabbath, till evening, that is, if sitting, that he keep sitting, or if lying, that he maintain this posture all day."

Abulfeda (14th century), in his Samaritan Chronicle, asserts of the Dositheans, that they held it unlawful on the Sabbath to drink from brazen or glass vessels, or to feed or water domestic animals: food and water must be placed before them before the Sabbath begins.

⁴³ Hausrath, 'Hist. of N. T. Times,' does not distinguish as to the time of both controversies. He names them together with the disciples' neglect of fasting and the conversing of Jesus with publicans and sinners (Mark i. 35-39), as having brought on the open opposition to him by the Rabbis of Capernaum. As in the opposition to his ministry the officials of Antipas had a common interest with the Pharisees, that writer further advances, that he was by this circumstance driven out of Capernaum (Mark iii. 7), and "his life was from that time a wandering one."

⁴⁴ The "deuteroproton" of Luke vi 1, which is in our English version rendered "on the second Sabbath after the first," is not yet sufficiently explained. Keim finds Scaliger's interpretation, that it meant "the first Sabbath after the second day of Easter" (Passover), as the most probable of all.

⁴⁵ Graetz, History, iii. third edition, makes a short cut of the relation in Matt. xii. 1-8. He declares the entire narration as a Pauline tendency-interpolation. For, reasons he, "if, as it is given out in v. 8, man is lord of the Sabbath, then the Sabbath is on the whole abolished." But, we protest (see our text), Jesus did in that verse not at all express a general human view, but an exaggerated Messianic one about himself. Graetz adheres to the notion, that Jesus "did not at all irritate the existing Judaism. Consistently with it he must pronounce all antinomian passages credited to Jesus, interpolated! So does he, indeed, declare the passage in which Jesus exalts himself above the Temple (Matt. xii. 6). In keeping with that notion is also his peremptory judgment, that "the authenticity of the Sermon on the Mount is more than suspicious," mainly because "it partly conveys Jesus' intention of opposing his own new doctrine to the Law."

⁴⁶ Keim, l. c p. 365, interprets the meaning of this sentence, that he wished to say, "here is a higher dispensator for the disciples than the temple is for the priests."

⁴⁷ In his claim of supernatural power in healing the sick and the possessed, Jesus proceeded on the pretension of his divine-like Messiahism. By virtue of this he presumed to have the faculty to forgive sins, and thus remove the cause of the disease.

Bodily ailments and maladies as well as suffering in general, were in ancient Judaism mostly regarded as afflictions for sin, or at least as Divine visitations for some object of discipline. The causal interconnection of sickness and sin naturally evolved from passages of the Pentateuch, such as Ex. xv. 26, xxiii. 25, Lev. xxvi. 14-16, Deut. vii. 15, xxviii.

15, sq. It is again markedly expressed in Isa. xxxviii. 17. And it has, further, been sagaciously supported by a Rabbi of the third century, from the parallel occurrence of both terms in Ps. ciii. v. 3 (B. Nedarim, f. 41). The ground-sentiment of the majority of the Rabbis of antiquity seems to have been, hakkol bide shamayim "all things are with and come from God," that is, are disciplinary dispositions of God. Diseases, all sorts of them, are included. Even those distempers originating, as it was believed, from stellar (fatalistic), or elemental (accidental), or even from magic influences (such as the evil eye, or the fiendish work of witches and demons), point to God as the first designing and dispensing Cause. This is the gist of Talmudical passages like those of B. Baba Metsia f. 107; Ketuboth f. 30; Nedarim f. 49; Baba Bathra f. 144; Cholin f. 7, and others. In the last place a Rabbi is even credited with the extravagant sentence, that "no one bumps his finger but it is so decreed in Heaven." In the name of the same Rabbi there is frequently produced in the Talmud the saying: "All things are dispensed by God, only affections of the body entailed by exposure to cold (and hot) air are purely casual," that is, independent of God's disposition.

(There is surely no consistency in the two quoted sentences of the same Rabbi. But they were evidently not intended to be strictly dogmatic. The Rabbi was happy to have found for each a corresponding Scripture accommodation, from which he could interpret either. This sufficed him for exhibiting his sayings as brilliant pieces of Scripture exegesis. That others should ever refer to them with a doctrinal view, was supposably far from his mind).

It may yet be mentioned that other Rabbis did evidently not agree with him on the hypothesis, that suffering from exposure to cold or heat is not ordained by God; see B. Ketuboth l. c. It may, farther, be pertinent to observe here that it is on the whole most difficult to positively decide how the generality of the learned Jews have, in the few centuries before and after Jesus, thought and believed concerning the various casualties and ills which flesh is heir to. While we prefer to assume from a number of Rabbinical passages, that those doctors disavowed the theory that bare accidents could, independently of God's Providence, cause bodily injuries or sickness,—and this would be in keeping with Scripture that characterizes even accidents as Divine causations; compare chiefly Ex. xxi. 13,—we are yet, on the other hand, confronted by contrary Rabbinical sentiments, also embodied in the Talmud. In Jer. Sabb. f. 14, the following is proposed: "In ninety-nine cases out of a hundred, it is not God's interference to which fatal bodily injuries and suffering are due, but mere accident, such as the effect of the evil eye, self-exposure to excessive cold or heat, or other indiscretions, referrible to man alone."

Jesus had evidently assimilated in his mind the pre-eminently Jewish view, that bodily suffering is inflicted by God, and that with a disciplinary purpose, chiefly in punishment of some offence committed against him. That sickness is the result of sin,—this idea underlies his argument in Matt. ix. 5, 6. See also Keim l. c. iii. 214, who says regarding the case produced there: "Jesus looked upon his illness as the result of sin," and quotes as recurrences of this sentiment, Matt. xii. 45, Luke xiii. 2, 11, John v. 14, ix. 1. (We have to note, however, that the last-named passage shows only its prevalence with Jesus' disciples, not with himself. He, on the contrary, disabuses their mind of the notion that the blindness of the man in question was due to sin). As a religious theory it was apparently in accord with the pious perceptions of his Jewish contemporaries, or, at any rate, of most of them. He only gave it an obnoxious turn by applying it to his pretension of being able to forgive sins, in his presumed capacity of the Messiah. As such, he conveyed in his argument, he could surely cure diseases. Their cause—sin —being once removed by the use of his supernatural power in dispensing pardon, the effect—sickness—must be lifted of itself. It was surely not difficult for his orthodox hearers to get at the drift of his argumentation.

As to his pretension of healing the possessed, that is, casting the evil spirit or spirits out of the victims on whom they had fastened themselves, this too had in his mind a Messianic bearing. By compelling the fiends, by the force of the spirit of God within him (see Matt. xii. 28), to leave the body, and thus beating Satan and diminishing his fatal sway, he claimed to pave the way to the kingdom of God and the exclusive rule of the Spirit of God, or, as it is indicated in v. 28, to have actually brought on that kingdom. See Hausrath, 'N. T. Times,' ii. p. 190, who observes on the expostulation in Matthew ib.: "It is his opinion that the casting out of devils by the Spirit of God proves the actual advent of the kingdom of God, and this assumption Jesus supports by the farther reference, that his breaking into the house of the strong man—the devil—clearly shows that the strong man had been previously bound, and that consequently the kingdom of the devil had come to an end."

[48] To accurately determine in such passages of Rabbinical free and easy exposition or narrative, whether the term Minean was to denote a pagan,—Roman or other,—or a Gentile Christian, will forever be a futile attempt. The Rabbinical relations were put down or transcribed with utter indifference to historical correctness. We have therefore to use the greatest caution in utilizing them.

How difficult it is to reach an authentic conclusion as to the meaning of Minean employed in the Rabbinical nomenclature, will appear from the following. Immediately after that colloquy between Akiba and Tinnius Rufus, the Midrash contains a dispute on the validity of the rite of circumcision, alleged to have been had between a Rabbi of the second century C. E. and a 'philosopher.' The objection which the latter raised to it was, that "if God wanted circumcision, it cannot be seen why he did not command it already to Adam?" From the juxtaposition of both the colloquy and this dispute we should judge that the 'philosopher' was likewise intended for a cultured or philosophically educated Roman, such as the governor Tinnius Rufus. And surely would we in the premises, from the title 'philosopher' which the olden Rabbis so often used interchangeably with 'Minean,' be justified to detect such a one in that personage. Yet when we, on the other hand, learn from external literature that the same argument attributed in the Midrash to the philosopher, was in substance, as it will appear by and by, frequently employed by Gentile Christians, we are at once determined to change our opinion and assume, that the personage styled there philosopher, was a Gentile convert to Christianity. We consequently become even further disposed to conjecture,—though there is no intrinsic cause for calling in question the arguments attributed in the Midrash to Rufus in his colloquy with Akiba; see also above p. 82,—that the narrator in that Rabbinical compilation of free and easy expositions had even in relating this colloquy no other impression on his mind, than the one which had come to him from actual hearing, or from the known fact, that Gentile Christians were used to attack both the Sabbath and circumcision with arguments such as he reproduced there. The reason why he connected Tinnius Rufus with arguments against the Sabbath, though he may have mentally alluded to Gentile Christians, is easily suggested to have been, because that governor was traditionally known as a frequent disputant on Jewish ritualistic and doctrinal subjects. By introducing him there as a questioner on the Sabbath, there would be gained the advantage of variation in the narratives. In reality, however, he may have alluded in his mind, in this instance as well as in the subsequently produced invective against circumcision, to Gentile Christians.

That this class frequently used the above-stated argument against circumcision, appears from Justin's Dialogue with Trypho, ch. xix. There, it is true, the objection differs somewhat in form from the one quoted above from the Midrash. It reads: "If circumcision were needed, God would not have created Adam uncircumcised." But this difference is unessential. The attack is substantially the same in both arguments. The validity of circumcision is in both accounts disputed on the ground, that God had not made it a law with the first man of Scripture. See also Otto's commentary in loco, who cites Tertullian, Cyprian, and Lactantius, as having reasoned in the same strain as Justin, in their polemics against the rite of circumcision.

[49] Hausrath, in ranking here the intercourse with publicans and sinners with the rest of Jewish ordinances, betrays a superficiality which we can only indulge in a Christian writer unacquainted with the old Rabbinical literature. There is, to our knowledge, not the slightest trace in that literature of an ordinance as to commerce with publicans. Nor is there a specific one to be found on the commerce with sinners.

Regarding the publicans,—a term used in the New Testament versions that would, however, be much more correctly rendered with the generic name tax-officials,—this averse notice only has come down to us, that they were hated by the ordinary Israelite for their frequent extortions, peculations, and other irregularities committed in their office. Whether Jewish or pagan, they were commonly associated in the thought of the Israelite, of the Phariseic sect and principles at least, with robbers; see especially Mishnah B. Baba Kamma f. 113. They are at times even named in one category and strain with highwaymen; see ib. f. 114, and Sifra f. 91.

That, besides, the heart of the truly religious and patriotic Israelite chafed and even revolted, at once on religious and economical grounds, at the several kinds of oppressive tribute imposed since the Roman institution of the census,—three kinds are named in the Pesikta, sect. Shekalim f. 11: gulgoleth " capitation-tax," arnona (read, annona) " land-tax," and demos, the nature of which is hard to decipher from the name, which has possibly come down in a mutilated form instead of telos " toll " (the last we presume to conjecture in spite of the authenticated frequent use by the ancient Rabbis of the term "demos" in various significance),—is reasonably set forth by Hausrath in the same work.

Even Jesus who, as the gospels bear witness, freely associated with tax-officials, and had even an apostle, Matthew, from this class, implicitly admitted their corrupt ways (Luke iii. 13), classifying them even directly under the generic stigma of sinners (Matt. ix. 13).

Nay, it seems to us that he had at the early part of his public life detested them as much as every other orthodox Israelite. For, in the Sermon on the Mount, he names them in one strain of speech in the category of Gentiles, that is, pagan polytheists; see Matt. v. 46, 47. (Luke has in this parallel, v. 32, "sinners" in place of either publicans or Gentiles). And even in the last days of his career, when he had already habitually been befriending them, he named them yet together with harlots (ib. xxi. 31, 32). This shows, that, though he then doubtless counted a number of publicans in the ranks of professors of his Messiahdom, as must appear from his awarding to them the precedence as to entrance into the Kingdom above the "chief priests and elders" of the Jewish people, he could, from the fact of their generally known and admitted corruption, not help combining them at least with fornicators. The natural conclusion from this juxtaposition of publicans with harlots would even appear to be that, notwithstanding the conversion of a number of publicans to the belief in his Messiahdom, the idea of their being as a class confirmed sinners, irrepressibly suggested itself to his mind and speech even so late as that. This conclusion would result from the bare circumstance of the harlots being placed by the side of the publicans. The former must at that conjuncture have been harlots still, or he would have designated them, as reformed and redeemed persons, under a different name, or at least with a vindicating epithet. So must the publicans, despite his efforts at gaining over a number of them to his Messianic creed, have then as a class practically been as corrupt as they ever were before.

With the generic name 'sinner' the critics of Jesus had, according to Luke xix. 7, branded also Zacchaeus, the chief of the publicans, with whom he had gone to lodge.

How it came that the tax officials were named and even identified with sinners, and in what general or special sense the Hebrew equivalent of this appellation was employed by orthodox Jews in speaking of them, is difficult of exact definition. Graetz (iii. third ed.), distinguishing three different lower and despised classes to which Jesus addressed himself in his public career, viz., the sinners, the custom officers and publicans, and the ignorant from the populace, suggests that those tax officials had "on account of abetting the Roman interests turned their back to the Law, and led a dissolute life." Where he collected this information, he does not state. We, on our part, would, to account for the combination and identification of publicans and sinners in the gospels, hazard the following conjecture.

We presume that in the days of Jesus the orthodox teachers or even laymen nicknamed those of the common people who were marked by habits of lawless violence or of defiant violation of religious laws, *baryone*. This word they probably adopted from the Greek 'barys,' Hebraizing it by affixing the ending 'on.' In two places of the Talmud (B. Synh. f. 37, Taanith f. 23) they are represented as impenitent religious and, doubtless, also moral recreants, and in a third place as a viciously vexatious set (B. Berach. f. 10), with whom the learned and pious would have no intercourse, nay, on whom they would often imprecate that God might take them from the world. Some, again, were charitable enough either to pray to God that he may cause them to repent, or to use personal suasion by which they hoped to bring them to their senses and a change of their evil conduct (see the quoted passages). In a fourth place of the Talmud (B. Gittin f. 56) even the zealots in the revolutionary war against the Romans are designated baryone. That they have drawn forth this stigma from the Rabbis who were mostly for peace and submission to the Romans, already during that war, should convincingly result from the introductory part of this last Talmudical relation, which bears a thoroughly historic stamp.

Now from all these passages combined we conclude that the 'baryone' were in the first centuries of the common era the synonyms for those abandoned sinners from the populace, who had not only rudely set at defiance the religious ceremonial of Israel, but also made no scruple to annoy and exasperate their pious and decent neighbors by different violent demonstrations, or even occasionally to assault their property and even persons. That they thus awakened the deep execration of all the righteous Israelites, and received from them that odious title in return, is not to be wondered at. We propose that it was this kind of violent sinners which the Pharisees ranked both in their thought and speech with the hated tax-officials, since these, too, passed with them, for their violent and fraudulent practices, as equal to robbers. And we further surmise that both the publicans and sinners stood coupled in the original of Matthew respectively as "mochesin" and "baryone." The translator of this gospel into Greek, meeting with the latter name which was neither Hebrew nor Chaldaic, but was adopted from the Greek to signify coarse and fierce religious and moral outlaws, found himself in a quandary how to render it, and resorted to the next best equivalent that should express the currently Jewish stigma. The generic word hamartoloi "sinners" occurred to him as such, and he put it down as the most suitable. While we give this as a mere conjecture, we yet claim for it a greater merit than can consist in Graetz's tracing the word sinners used with publicans in the gospels, to 'abaryanim,' as denoting "violators of the Law." We do not believe, from the very rare occurrence of this later Hebrew word in the Rabbinical literature, that it had gained currency with the learned of old to brand with it Judaic Law-breakers. Why not rather think of the pure Hebrew word "reshaim" or "posheim," as corresponding to those sinners? The word reshaim was currently used by the ancient Rabbis as the opposite of tsadikim "righteous," or kesherim "worthy." Graetz's further proposition that those sinners were "such as had been expelled from the Jewish society for religious transgressions," is destitute of all warrant.

If our above conjecture should be deemed too hazardous, we advance yet another original Jewish concept, as possibly embodied in the hamartoloi "sinners" of the gospels. We allude to the am ha-arets "common people," or, as the olden Rabbis were used to employ this term, an individual of the common people,—provided, of course, that these were already in Jesus' time despised by the learned for levity as to questions of religious purity, the tithes, and the Sabbatic year. Space forbids us to treat at length of the interrelations of the "am ha-arets" and the learned, in the several centuries before and after our era. It would be of great interest at once to the Jewish and Christian intelligent world, if a competent writer undertook to furnish a lucid, critical description of them. We will here briefly state that it is quite possible, that the common people were already in Jesus' time signalized and shunned by the Pharisees as suspects with regard to those three points.

Whether the rule existed already then, that the clothes of an am ha-arets defile a Pharisee (Mishnah, Chagigah ii. 7), to the extent that he would, after coming in contact with them by touching, suspending, carrying them, or by sitting, lying, standing, or leaning on them, be religiously polluted till evening, both in person and as to his own clothes, we do not know. The reason why the clothes of the am ha-arets should be impure to a Pharisee, is in the Talmud stated to be, that his wife might in her own defilement have sat on them. Naturally this rigid restriction must have prohibited any close intercourse and meeting by a Pharisee with an am ha-arets, even in a public place, not to say, at the table. Jesus, having doubtless been held and treated as a "Chabher,"—this as well as the term "Chasid" was the distinctively honorable title of a Pharisee or Pharisaic doctor of the Law, in the mouths of the later Rabbis at least,—would accordingly have properly been censured for sitting down to eat with any of this unlettered class.

Again, we meet with a relative restriction in the Talmud, called forth by the suspicion cast on the am ha-arets for wanting a sufficient seriousness as to tithes. It is: "One must not make converse with an am ha-arets, for fear he would at length give him to eat things from which the tithes had not been separated" (Nedarim f. 20). Yet there is no certainty about the existence of this injunction in Jesus' time, either.

Now, though we cannot adduce any direct evidence from the Rabbinical literature that, on account of various more or less grave suspicions of ceremonial levity resting against the unlettered Jewish people, a decided and open antagonism to these prevailed with the learned already at that early period, we are warranted to infer it from relative gospel accounts. That the Pharisees were then most austere concerning rules of ceremonial purity and the widely ramified tithing, is clear from various statements produced by the evangelists; see especially Matt. xxiii. 23, 25. From this it is fair to conclude that the common people will, at least as to the intricate rules of purity, not have succeeded, even if they had a mind to, to come up to the stern demands of purification as exacted by the Pharisees. These will consequently have been impelled to keep aloof from them as much as possible. The association with them was unavoidably fraught with a continuous doubt of religious purity and apprehension of defilement. That they regarded them as 'sinners' with whom no Chaber should sustain company, is therefore not impossible. This stigma may, then, have been fastened on the common people in the time of Jesus, so that reference was made to them in the reproaches of the Pharisees about his close association with them.

A third interpretation of the 'sinners' whom Jesus had befriended, is yet possible. It is well known that the sick were in the gospels often represented as sufferers on account of sin. In Luke vii., a Pharisee takes exception to Jesus allowing himself to be attended by a female 'sinner,' in the manner set forth in vv. 37, 38. This woman was perhaps known to the Pharisee as afflicted with a disorder like that mentioned in Matt. ix. 20. In this case her touch was ceremonially polluting, and the Pharisee had, from his religious legal standpoint, a perfect right to call Jesus to account for that attendance. Some men and women with such like physical disorders, whose impurity fell partly under the head of direct Mosaic inhibitions, or were partly rigidly construed by the Pharisees from the respective texts of the Pentateuch, may many a time have addressed Jesus with the entreaty to cure them. The healing involving at the same time the forgiving of the sins in punishment of which the bodily affliction was believed to have been visited, it may fairly be supposed that the sinners, named as such with publicans or separately, were meant to be that sort of diseased people.

⁵⁰ Jesus wished to set forth by the illustration in Matt. ix. 15, merely the inconsistency of allowing mournful sentiments to intrude themselves on Messianically transported and exulting souls, such as he implicitly represented those of his disciples to be. The two similitudes following in vv. 16 and 17, Jesus chose with the view of strengthening the illustrative force of the main contrast, in the previous verse, of groom and gloom. He aimed by them to impress more vividly on the criticising disciples of John the impropriety of mixing opposites in the sentiment and usage of life. The illustration in v. 15, should characterize the nuptial feast and the fast as sharp opposites. The two subsequent ones were meant to be nothing but similar instances of striking contrast. He added them as corollaries in the fluency of speech, to show yet more convincingly the correctness of his and his followers' position. That he should have propounded them with any doctrinal purpose, as Canon Farrar opines in his 'The Life of Christ,' ch. xxiv., is unwarranted. This author proposes that the two metaphors in vv. 16 and 17, were to point the dogma, that "the new spirit was to be embodied in wholly renovated forms ; the new freedom was to be untrammelled by obsolete and meaningless limitations ; the spiritual doctrine was to be sundered forever from mere elaborate and external ceremonials."

All this is a mere waste of words, and another example of that author's pompous and profuse diction on the one hand, and, on the other, of his fixed effort at the apotheosis of Jesus with regard to any of his sayings and acts. It is surely going too far to find every metaphor used by Jesus pregnant with the deep meaning of "spiritual doctrine." To contrast old and new by the simile of new wine put in old skins and the reverse, was evidently common among the olden Jews. See Pirke Aboth iv. 27, where the " new skin full of old wine " is to convey the moral, that one's age ought not to prejudice us for or against him in our judgment on his knowing faculty ; for there is often found a youthful person with profound understanding and insight, clearly settled views, and a large fund of well assimilated objects of knowledge, whereas many a full grown or aged one is deficient even in that wisdom, which the experience of many years is expected to impart. The meaning in this simile is, indeed, totally different from that used by Jesus. But the Jewish habit of employing this kind of homely metaphors for contrasts, is not the less shown forth in that Rabbinical sentence. The kindred one attributed to Jesus suggested itself to him in the same way, namely, through common Jewish usage. Such and the like metaphors were readily and easily formed by reflecting persons in a country, where wine-growing was such a prominent pursuit. There is nothing exceptional in the sententious application of them. Nor is there any hidden allusion to Jesus' own spiritual doctrine to be detected in the one employed by him in his reply to John's disciples.

[51] The phrase used here for the performance of the magical cure is, "abad milla." It occurs in the same sense also in B. Synhedrin f. 101. It means essentially, in the Rabbinical phraseology, to 'do a thing that cures.' The ancient Rabbis employed it also for bleeding,—a surgical operation the sanative virtue of which they held so very effectual ; see B. Sabbath f. 129. In the Midrashic passage under notice, as well as in that of Synhedrin l. c., the use of a formula of exorcism is doubtless to be understood by that phrase. The Minean curers—those, namely, of the Christian sect, for there were Essenic ones as well—were Christians of Jewish or other descent, against the medical treatment by whom a Rabbinical prohibition had been passed ; see B. Abodah Zarah, f. 27. Its chief cause was, we hold, because they employed the name of Jesus as a divine being in their healing practices and exorcisms ; comp. Jerus. Sabb. ch. xiv. We treat of all this at large in our work on the Mineans, in the division, ' The Christians as Mineans.'

[52] This sage, Jose, was one of the presidential pair of the theological school of Jerusalem in the Maccabean times. He was one of the sixty Scribes—interchangeably called Chasidim in 1 Maccabees—who were singled out of the

rest of the suppliant delegates pleading before Bacchides and the Jewish high-priest, Alkimos, for justice and peace, to suffer death on one same day (1 Macc. vii. 12-17). It is indeed quite possible that his unscrupulous and pitiless nephew, this same Alkimos, derided him in the manner mentioned in the Midrash. He had when high-priest, as it is said in 2 Macc. xiv. 3, "defiled himself willingly in the times of the intermixture" (namely, with pagans). He had also maligned the adherents of Judas Maccabeus to Demetrius (ib. 6). His uncle, Jose, was his extreme opposite in piety. As a "Chasid of the priesthood" (see B. Chagigah f. 16), he was austere as to ceremonial purity, and surely also very strict in all other Jewish observances. He may, too, have frequently rebuked his nephew for his loose, Hellenizing manner of life. This may have aroused his indignation, which it is to be supposed that he vented on his uncle on the day when he was to suffer martyrdom with the rest of the doomed Scribes, in the mocking way described in the Midrash. Alkimos' appearance on horseback on the Sabbath, as related there, we may safely combine with the affair reported in the before-quoted first book of the Maccabees. He may then have been high on horse in the attendance of the Syrian commander, and designed to make that mockery doubly sensitive to his uncle, by the offence he would give him by such demonstrative disregard of the Sabbath : all this, we surmise, to wreak his vengeance on the rigorous uncle for his former reprobations of his wanton Grecianizing departure from orthodox Judaism.

EXCURSUS A.

Strauss (A New Life of Jesus, i. 291 sq.), who does on the one hand not own an Essenic, that is, ascetic and dualistic standpoint of Jesus, is yet strongly inclined to discover in these instances a spirit of set opposition to the ceremonial service of the Temple : first, that he is not reported to have ever taken part in the Jewish sacrifices, with the exception of the Paschal lamb ; secondly, that he acted, as he did, in the Temple (Matt. xxi. 12 sq. and parallels) ; and, mainly, that the witnesses had testified his disparaging utterance about it (Matt. xxvi. 61). He further supposes, with reference to this utterance, that " it might very easily be the case...that the Jews understood only too well the expression of Jesus about his reforming purpose, and that in this (viz., the purpose of rejecting the material worship of the Temple; and commending and, perhaps, attempting to introduce a spiritual one instead) lay the ground of the accusation against him and of the condemnation of him." Keim, History of Jesus, vi. 20, contends with reference to John iv. 21, that the latter sentiment is a late, unhistorical assertion, and that—Stephen and Mark notwithstanding—Jesus never announced the definitive end of the national worship. In a Note there he suggests that Mark xiv. 58, is copied from Acts vii. 48.

This hypercritical judgment can, however, not stand the test of historical inquiry. Jesus' antagonistic attitude to the established national worship of the Jews, is too well attested for any one to challenge the historicity of his disparaging threats of its cessation or overthrow. We have, in our text, adduced incontrovertible proofs of this antagonism. Let us here bring forward yet another point particularly worthy of note, and which furnishes a very strong additional evidence of it, though only circumstantial. It is, the obvious systematic transmission of it, as though of a typical mark of heredity, through the entire Jewish and Gentile Christian literature, the earlier as well as the later. The opposition to sacrifice being peculiar to, and significant of, the entire body of Christian sectaries of the apostolic and post-apostolic age, it unmistakably points to the original head as its doctrinal author.

That Jesus had really uttered the denunciation with which he was charged by the witnesses (see above), or "one similar in import" (so Edward Zeller), would first of all appear from its repetition by Stephen, a year or two after Jesus' death, in the form reproduced by the witnesses against him: "this Jesus of Nazareth shall destroy this place," viz., at his Parousia. Admitting even provisionally with Zeller and Baur, that the entire narrative of Acts vi. 9 to vii. 60, is unhistorical, and the bare fact of Stephen's execution alone indisputable, are we not at all events justified to trace in Stephen's speech at least the *tradition* of the disparagement by Jesus of the Jewish national Temple service, which the Pauline author of Acts utilized?

That this tradition differed in form in its various reproductions, as will be seen from the following, can surely not detract aught from the merit of our view, that the opposition to the Temple service was *continuous* in Christianity from Jesus onward.

Let us now survey the course of this tradition. The Hellenist Stephen, or the author of Acts speaking in his name, has given forth his relative diatribe in the above-noted narrative of Acts. It is to be remarked, however, that he has not correctly echoed Jesus' sentiment about the Temple. Jesus never thought of assailing the Temple as such, that is, as the central institution of Israel's worship. He held it in awe,—as we have set forth in another paper published a few years ago,—opposing only the sacrificial rites carried on in it. Whereas Stephen's attack is directed against the hand-made Temple, the national-religious edifice, as such. He condemns Israel and with them Solomon himself, for rearing a structure called house of God, for worship, as well as for rejecting the holy Spirit that had spoken through Isaiah (see ib.).

Of about the same tenor as Stephen's may have been Paul's teachings against the Temple, of which the Asiatic Jews accused him (Acts xxi. 28). He propounded at least the same sentiment of "God not dwelling in temples made with hands" (ib. xvii. 24). God dwells to him in the temple of the heart (2 Cor. vi. 16).

These Hellenists have, then, evidently gone in their assaults upon the Temple much beyond Jesus, whose thought was not so far swayed by philosophical speculations, that he should have disdained to employ the Scriptural expression of God dwelling in the Temple (see Matt. xxiii. 21). Yet we may, on the other hand, lay it down as reasonably certain, that they would not have made such polemical onslaughts against it, had they not found a warrant for it in Jesus' authenticated antagonistic attitude towards it. As little as we can believe that Paul would have dared to fiercely derogate and declare as abolished the whole Mosaic Law, had he not found the outlines for such assumption and some single facts of opposition to it in the life and teaching of Jesus, as known to him from extant accounts, so little can we disconnect the Hellenistic Jewish Christian attacks on the Temple from the kindred ones made before by Jesus.

But this opposition was not characteristic of Hellenistic Jewish Christianity alone: It was avowedly one of the cardinal points of heretical doctrine with the Ebionite section as well, and prominently so.

It deserves especial notice that their reverence for the Master was unsurpassed by any sect that ever followed a leader or head. They referred to Jesus and to his spoken word and example, in every question of tenet and usage. In their well-known implacable opposition to sacrifice they adverted to him, too. The later members of this sect, to which the author of the Clementine Homilies unquestionably belongs, quoted him as authority not only against sacrifice, but once even, in the manner of the before-named two Hellenists, Stephen and Paul, against the notion that God was in the Temple (Hom. iii. 49-56). Jesus having to this sect been the "true prophet," his directions had in all questions to be sought, and were actually sought, by them. This was, in truth, a dogmatic rule with them.

Now it may be said that the Ebionites, in their intense Essenic detestation of animal sacrifice, may not have shrunk from many exaggerations relating to Jesus' real position towards the Temple service. This is possible, indeed. Yet for all that is it to be conceived that their reference to him at all as to his hostile attitude to it, was unfounded and false? By no means is such supposition admissible. The real affinity, which may perhaps rightly be called consanguinity, that existed between them and Jesus, the Master, at once precludes it.

We have positively to affirm that for all the eclecticism with which Jesus entered into the body of the Essenic views, doctrines, and customs, with which he familiarized himself either at his stay with the Baptist (even Strauss who very decidedly rejects, l. c. p. 292, an Essenic doctrinal opposition of Jesus to sacrifice, suggests on p. 265 ib. that "Jesus might have learned much from him"), or by reading some works of that sect, which, while its members were bound by oath to the greatest secrecy about their sectarian books (Jos., Wars ii. 8, 7), could yet not hinder novices who left their monkish retreats after the first year, from carrying away with them some copies, and making that use of them which they deemed practicable (comp. Hausrath, N. T. Times, i. p. 165),—it admits of no doubt that he stood in real spiritual sympathy with Essenes and other theosophists of similar principles and tendencies.

That Essenism was, further, well represented in the early Church, will be difficult to dispute. Not only Epiphanius dates the existence of the Ebionites—the Christian Essenes—to the apostolic age (Haer. xxx.), but Paul's polemical references in Ep. Col. ii. seem to Baur (Paul ii. 28) and others, to point to the same sect. Even Ewald, who adheres yet to the notion by which the learned Frankel, too, was captivated, that the Essenes were distinguished by a heightened legalism (see Hist. of Israel, vii.), is of the opinion that there entered into the young Church, in Paul's missionary period, a number from this sect, by which circumstance was brought forward a new influential form of Christianity, viz., Christian Essenism. Allusion to devotees of this new Essenic faction he finds in 1 Cor. vii., Rom. xiv. 2, Col. ii., and suggests also as likely in 2 Cor. x-xiii.

On the marked Essenic traits of James the Just, Jesus' brother, and even of the previous James, the apostle, both of whom were leaders of the early Church, the former having repudiated flesh meat and the latter having, as we tried to demonstrate in Note 34, in the three out of the four apostolic decrees, implicitly coincided in such repudiation, which, again, was sympathetically connected with the rejection of sacrifice, we refer the reader to that same Note. These striking features of early Christianity, showing forth, here directly and there indirectly, a decided, uncompromising opposition to sacrifice, point, to our mind, unmistakably to Jesus as its author and champion within Christianity. From his mouth the disciples undoubtedly inbibed it. And strenuously, too, we hold, they transmitted and propagated it within the fold of the crescent Church.

That also the Nazarenes had adopted Jesus' antagonistic attitude relative to sacrifice, we may take for granted, from our safe apprehension of this sect as close adherents of the Jesus-religion, and withal on the ground of systematic continuity from the Master.

EXCURSUS B.

Religious philosophy as the seat of which we are used to regard Alexandria, had, in the century of Jesus, and doubtless already in the two previous centuries, occupied itself preeminently with clearing Scripture by speculative methods of the anthropomorphic personalism of the Deity, which the plain letter of its numerous passages would convey. We may divide the theories of the Jewish theosophists on this problem into three classes. The one was Philo's, which we will illustrate immediately. The other that adopted by the Hellenistic Jewish Christians of the type of Stephen and Paul, and also by some Gentile Christian Gnostics. The third that of the Ebionites, of the kind to which the author of the Clementine Homilies belonged, who declared all anthropomorphic expressions and, besides, those parts of Scripture incongruous with his religious philosophy, as spurious.

I. PHILO'S POSITION.

Philo was both as to his metaphysical, theistic speculation and that upon the authority of the Law, in striking variance with the simple orthodox standpoint held by the non-philosophical, pious Jews of his age. We will here set forth both his relative views, though the former does not directly bear on our present subject. It will yet essentially aid us in characterizing that celebrated Alexandrian Jewish philosopher.

Philo has by his conception of God as the Absolute, and as being totally abstracted from the finite world and out of any direct relation to it, practically volatilized almost the entire purport of the Mosaic dispensation. His speculative system rested mainly on the then dominating Platonism. But he called to aid also the Pythagorean numbers and other notions of this philosophical school, as well as various Stoic concepts. The name of his Logos—standing for divine Reason or Word—was as well as some other of his theories borrowed from the Stoic sect. His aim was to adapt the Hebrew Scripture to the flourishing Greek philosophy and harmonize both with each other by the way of allegory, just as the renowned medieval philosopher, Maimoni, attempted, in his "Moreh Nebhuchim," to clothe Mosaism in the then stylish garb of Aristotelism and

Neo-Platonism. To remove from Scripture interpretation all traits and traces of human-like action of God, and to insure God's absolute unchangeableness and utter distance from the material world, was the task he, the same as other Jewish religious philosophers before and after him, had set himself to. In order to it he invented, or rather utilized, the philosophical theory of dynameis "divine powers," evolved from, and kept in a certain continuous reflux to, God. These divine powers were to him the intermediate agents between the Creator-Father and the world and mankind. The Logos was the highest of them,—the idea of ideas, the archangel,—in a word, their original complex. God used this Logos, Philo theorizes, in creating the world (Alleg. iii. 31 ; On the Cherubim, xxxv ; Confus. of Lang., xiv., end). While other celestial powers had assisted God in making man (Creation of the World, xxiv.), the Logos remained yet the chief organ of God's creation. He was nearest to God, and his direct image. He was the Father's "first-born son" (On Dreams, xxxvi ; On the Tilling of the Earth, xii.), or his "eldest son" (Conf. of Lang. xiv.). He was assigned the highest rank and function of all the divine powers,—the rank of the archetypal world-mind and great governor of the cosmos, "being in a manner its God" (On the Creation, xxiii.)

This latter quality is, indeed, somewhat reduced again in 'On the Tilling of the Earth,' xii., where he characterizes the Logos only as superintendent, next to the supreme governor, God. Yet a very high degree of divinity Philo nevertheless reserved to the Logos. This appears most readily from the Fragment preserved by Eusebius, in which he is pronounced the "second God." The genuineness of this passage is borne out by another in Allegories, ch. lxxiii., where Philo speaks of the Father of all as the "first" God, and of the Logos as inferior, yet sufficient to be the ordinary, imperfect man's divinity. If this is not a real sublimation of the Logos to a substantial sameness, nor even a nominal identity, with God, but merely an hypostasis; especially since, as Schmidt, 'Libellus, etc.' argues, the angels too are by Philo denominated Gods : it can yet not be gainsaid that such daring speculative attempts were fraught with serious perils to true Monotheism.

No matter that Philo was not strictly consistent in the divine personification of the Logos, representing him about as often as the abstract Reason-Word of God, as he attributes to him a distinct, substantial existence. He perpetrated none the less a grievous departure from orthodox Judaism in those places where he does personify him. Even where he presents the Logos only in the character of God's Reason, the impression he gives us is, that this Reason is in some manner dissociated from God. And surely is such departure noticeable in his proposition, that service is due the Logos next to God (see Gfroerer, 'Prim. Christ.,' i. p. 272, end). Above all must his suggestion be pronounced an irreconcilable departure, that those "having knowledge of the one God are properly called sons of God,"—meaning thereby, as will appear from the following, the knowing ones or Gnostics. True, he has immediately after restricted the sweep of this theory, saying that none may so far have attained that perfect wisdom and goodness which yields that title. Nay, from his further remark, that one should at least endeavor to be adorned with the name "son of the Logos," we should judge that he meant, that no ordinarily aspiring wise man (be he even of Philo's philosophical acumen and ethical refinement!) can well succeed in reaching the state in which he may justly bear the name "son of God." But has he not at all events allowed the possibility of reaching it, how late soever in a wise and holy man's life this might be? Has he not, by avowing that virtually a man out of thousands may reach it,—deducing this even from a pretended Scriptural indication,—opened the door to claimants of it, whose grade of perfection would not only rest on the lofty self-consciousness of the individual, but on a popular assenting and sanctioning vote? [For further information of the reader about Philo's theory on the ideal man, we refer to Allegories, lxxiii., where he brings forward the sentence that "the imperfect (i. e. the average aspirers after wisdom and goodness) may be content with having the *name* of God (identical with the Logos) as their God; it is only the wise and perfect who can have the 'first' (that is, God, the invisible Father of all) as their God." Compare also Migration of Abraham, ch. xxxi., where the Logos is assigned to the imperfect man as his divine guide, until he have achieved the "highest wisdom," when he, having caught up with the Logos himself, will be his peer, and "both together become attendants of the All-guide, God."]

That such theories advanced, we own, with great reverence to the God of Israel, but nevertheless impairing his character as rendered in Scripture, must have been held as heterodox by all Palestinian orthodox Israelites who should have heard them, will readily be conceded. That his "divine powers" must have appeared to them as strongly tinctured with a sort of compromise with the ethnical polytheism, is likely enough. At any rate must he by his Logos-doctrine have laid himself open to the suspicion of ditheism or diarchy, in the same manner that the later heresiarch, Elisha ben Abuyah, was suspected of ditheism for his Gnostic attachment and the construction of the Metathron of Jewish mysticism—the cognate of the Logos, comp. Philo's Migration of Abraham, xxxi., towards end, with B. Synhedrin, 38, 3, towards end—into a second God; see on this B. Chagigah, f. 15. We know that Philo was all along emphatically affirming the unity of God, whom he has, moreover, in divergence from Plato, positively hypostasized and exalted above the latter's God, who was merely the Idea of the good; see on this Schmidt, as above, and comp. Doellinger, "Gentile and Jew," etc. But his theosophy nevertheless partook as much of pagan philosophy as of Jewish religious belief. He made such vast concessions to the former, that it can never be claimed for him that he was an exponent of the pure Jewish Monotheism, as bodied forth in Scripture and conceived by his orthodox contemporaries. He was assuredly, if not the only one, at least one of the theoretical originators of Gnosticism, that proved so baneful alike to Judaism and Christianity. And we truly believe that, had his theosophical theories come to the cognizance of the orthodox Palestinian authorities, he would have promptly been denounced by them as heterodox and branded with the stigma of 'Minean,' his outward pious conformation to traditional Judaism and fervid Jewish national attachment notwithstanding.

That in a system like Philo's, in which God's rigid abstractedness from the material world was taught with such emphatic assertion, and the great-power, Logos, devised to be the active link between God and men, a legislation for Israel by Jehovah had very little or no room at all, is thus easily recognizable. Indeed has he accorded direct promulgation by God only to the Ten Commandments. The rest of the Mosaic enactments were to him enunciated directly by Moses. They were "divine oracles," it is true. But they were such only by virtue of *inspiration.* For, as he urges with reference to the delivery of the Decalogue, "let no such idea ever enter your mind that God was himself uttering some kind of voice." Those oracles he divides into three classes: the one, in which Moses acted as interpreter of God, delivering the decisions himself, though the Pentateuch attributes this act to God; the second, put in the form of questions and answers between God and Moses; the third, constituting by far the largest body of precepts, which were "delivered by Moses in his own character as a divinely prompted lawgiver, possessed by divine inspiration" (On the life of Moses, xxiii.), or, as he gives it at another place, "the lawgiver, who is a prophetic spirit" (On the Festivals, vii.).

It is only to the Decalogue that he awards a sort of really divine authority. Its revelation was accomplished, he proposes in 'On the Ten Commandments,' ch. ix., by a new creation. God brought forth an "invisible sound" in the air, animate with a "rational soul." This "sounded forth a voice like a breath passing through a trumpet." It was a "visible voice," as he sets forth in 'On the Life of Moses,' ch. xxvii., "which affected the eyes of those who were present even more than their ears." These eyes were, however, not those of the body, but "of the soul," as he asserts in 'Migration of Abraham,' ch. ix., pressing there, moreover, the literal sense of some figurative expressions of the Pentateuch for his purpose of illustrating, that the voice of God giving forth the Ten Words was not one of a material nature, but "a most exceedingly brilliant ray of virtue, not different in any respect from the source of reason." The gist of all these reasonings is, that on the occasion of the delivery of the Ten Words it was the rational soul specially created by God, that communicated them to the rational souls or minds of the then assembled Israelites. The revelation of the Decalogue was, then, a totally immaterial act. And it was too the only portion of the Mosaic code that "God had uttered without the intervention of the prophet" (comp. 'On the Life of Moses,' l. c.).

II.

Another class of religious philosophers of the days of Philo and Jesus, attributed all the announcements and commands of the Mosaic code to angels. This angelic authority was resorted to from the same motive that animated Philo,—to avert from the supreme God every anthropomorphic and anthropopathic imputation. Philo, however, had yet for all his denial of the immediate Divine authority of all the Mosaic laws but the Decalogue, reverently ascribed at least an indirect divineness and religious obligation to all of them. He had, for all his love for allegory which he had elevated above the material meaning of the letter of the Law (calling the former the soul and the latter the body), urged with sincere piety the practical observance of all of them, warning seriously against their omission in the proud self-sufficiency, which the wise might feel in the speculative process of symbolical interpretation.

An entirely different set were those who assigned the whole Mosaic legislation to angels. In the case where angels were given out as the real authors, the unalterable obligation of its laws was surely out of the question. One of these men, Paul, had, indeed, come to teach the total abrogation of the Mosaic Law. There was consistency, too, in such negative position. For, why should commands coming from angels have binding force for men who have rational souls like them, though of some degrees below theirs? Among that class are to be numbered Stephen and Paul, as also some of the Christianizing Gnostics of Samaritan, Jewish, and Gentile descent.

Stephen gives out "the angel" as having spoken to Moses on Sinai, imparting to him the "living words" for Israel (Acts vii. 38). This angel was doubtless to represent the "Elohim" in Ex. xx. 1. In v. 53 of the same chapter Stephen reproaches all Israel, alike of the past and the present, with disobeying the Law which they received "according to the commands of the angels." The plural is here probably used because he alludes to all the ordinances of the Law, and not only to the Decalogue; they being manifold, may have been thought by him as having a variety of angels for authors, or, at least, promulgators. Corresponding to Stephen's phraseology is that employed by his doctrinal successor, Paul. In Gal. iii. 20, he reflects on the Law as "commanded (or appointed) by angels, in the hand of a mediator" (i. e. Moses).

Underlying these expressions was indubitably the philosophical notion, that God must not be degraded to the rank of human-like lawgivers. His enunciation of commands as represented in the Pentateuch, had consequently to be corrected into the perception, that they had an angelic origin. The philosophical theorists who brought out that notion may, we suggest, have drawn a support for it from the peculiar translation by the Septuagint of the last part of v. 2, ch. xxxiii. of Deuteronomy into: "from his right hand angels with him." This was indeed a radical alteration of our transmitted Hebrew text. We are at a loss to account for it, or even only to guess at the corresponding words which the sages composing the Greek version had in their own original text. This decided variance of the Septuagint had yet not struck the Grecian Jewish philosophers of those latter days as anything abnormal and strange. For to them the Hebrew original was mostly a sealed book, and the Septuagint version the all-sufficient, venerable oracle. Well can it, then, be supposed that they discovered in that translation a confirmation of their anti-anthropomorphic apprehension, that it was only spirits, and not God himself, who imparted to Moses the sacred enactments. [We deem it proper to refute at this place the opinion of those modern writers who rank the passage of Josephus, Ant. xv. 5, 3, with those others purporting to represent angels as promulgators of the Law. Josephus reproduces there a speech delivered by Herod before a Jewish multitude, in which he among other things exalts the dignity of ambassadors, arguing: "we ourselves having learned the most excellent of our doctrines and the most holy things contained in our laws ' through angels from God.' " It is positively a gross error to think here of real angels. Herod merely alluded to *prophets* as ambassadors of God, being such either by direct appointment, or by means of inspiration; compare on the latter, Against Apion, i. 7. We hold, farther, that if the word "laws" in that speech is to be taken strictly, in the sense of Mosaic, the speaker may have referred to Moses and Aaron and, possibly, to other pious ancestors anterior to them, whose utterances are recorded in the Pentateuch, and this in the point of view of their having been messengers of God; compare Ps. cv. 17, 26. If Scripture at large be meant by the term "laws," then, we propose, all the accredited prophets occurring therein are readily suggested as objects of that allusion made by Herod. The same meaning of *prophets* we assign to the "angels" in Ep. Hebr. ii. 2. Not that this Pauline epistolator was not capable of bodying forth the heterodox philosophical notion of angels having been the promulgators of the Mosaic Law. By no means. But the context does not require such construction being put on the word. Contrasting that passage with ch. i. verse 11, we find it more reasonable to suppose that he referred there to prophets, too, as having delivered the divine appointments to the Israelites. The prophets, then, he called angels, in the sense of messengers of God to men.]

We will now produce some corresponding views on the origin of the Mosaic Law, held by Gnostics properly so called, that is, those Christianizing religious philosophers whom the Church denounced as execrable heretics. It is well known that they assumed more than one God, lowering the Demiurgus (Creator, or, rather, Fabricator or Fashioner) of Plato and Philo to a degree below the supreme God, the Father. We cannot here enter in detail on the question of how much of Gnosticism there was virtually adopted by Paul in view of his supernal Christ, or by Philo with regard to his highly exalted Logos. We will only say in brief, that Philo has at all events never transferred the title Demiurgus from God to the Logos. Whereas Paul held forth his Christ as the Creator proper of all things, visible and invisible, by the side of the "invisible God," in Col. i. 16; comp. 1 Cor. viii. 6. (Possibly, however, Paul attributed to his Christ, the Son, even in the former passage, no more than the same dignity which Philo did to his Logos,—that he was the instrument of the creation of this world. Not only does the contradistinction he employs in the latter-quoted passage admit that he pointed out such a perception; but Philo, in his "Allegories," i. 13, and 'On the Cherubim,' xxxv., offers an analogy by which that supposition gains a fair support. Philo distinguishes there between "hypo" and "dia," in connection with the Divine creation. His view, taking the one passage with the other, is, that the latter preposition is expressive of immediate production by God, whilst the former denotes only God's causation. Similarly may Paul have meant to convey by "dia autou" in the just quoted passages no other idea than that Christ was the instrument of the creation, and by "ex hou" in Cor. l. c. no other than what Philo implies in "hypo" as relating to the Creator-Father, viz., that he was the *cause* of all things). Thus he had no right to inveigh, in Tim. vi. 20, against the false Gnosis as compared with his own, which he claimed to be the only true one; see 1 Cor. viii. 7. For, strictly considered, there was very little difference between the Gnostics so called, who were decried as heretics for holding a Creator distinct from the absolute Principle, God, and himself. He too invested his Christ with the title of Creator,—though at the same time nominally avowing the "one God, the Father" (Cor., as before).

Now as to those Gnostics we will say, that Simon of Gitta, in Samaria, nicknamed the Magician, who is by the Church fathers treated as the originator of heretical Christianizing Gnosticism, is by Hippolytus, Ref. Haer. vi. 14, credited with asserting, that "the angels who created the world, made whatever enactments they pleased." The origin of the Mosaic Law was thus attributed to angels. To this Samaritan school of Gnostics belong Menander, Saturnilus, and Basilides, all of whom held about the same doctrine. The two last-named, flourishing in the earlier part of the second century C. E., assumed next to the first Principle, God, seven world-making angelic gods, one of whom was the God of the Jews and of the Hebrew Scripture. Basilides called this Divinity the Archon (or, as

Hippolytus represents it, one of the two Archons, of whom the first ruled from Adam to Moses, and the second from Moses onward). To all of these Gnostics the Mosaic enactments were of angelic origin.

Of Jewish Christian Gnostics who had embraced the same view, Cerinthus is to be mentioned. He was schooled in Alexandria, and flourished in Asia Minor in the latter part of the first century C. E. According to a number of modern Church authorities he was the first of the real heretical Gnostics. He taught that the material world was created by angels, and that the God of the Hebrew Scripture, at the same time the God of Israel, was one of them. Some ancient Church writers state about him, that he held angels in general as the authors of the Mosaic Law.

There is in this connection to be noted a Gentile Christianizing Gnostic of Marcion's school, Apelles. Marcion was notoriously the fiercest of all the enemies of orthodox Christianity, alike the Jewish and Gentile portion of it. He assumed two co-eternal and opposite principles, the supreme, good God and the Demiurgus—the latter imperfect and the God of the Old Testament, which Testament he contemptuously rejected besides. Jesus he set down as a mere semblance, but Christ as the revealer of the new Deity, the true, supreme God, the Father. Apelles was his most prominent disciple. He aimed to soften the harsh dualism of the master by making of the Demiurgus a celebrated angel, brought forth by the supreme, good God. He also taught a third God or superior angel, of fiery nature, who was the God of Israel and of the Law; see Hilgenfeld, Hist. of Heret., etc., p. 536.

In all the above instances the theory is maintained that the Mosaic dispensation came from angels. Greatly different from one another as the general doctrinal positions of all those personages were, there is yet one common original cause to be upheld for that theory—that God must be regarded as totally divided from the world of sense, and as having no contact and communication with men.

III.

A specimen of a third position on the origin of the Mosaic Law is held forth in the pseudo-Clementine literature. It is of Ebionite origin, of about the middle of the second century C. E. The polemics set forth therein is supposably in the main directed against Marcion, yet partly also against Paul, and this in a disguised and indistinct conjunction with the above-named arch-heretic, Simon of Gitta. Baur, "The Christian Gnosis," classes the pseudo-

Clementine system, too, under the name of Gnostic, ranging it as the Judaizing form of the (Christian) Gnosis. Ebionism, that is, Christian Essenism, is in modern days admitted to be the ground-tone of those writings.

In the Homilies God is stanchly defended as the real, only Creator. Rigid Monarchist as their author was, he would not, like Philo, introduce the Logos or the Wisdom as the instrument in creating the world. For polemical argument's sake, it is true, he once averred that Wisdom—a half-impersonated divine power of the kind of Philo's Logos—assisted God in creating man. But on the whole he adhered to the orthodox Jewish standpoint in regard to the creation of the world. He pronounced the four elements—the original component parts of this world —as generated by God. Unlike the Platonic Philo who held matter pre-existent, he, on the contrary, avowed it originally created by God. For it was to him not at all incongruous with the sublime idea of God, to believe him coming in contact with matter.

Yet for all this firm monotheistic attitude, he was most radically heterodox as to the authority and venerableness of the Pentateuch and Scripture in general. He put up a distinction between a primitive religion which was even anterior to Adam, and the later Mosaic. The Mosaic religion he declares as a mixture of true and false things. The true things are, he argues, "from the tradition of Moses." He was a true prophet and the prophet of truth. (Prophecy is, by the way, extremely exalted by our author, in a genuine Pythagorean-Essenic manner.) He was continuously possessed of the spirit of God, as were Adam, Noah, Enoch, Abraham, Isaac, Jacob, and, after these, Christ, in whom, again, the prophetical Spirit of all of those saints was collectively united.

Moses, he further theorizes, gave the law of God, "by the order of God and with explanations," without writing, to seventy men, to be handed down to posterity. [It is curious to note the "mystery of initiation" by which, according to the alleged letter of Peter to James attached to the Homilies, those seventy men were in the mystical Essenic-Ebionite sphere represented to have received that law. They had to stand by the living water, it is asserted there (water was so loftily rated by the Ebionites, because they claimed that it received its motion from the Spirit, and this, again, had his origin from God), and "not to swear, for that is unlawful, but to adjure and say : 'I take to witness heaven, earth, water, in which all things are comprehended, and in addition to all these, the air also which pervades all things, etc.'" This impresses us, in passing, as having been the usual Essenic adjuration, in the place of oaths prohibited with them.] But after Moses was taken up, it was written by some one, "the wicked one having dared to work this." (By the wicked one the evil Spirit is meant, to whom, as our author's further doctrine was, God had assigned the rule over this world and also the punitive jurisdiction over men.) It was not written by Moses. For how could he himself have noted down that he died? About five hundred years after him the Law was found lying in the Temple, and about five hundred years more it was carried away and burnt in the time of Nebuchadnezzar (compare as to the latter notion the apocryphal Fourth Book of Ezra, xiv. 21, where this holy man is made to reply to God: "For thy law is burnt, therefore no one knows thy deeds of the past or of the future.").

How much of all this fantastic theory belonged already to the earlier Ebionites, is very difficult to trace out. In substance, we incline to think, it reaches back to them. And we farther believe, that the Essenes were not alien to it, either.

As to the written Mosaic Law which our author pronounced as containing confusedly true and false things, he put, concerning its true and genuine parts, in the mouth of Peter the affirmation, that "God had a written law from Moses to the present times" (Hom. xviii. 3). These parts were to him, then, in a sense, Divine. They were in his mind presumably the Decalogue (minus the third commandment, to be sure), and all those other Mosaic precepts which the Essenes had held obligatory, modified though to the religious views and practice of Jesus.

The direction of Jesus, the prophet and teacher, our author religiously maintains, is wholly to be followed. It was, in general, that one should use his own judgment as regards Scriptural sayings,— an imputation to Jesus which he attempts to verify by his (alleged) admonition: "Be ye prudent money-changers." Jesus, he argues, had himself admitted the existence of false things in Scripture. He bases this assumption on Matt. xxii. 29, where his reading was: "Not knowing the true things of the Scriptures," instead of the canonical, "not knowing the Scriptures." This, he contends, is further proved by the circumstance, that Jesus had once declared, "I am not come to destroy the law," and that he had yet appeared to be destroying it. By this seeming contradiction the prophet-teacher, Jesus, intimated, so he concludes, that the things which he did destroy had not belonged to the Law.

And now our Ebionite author goes on to prove from Jesus' utterances, what the respective true and false parts of the Mosaic Law are. That sacrificial ordinances were not included in its original composition, he tries to support by Jesus' saying: "The heaven and the earth shall pass away, etc." (Matt. v. 18), arguing therefrom that, as sacrifices had (at his own time) actually ceased, they must not have formed part of the Law of the God-inspired Moses, but been added later. To show that the sacrificial ritual was interpolated, he refers, besides, to Jesus' saying in Matt. ix. 13.

Against the insinuation that God swears, instances of which occur in Scripture, he produces Jesus' admonition: "Let your yea be yea, etc." Against the Scriptural imputation that God tempts, he holds out Jesus' assertion (not to be found though in the extant gospels): "The tempter is the wicked one." False things in Scripture are to him also the representations, that Adam was ignorant, or a transgressor of God's command, for he was, in his view, "the sinless, true prophet of God;" or that Noah got drunk; that Abraham had three wives, and Jacob four, two of whom, besides, sisters; that Moses slew a man, or once accepted advice from an idol-priest, etc.

False are to him, in fine, any statements of Scripture attributing to God, directly or by implication, any evil or want of foreknowledge, ignorance, reflection, repentance,—all of which misconceptions must positively be cleared off from man's apprehension of the Deity.

According to all the foregoing, we have to judge that the volume of the Mosaic code of our Ebionite author, after being purged of the many portions which were to him ungenuine, had very diminutive proportions, indeed. And so there were likewise, in his system, very few of the ritualistic laws, to which he assigned a truly Mosaic origin and Divine inspiration and, consequently, perpetually obligatory force. Which these were, this we cannot discuss here.

Concerning the primitive, unwritten law of God, our author has not left us entirely in obscurity as to what he had decided to be such. He meant by it that law, "illustrated by God's creation," namely, that "there is one God and Creator whom man has to love and fear, and for whose sake he has to be righteous and kind to his fellow-men, as thereby he honors God's image: man." This is evidently the moral law of the natural religion. That he construed the primitive law as such, we deduce especially from a passage in Hom. viii. 10, where he proposes: "God having made all things well, and having handed them over to man... , appointed a perpetual law to all, which neither can be abrogated by enemies, nor is vitiated by any impious one, nor is concealed in any place." That this perpetual law was to him no other than the moral, appears yet from another point of his Homilies, viii. 27: "the will of the righteous One is, that you do no wrong ; that is, murder, hatred, envy and such like."

EXCURSUS C.

To supplement our proposition advanced in that dissertation, we will remark that it was not at all alien to the Sadducean party to judicially proceed against accused persons by way of deduction from Mosaic ordinances, and of logical combination. For all their noted literalism which, according to Megillath Taanith, they applied also in cases falling under the head of the Mosaic retaliation laws, they yet used their own discretion in interpreting various judicial appointments of the Mosaic code, going at times even beyond the rigid letter of the Law. This does not only appear from the chapter of that Megillah in which the Sadducean codified "book of decisions" is characterized as containing classified sections for cases requiring capital punishment, "for which they could, however, not bring forward any evidence from the Torah ; " but is attested by the following instance which may be regarded as typical of their whole juridical course.

Josephus relates in Ant. xiii. 10, 6, the conflict of John Hyrcanus with the Pharisees; see the details there. We find in that representation the Sadducees disposed to inflict capital punishment for an offence to which, however, the Law had attached no penal visitation; see Exodus

xxii. 27. This instance does not only clearly exhibit the Sadducees as "very rigid in judging offenders above all the rest of the Jews" (Ant. xx. 9, 1), but even as arbitrary tyrants in judgment.

What wonder, then, that the Pharisees rejoiced and established a feast for the day on which they succeeded, under the queen Salome Alexandra, in abolishing the Sadducean "book of decisions?" It was doubtless replete with self-construed points of judicial law, and contained in particular many provisions of severe penalties even on those transgressions, to which the Mosaic code had annexed no deterrent threat of penal visitation. Possibly that Draconian book was re-introduced when they, after Herod had slain the Synhedrin, regained more and more the ascendency and certainly the majority in the national senate, in which indeed they sustained themselves from thence till the latter days of the State. (At the time of Herod's trial before the Synhedrin, this body were yet for the most part, it seems, composed of Pharisees. This may be inferred from the ultimate assent of the whole Synhedrin to the opinion of the Pharisee, Sameas, that Herod was liable to the penalty of death; see Ant. xiv. 9, 5). Especially can such revival of that book be presumed from the time when the political government was ultimately taken entirely from the hands of independent Jewish rulers, and exercised by imperially appointed procurators. With this epoch the Sadducean power and prestige in the Synhedrin must have markedly increased, probably suffering no essential diminution even in the few years of the reign of Agrippa I.

It is consequently also possible that the severe judgments inflicted on some Jewish Christians after Jesus, were chiefly due to the excessive rigor the Sadducees exhibited in the execution of penal laws. For, as to the Pharisees in the national council, it occurs to us that, whatever participation is, according to the N. T. sources (see Matt. xxi. 45, 46; xxii. 15, 16; xxvii. 62), to be assigned to them in the doom of Jesus, they manifested in all other accusations of Jewish Christians that judicial moderation and leniency which are variously attested of them. Jesus' cause with its complex nature of aggravation, alike Jewish religious and Jewish national, or rather political, may have appeared to the Pharisaic members of the Synhedrin too exceptional, not to co-operate with the Sadducean majority in his prosecution. Apart from that objective aggravation, Jesus had given the Pharisees ample cause for personal offence, nay animosity, against him. For he had unsparingly and unrelentingly been venting his scorn and abuse against them as a class in public, whereby their minds must have been odiously excited and imbittered against him. In the causes of all the other accused Jewish Christian professors after him, however, it may reasonably be supposed that they exhibited the spirit of mild judgment, for which they are known from authentic sources. That they did possess and ordinarily bring to bear this quality, is testified in many places of the extensive Rabbinical writings, as well as by the notable account of Josephus, in Antiquities, xiii. 10, 6. We propose, in the following, to adduce two more relative points of confirmation.

First, we refer to Gamaliel's reported interference in behalf of the apostles at the conjuncture of their alleged second persecution (Acts v. 17-42). As to the criticism on this whole account, we have to direct the reader to Baur and Edward Zeller in their respective treatises, 'Paul' and 'The Contents of Acts.' These authors put forth very strong arguments against the genuineness of Gamaliel's speech, one of which is the glaring anachronism regarding Theudas. There is, indeed, no gainsaying the mythical character of that entire narrative of Acts. And yet it strikes us as proper—to negatively use Baur's verdict—that "Gamaliel should not be given up." We mean, not wholly. We aver that it is not at all unlikely that the apostles were, not only twice but even more often, brought to Jewish justice to answer for their wonder-working in the 'name' of Jesus, and otherwise for teaching their doctrines about him. Accordingly, though criticism finds the relative report produced in Acts deformed by repellent mazes of fiction and exaggeration, its essence at least commends itself to our acceptance. We hold, therefore, that it is safe enough to retain as authentic the bare notice of Gamaliel's intercession, which may be put down as having occurred at some meeting of the Synhedrin before which the apostles were cited : so far at least, that he put in for them a determined advice of 'nolle prosequi,' and this from his moderate sectarian tendency in judgment.

As to Zeller's objection to assuming such moderation in Gamaliel, on the ground of the general hostile attitude of the Pharisees toward Jesus, it is, we suggest, easily lifted by our above remark, that the cause of Jesus was an exceptional one. His other objection that, as Paul who was a disciple of Gamaliel had, before his conversion, persecuted the Christians, it cannot be perceived that this teacher of his was so tolerant as he is represented in the account of

Acts, is very slender, indeed. Is it conclusive, we ask, that, because Paul acted the myrmidon for the Sadducean high-priest and other ex-high-priests of the same persuasion (see Acts ix. 1, 21), he must have learned his lesson of persecuting the Christians from his teacher Gamaliel? If it were, we would surely also be entitled to draw from the fact—if it be at all a fact—that he had formerly attended the latter's school, the ultimate consequence that his later fierce antagonism to the Mosaic Law had its mainspring in the theories propounded by the same theological instructor. But that such consequence would be the height of absurdity, will readily be allowed by every judicious reader.

Our second point of confirmation of the reputed judicial fairness and clemency of the Pharisees, we educe from Josephus' relation of the condemnation of James the Just and some others, in Ant. xx. 9, 1, which we have already before surveyed at length as to James. This relation is to us most worthy of serious notice. It offers, if rightly construed and understood, another important testimony that the Pharisees were indeed possessed of that noble quality. On the criticism of Baur and Zeller, both of whom assume in it a Christian gloss, it is beside our present purpose to enter. What we wish to bring out here is, that Josephus meant by those who reprobated the sanguinary act of the Synhedrin convened by the high-priest and president, Ananus, no other class than the Pharisees. He says (we give it in our own translation, having to reject Whiston's on grounds to be hereafter stated): "But those who seemed the most equitable of the citizens, and exact with regard to the laws, bore that matter ill, etc." The Greek original of "exact" is "akribeis." This epithet appears to us to point unmistakably to the Pharisees. Josephus uses the noun of the same etymological stem when speaking of this sect in Ant. xvii. 2, 4, as "valuing themselves highly on the exactness as to the Law of their fathers," and does so likewise in 'Life,' sect. 38, when he characterizes Simon, the son of the before-noted Gamaliel, as being "of the Phariseic sect, who seem to be distinguished from the other people by the exactness in the ancestral customs" (or "laws"). In view of this double recurrence of this epithet in connection with the Pharisees, we reckon it most probable that it prevailed in Josephus' mind and was, as it were, stereotyped with him in his reflections on this sect. The same combination, we assume, he had before his mind when speaking of those "exact with regard to the Laws,' who condemned the action of Ananus' court. It was the Pharisees whom he here thought of. They, were, indeed, best marked by their exactness in the laws.

Yet this exactness is not, as Whiston renders it, in Life, with " accurate knowledge," and in Antiquities, with "exact skill," but an exactness alike in the understanding and practice of both the written and oral laws of Israel. We even prefer to think that the point of view of the exact religious *practice* of the Pharisees predominated in Josephus' mind on noting the peculiarity of this sect. For they, in truth, stood out for their punctiliousness in religious observances, in especial those of ceremonial purity, the tithes, and the Sabbatic year. But whether or not he alluded rather to their exactness in the observance of the Jewish ceremonial, thus much is sure beyond any shadow of doubt, that it at least formed part of his thought when reflecting on the Pharisees. It is accordingly imperative not to construe that epithet in the only meaning of exactness in the knowledge of Israel's laws, as Whiston erroneously does. What we have yet to notice as most curious in this translator, is his awkward and misleading version in the passage at issue, in Ant. xx. 9, 1. He gives it: "But as for those who seemed the most equitable of the citizens, and such as were the most uneasy at the breach of the laws, they disliked what was done." Evidently is the second clause of this translated sentence to carry the sense, that the persons spoken of were a different class from the equitable ones of its first part. Yet the Greek original does not in the remotest way intimate the purport which Whiston has imputed to it, viz., "the most uneasy at the breach of the laws." All Josephus' respective words in the original are : "exact with regard to the laws." There is actually no mention of " the most uneasy at the breach."

To resume we would suggest, especially on the strength of the just reviewed remarkable passage in Josephus, that the Pharisees were in all the inquisitory cases of Jewish Christians after Jesus—save, perhaps, in those of Hellenistic defiers—not minded to severe measures being employed against them. And with the Pharisees, that is, the pious doctors of the Law and their disciples, who were in the apostolic period, as likewise afterwards, mainly divided into the schools of Shammai and Hillel, we may safely range the bulk of the Jewish people. For the same historian delivers also this information, that "the Pharisees have the multitude of their side" (Ant. xiii. 10, 6).

EXCURSUS D.

The summary treatment of the apostates in the time of the Syrian persecution by Mattathias and his son Judas, cannot well be held out as counter-proofs. For in those days of the remorseless rule of idolatrous Syria, in which the religious susceptibility of the pious was, for the enormous national-religious infidelity that had crept into the Jewish community, driven to the sorest tension, a regular institution of proceedings by the legally constituted courts was scarcely to be expected; though there is, on the other hand, no evidence whatever that the zealous leaders and pious avengers had not, in the chastisement of those malefactors, acted by authority and concurrence of the Senate. That such a supreme council existed in that period, is to be gathered from 2 Macc. iv. 44; compare also ib. xi. 27, and, for the reign of Antiochus the Great, Ant. xii. 3, 3.

Of a different character is, however, the proposition in the Mishnah, Synhedrin ix. 6, that against certain transgressors individual religious zealots—of the type of Phineas; see Numb. xxv. 6-8—may get up to visit on them a prompt infliction of death. One of the offences named there as coming under this head is, blasphemy of God, aggravated by a resort to polytheistic sorcery.

It appears to us as very probable that the author of the Mishnah has incorporated this proposition, which at the first glance contradicts the traditional leniency of judgment of the Pharisees (Ant. xiii. 10, 6), as a transmitted point of law, having for its historical background the days when those who had assumed the title Kannaim "zealots" were flourishing.

Waiving the question as to the exact point of time when these zealots, the revolutionary haters of the Roman government, as whose head Judas of Galilee is known in history, first adopted this their title, we may state thus much for certain that it was largely in vogue with the increase of those revolutionists styled Sicarii. This was under the procurator Festus; see Josephus, Ant. xx. 8, 10. Yet the existence of the zealots as a set of desperate anti-Roman insurrectionists is surely to be put on a much earlier date. Now as to those Sicarii who were without doubt only a faction of the "zealots," we have to say that their many acts of extreme violence were, judging by the account of Josephus (Wars vii. 8, 1), committed only against those of their countrymen supposed to be willing and ready to tamely submit to the Romans. Their view, also stated by that historian, was, that such were false brethren, "not differing at all from foreigners" (heathens). In their intense, exorbitant patriotism they denounced all such temporizing fellow-religionists as Nochrim, "heathen foreigners." Their ultimate motive, misdirected as it surely must appear, was to avenge what they held to be a *national apostasy*, which at the same time implied to them—really or only pretendedly—a religious apostasy, a fraternization with the "sons of alien gods" (comp. Mal. ii. 11).

According to the foregoing we may reasonably assume that the author of that Mishnah had in view and re-echoed an occasional lynch practice resorted to in the excited days of terror which those Sicarii had caused. Possibly he thought of the whole period of the Gaulonite revolutionists, that is, from the second decade of the first century C. E. till beyond the ruin of the Temple, along which time exemplary lynch law, in the cases enumerated there, was held applicable.

That reminiscences of actual occurrences of this kind of self-assumed justice underlie that Mishnah, would appear to us from its additional mention of priestly lynch law, though, too, only in the form of a proposition. This certainly points to the Temple times. The author must accordingly have referred to the period in which the Synhedrin flourished as the constitutional supreme power of the nation. There are, then, even from this period, looming forth some indications of self-constituted power of single religious zealots to inflict death on certain offenders, reflecting temporary departures from the norm of regular Synhedrial trials!

Whether by the "zealots" of the Mishnah the real Sicarii of Josephus are meant, or in general merely Phineas-like enthusiasts for the purity of religion, at any rate will the supposition that occasional lynch justice was not entirely foreign to the Jews of the first century C. E., find a fair support by that Rabbinical paragraph.

www.ingramcontent.com/pod-product-compliance
Lightning Source LLC
Chambersburg PA
CBHW030743230426
43667CB00007B/828